D1602881

Buzzards Bay

Weweantic River

Wareham

Agawam River

Buttermilk Bay

Cape Cod Canal

Onset Bay

Back River

Bourne

Pocasset River

Pocasset Harbor

Redbrook Harbor

Marion

Bird O.

Sippican Harbor

Megansett Harbor

Mattapoisett River

Mattapoisett

Tucoot Cove

Wild Harbor River

Wild Harbor

Falmouth

Acushnet River

Fairhaven

Mattapoisett Harbor

West Falmouth Harbor

New Bedford

Ram O.

Nasketucket Bay

Quisett Harbor

Westport

Apponagansett River

Clark's Cove

New Bedford Harbor

Buzzards Bay

Woods Hole

Dartmouth

Apponagansett Bay

Elizabeth Islands (Gosnold)

Naushon I.

Vineyard Sound

Westport River E. Branch

Slocums River

W. Branch

Penikese O.

Pasque O.

Marthas Vineyard

Cuttyhunk Pond

West End Pond

Cuttyhunk O.

Nashawena O.

N

Atlantic Ocean

Nomans Land

DANIEL SHELDON LEE

Buzzards Bay

A Journey of Discovery

COMMONWEALTH EDITIONS—BEVERLY, MASSACHUSETTS

FOR MY WIFE, LAUREN

Copyright © 2004 by Daniel Sheldon Lee.

Library of Congress Cataloging-in-Publication Data
Lee, Daniel Sheldon, 1966-
  Buzzards Bay : a journey of discovery / Daniel Sheldon Lee.
     p. cm.
  Includes bibliographical references and index.
  ISBN 1-889833-64-9
  1. Natural history—Massachusetts—Buzzards Bay (Bay) 2. Buzzards
Bay (Mass. : Bay) I. Title.
  QH105.M4L44 2004
  508.744'9—dc22

                                    2004002645

Design by Ann Conneman, Peter King & Company
Jacket photo: Brian Smith
Frontispiece map: Jeffrey M. Walsh
Printed in Canada

Published by Commonwealth Editions
an imprint of Memoirs Unlimited, Inc.
266 Cabot Street, Beverly, Massachusetts 01915
www.commonwealtheditions.com

Contents

Acknowledgments

I HAVE READ that no book is written by one person alone. That is doubtlessly true of this one. Many of the ideas and even some of the words contained herein were generously offered to me by others. Countless people around Buzzards Bay contributed to this work, only some of whom I have the opportunity to thank here. Although I have, for the most part, chosen to omit professional titles here in order to address as many contributors as I can, many of the men and women mentioned below are distinguished scientists or other professionals.

I am most indebted to George Hampson, Oceanographer Emeritus of the Woods Hole Oceanographic Institution (WHOI), the Woods Hole Group, and the UMASS-Dartmouth School of Marine Science and Technology (SMAST). Without George's introductions to key members of the Buzzards Bay scientific and environmental communities, and his endless assistance in every other matter conceivable, there simply would have been no book.

Much of the research on which this book relies is the work of Brian Howes and his team at SMAST. Joe Costa of the Buzzards Bay Project referred me to many competent professionals and was also an important contributor to several parts of the text. Mark Rasmussen of the Coalition for Buzzards Bay was untiring in his commitment to my cause. Bob Rocha of the coalition proved to be an incredibly helpful person. Seth Garfield of Cuttyhunk Shellfish Farms offered many important concepts and answered many requests for information. Ben Baker, of Baker Books in Dartmouth, provided insight into the workings of the Bay and was in other ways supportive of my efforts.

For the birds chapter, I would like to thank Ian Nisbet, formerly of Mass Audubon, for his expertise on terns, and Simon Perkins of Mass Audubon for his help with winter bird species and related environmental issues.

For the chapter about the Elizabeth Islands, I am grateful to Seth Garfield and his family for welcoming me to Cuttyhunk Island, and to John Richardson of

Hingham for pointing me in the direction of key people there. Toby Lineaweaver and Tammy Barboza of the Penikese Island School offered me the use of their facilities and gave me the run of Penikese Island on several occasions. Thomas Buckley, author of *Penikese: Island of Hope,* reviewed the historical aspects of my discussion of the island.

John Ghiorse of NBC 10 in Providence helped me with the technical aspects of the hurricanes chapter. I am also indebted to the hurricane research of William Gray of Colorado State University. Alice and Frank Miller and Bradford Tripp shared eyewitness accounts of hurricanes, for which I am grateful.

For the wildlife chapter, Marc Mello of the Lloyd Center for Environmental Studies educated me about seals. Bob Prescott and Don Lewis of Mass Audubon provided their expertise about diamondback terrapins. Steve Hurley of Mass Wildlife took time out of his busy schedule to teach me about trout.

Dick Backus, formerly of WHOI, provided his research and a guided tour of Penikese flora for the plants chapter. Mario Digregorio similarly donated his expertise about wildflowers and other local plant species. Joe Costa and George Hampson taught me about eelgrass.

Greg Swanzea, Amanda Madeira, and Traudi Coli of the Schooner Ernestina educated me about sailing and the city of New Bedford. Steve Vaitses and the students at the New Bedford Community Boating Center helped me understand the meaning of boating, as did Ben Baker. Rick Gurnon and John Muldoon provided me with insight into the mission of the Massachusetts Maritime Academy.

For the fisheries chapter, I am grateful to Andrew Kolek, formerly of the Massachusetts Division of Marine Fisheries, for his information on sport fishing; Bruce Estrella of Marine Fisheries for his expertise on lobsters; and Henry Cebula, lobsterman, for allowing me into the world of the fisherman. Dave Whittaker of Marine Fisheries taught me about shellfish management and provided me with important contacts and technical documentation. Dale Leavitt of the Southeastern Massachusetts Aquaculture Center helped me understand aquaculture, as did Seth Garfield, who showed me how oysters are farmed. John O'Neil of Hingham lent me his dry gear to go out on the Bay in December, a courtesy which at the least saved me from a bad case of pneumonia.

For the conservation chapter, George Hampson, Mimi McConnell, formerly of the Coalition for Buzzards Bay, Chris Reddy and Bruce Tripp of WHOI, and Mark Rasmussen taught me about oil pollution. Tony Williams of the coalition and George Heufelder of the Massachusetts Alternative Septic System Test Center contributed to the piece on nutrient loading. Bernie Taber of the U.S. Department of Agriculture educated me about fecal coliform bacteria contamination. Dave Dickerson of the Environmental Protection Agency offered his insight into the PCB cleanup in New Bedford Harbor. Graham Giese at WHOI, Jeff Williams of the United States Geological Survey, and Jim O'Connell of WHOI's Sea Grant program provided expertise on the subjects of sea level rise, erosion, and global warming.

I would like to thank my publisher, Webster Bull of Commonwealth Editions, for giving me the opportunity to write this book. Penny Stratton, my editor, and Joanne Crerand, my copyeditor, labored exhaustively to forge the raw manuscript into something focused and readable, for which I am very grateful. Brian Smith's professional excellence led to a cover photograph that captures late summer on the Bay.

I also wish to express my appreciation to the Hansel family, who donated the study room at the Hingham Public Library, which provided me with that most precious of things for a writer, a silent space in which to think and write.

My brothers, Brian and James Lee, were an enormous source of moral and other means of support while this work was in progress, as was my mother, Lennie. The same can be said of my father-in-law, Bradford Tripp, and his wife, Jane. Most important, I wish to express my deepest appreciation to my truly wonderful wife, Lauren, for her unswerving support of my efforts to complete this book. She believed in me.

Gosnold at Smoking Rocks, by William Allen Wall, 1842,
Courtesy of the New Bedford Whaling Museum

This painting depicts Bartholomew Gosnold landing at Smoking Rocks in 1602.
Smoking Rocks was located on the New Bedford coast opposite Palmer Island,
which is just north of the hurricane barrier.

Introduction

BUZZARDS BAY WAS discovered in 1602 by Bartholomew Gosnold, a
wealthy private explorer. Gosnold sailed in search of adventure and profit
and also with the hope of establishing England's first permanent colony in
the New World. He left Falmouth, England, in the *Concord* with thirty-two
men on board and headed directly for New England. The *Concord,* which left
England on March 26, was blown south of her course by unfavorable winds
to the Azores and did not make landfall in New England until May 14, later
than expected, on what was probably the southern coast of Maine. The
explorers then sailed her south and rounded Cape Cod, which Gosnold
named, along the offshore islands, around the tip of Cuttyhunk, and
dropped anchor in Buzzards Bay. What Gosnold's men found there can be
described only as paradise.

The Englishmen settled on Cuttyhunk Island and for about three weeks
used it as a base for forays to surrounding islands and the mainland before
abandoning their plans for a permanent settlement and departing for home.
Two members of the voyage, John Brereton and Gabriel Archer, recorded
separate versions of the *Concord*'s journey. Both Brereton's and Archer's
accounts, called *Relations,* were later published. Brereton's *Relation,* printed
in 1602, officially became known as the earliest English book relating to
New England. In their journals, both Brereton and Archer, with varying
attention to detail, faithfully recorded the Englishmen's observations of the
ecology of Buzzards Bay and their experiences with the native people they
encountered there. Upon rounding Cuttyhunk Island into Buzzards Bay,
Archer wrote: "We . . . came to anchor in eight fathoms, a quarter of a mile
from the shore, in one of the stateliest sounds that ever I was in." Of the
mainland of the Bay, an area believed to be near the Acushnet River in New
Bedford that the party later explored, he said: "This main is the goodliest
continent that ever we saw, promising more by far than we any did expect
for it is replenished with fair fields, and in them fragrant flowers, also
meadows, and hedged in with stately groves, being furnished also with
pleasant brooks, and beautiful with two main rivers that (as we judge) may

haply become good harbors. . . ." In his description of the offshore islands, Brereton, after a frustrated attempt to describe the seemingly endless array of animal, plant, and fish species found in the area, concluded: "But not to cloy you with particular rehearsal of such things as God and Nature hath bestowed on these places, in comparison wherof, the most fertile part of al England is (of it selfe) but barren." Quite simply, the journals of Brereton and Archer reveal that the well-traveled explorers of Gosnold's party had never encountered a place of such overwhelming natural beauty as existed at that time on Buzzards Bay.

Today, more than four hundred years after Gosnold's voyage of discovery, the natural beauty of Buzzards Bay remains largely unspoiled. The clean waters of the Bay are treasured by countless people for swimming, fishing, boating, and other recreational activities. The Bay also supports healthy commercial fisheries and provides a rich habitat for diverse plant and animal species. In this respect, it is nearly unique among its peers. Mariners who have sailed between ports from Maine to Florida will not hesitate to tell you that Buzzards Bay is one of the last clean bays on the East Coast of the United States. While other major bodies of water, such as the Hudson River and Chesapeake Bay, have been seriously degraded by pollution, Buzzards Bay remains, for the most part, healthy.

In recognition of this fact, in 1985 the federal government designated Buzzards Bay an "Estuary of National Significance" under the Clean Water Act. This designation was reserved for a limited number of embayments around the country that were deemed nationally important ecological areas in danger of environmental degradation. This designation qualified the Bay for substantial federal funds and led to the establishment of the Buzzards Bay Project, an organization that develops strategies for protecting the Bay's natural resources. The Buzzards Bay Project works closely with local scientists and with the Coalition for Buzzards Bay, a citizens' group, in their conservation efforts.

Buzzards Bay is now poised at a critical juncture in her history. The greatest threat to its future lies in the water pollution from septic systems, known as nutrient loading, that accompanies the massive residential development currently taking place on its shores. Southeastern Massachusetts is the fastest-growing region in the state. According to the Coalition for Buzzards Bay, the population in the Bay's watershed (the land area surrounding the Bay that drains into it) has increased by more than 50 percent over the past fifty years. Today, there are currently about 360,000 people living in the eighteen communities that fall completely or partially within the Bay's watershed. By 2020, it is estimated that an additional 200,000 people will call this area home. The way in which this development is managed will largely determine the Bay's future.

Another major threat to the ecology of Buzzards Bay is oil spills, as was recently highlighted by the *Bouchard 120* spill in April of 2003. At nearly 100,000 gallons, the spill ranks as the Bay's second-largest oil spill ever. Our ability to safely manage the immense amount of oil transported through the Bay and thus avoid disastrous tanker spills will also prove critical to the Bay's survival.

This book is the story, or "relation," of a modern journey of discovery of Buzzards Bay, one undertaken four hundred years after Gosnold's. Like Gosnold's journey, it is essentially an attempt to survey and describe a place through travels among its ecosystem and its people. Unlike Gosnold's journey, however, this modern one was undertaken not in the spirit of conquest and plunder prevalent in Gosnold's time, but rather in the spirit of cooperation and conservation that has become essential to our own. The journey was an attempt to learn what makes Buzzards Bay a special place, and to understand some of the challenges it faces as an ecosystem and a community. I hope this "relation" will help inspire and foster cooperation among the various groups and individuals who share a common interest in the Bay's survival. In a broader sense, the story of this journey of discovery is only a part of an ongoing, community-wide effort among scientists, conservationists, and everyday citizens around the Bay to ensure that our children and grandchildren will enjoy this "stately sound" as much as we do.

Native Americans

These people, as they are exceeding curious, gentle of disposition, and well conditioned, excelling all others we have seen; so for shape of bodie and lovely favour, I think they excel all the people of America; of stature much higher than we. . . . They are quicke eied, and stedfast in their looks, fearlesse of others harmes, as intending none themselves.

—BRERETON, ON THE NATIVE AMERICANS FROM THE MAINLAND OF BUZZARDS BAY

THE NATIVE AMERICANS who originally populated the shores of Buzzards Bay were members of the Wampanoag tribe. As one of the first tribes to come in contact with white colonists, the Wampanoags were among the first to be physically and culturally decimated. Today, the largest Wampanoag communities left are the Mashpee tribe on Cape Cod, with about twelve hundred members, and the Aquinnah tribe on Martha's Vineyard, with about three hundred members. Smaller Wampanoag tribes in the area include the Assonet (New Bedford to Rehoboth), the Herring Pond (Wareham to Middleboro), and the Nemasked (Middleboro). According to national census information, the total number of people claiming Wampanoag descent is around three thousand; most reside in southeastern Massachusetts, in Barnstable, Plymouth, and Bristol Counties.

The Wampanoags passed down their history orally, leaving no written records. As a result, knowledge about them must be gleaned from the records of early European explorers, the English colonists, a few recent works by Native Americans, and existing tribal memory. This unfortunate situation necessarily leads to a good deal of uncertainty and guesswork in any account that describes Wampanoag culture as it existed before European contact.

To the best of our knowledge, there were nine major subtribes of the Wampanoags originally living on Buzzards Bay. These tribes were ruled by the sachem, or chief, Massasoit, from his capital in what is now Warren and Bristol, Rhode Island. As a whole, these tribes were considered powerful, capable of raising three thousand warriors, a figure from which we might extrapolate the total native population originally living on the Bay. The Wampanoags established themselves as a tribe in the Woodland period, one of the four Native American cultural periods recognized by archaeologists in the Northeast. This period spans from 3000 BP (before the present) to the sixteenth century. The Woodland period directly preceded the moment of European contact. It is characterized by an influx of technology from tribes to the south, including the art of making pottery, use of the bow and arrow, and farming. Agriculture made it possible for the Wampanoags to settle in semi-permanent villages and for their population to increase. According to this version of Native American history, the people whom the colonists found living on the Bay had existed there in a similar fashion for at least twenty-five hundred years.

The Wampanoags, whose name means "eastern people," or "people of the dawn," were the easternmost representatives of the Algonquin Nation of the eastern forests. These tribes were united by language. All tribes of the eastern seaboard above South Carolina spoke some dialect of the Eastern Algonquin tongue. The Wampanoags and their neighboring tribes spoke the Massachuset dialect, from which is derived the name of the Commonwealth. The Wampanoags' territory abutted that of their allies, the Massachusetts tribe to the north and the Nausets of lower Cape Cod to the east; and their enemies, the Narragansetts of Rhode Island to the south.

Accounts from early European explorers indicate that Native American civilization was thriving on Buzzards Bay around 1600. John Brereton, who documented the Englishman Bartholomew Gosnold's voyage of discovery to Cape Cod in 1602, described the Elizabeth Islands as "all having large cleared spaces" for agriculture, with some natives living there. He also noted that Martha's Vineyard supported a large colony of natives.

Two years later, in 1604, Samuel de Champlain, a French explorer, described the natives of Cape Cod as good fishermen and farmers, growing corn, beans, squash, Jerusalem artichokes, and tobacco. At the time of

Champlain's voyage, the Wampanoags numbered at best forty thousand people. By the time the *Mayflower* arrived in 1620, their population had declined to around four thousand. There are two generally accepted reasons for this population decimation. It appears that around 1615 to 1616, the Wampanoags were brutally attacked by a tribe from the north called the Tarratines (who were probably the Penobscots). Then, around 1617 to 1619, they were victimized by European disease, most likely smallpox or bubonic plague. The natives described this disease as turning the afflicted and their blankets yellow.

These events, which the English later ascribed to "divine providence," cleared the way for European settlers. In 1621, a small party of Pilgrims traveling around Buzzards Bay, on their way to a meeting with Massasoit in Rhode Island, reported seeing ghost towns. They described seeing deserted villages, which once had sheltered "thousands of people," surrounded by silent fields. That same year, Massasoit signed a peace treaty with the English, saying, "Englishmen, take that land, for no one is left to occupy it."

The few Wampanoags who survived the physical decimation wrought by war and disease were subsequently the focus of intense cultural conversion efforts by Christian missionaries, most notably Thomas Mayhew and his descendants on Martha's Vineyard and Richard Bourne in Mashpee. These missionaries, whom the Wampanoags considered their friends, sought to make "Christian Indians" who lived as closely as possible to the white man's way of life. They ultimately succeeded in making the Wampanoag tribe more "civilized" than Native Americans anywhere else in the country.

Ironically, although the missionaries helped the Wampanoags obtain lands such as Mashpee and otherwise aided them amid a sea of unsympathetic settlers, they were also instrumental in destroying what remained of Wampanoag culture. The Aquinnah tribe on Martha's Vineyard held out the longest against Christianity. They held traditional religious beliefs until 1693, when Thomas Mayhew converted their sachem, Mittark, to Christianity. As it was historically, today Aquinnah is still the stronghold of traditional Wampanoag religion. As a result of this series of traumatic events, by the middle of the seventeenth century, when we had obtained only a fleeting glimpse of Wampanoag culture in its unspoiled state, it had vanished.

In 1660, Passaconaway, an elder statesman of the Wampanoags, made a speech of peace at his hundredth birthday, saying of the whites, "We are few and powerless against them." Shortly after, Massasoit's son, Metacomet, known to the English as "King Philip" for his haughty manners, began trying to convince the Wampanoags to start a last-ditch war to reclaim their lands. He told John Borden, his English friend, "But little remains of my ancestor's domain. I am resolved not to see the day when I have no country." In 1675, Metacomet's brief but remarkably bloody war against the whites resulted in the final destruction of his people. The tribes on Buzzards Bay were split during the conflict. To the west of the Bay, the tribes fought on the side of Philip: Weetamoo, the great female leader of the Pocassets, sent three hundred men to join Philip, as did other tribal leaders. To the east, the Wampanoags of the Cape and Islands did not rise against the colonists. As a result, the Mashpees and the Aquinnahs were the only tribes that survived Philip's conflict intact. The other remaining Wampanoag bands were scattered after the war and eventually died out. Some individual survivors migrated to, and were absorbed by, the Mashpee and Aquinnah communities.

The Mashpees and Aquinnahs subsequently mingled with local populations, a process accelerated by their policy of encouraging nonwhites to settle in their communities. By 1807, a visitor to the Mashpee Reservation reported only twenty pure-blooded Native Americans out of four hundred. The rest were of mixed descent, including African American, English, and Hessian. Hessians were German mercenaries, hired by the English during the Revolution to fight the colonists. Hessians captured by the colonists were sent to oversee Native American workers employed in the saltworks at Mashpee, and some settled there. Visitors to Gay Head on Martha's Vineyard around 1807 noted about twenty-five purebloods out of 240 people; most of the rest were partly descended from African Americans. The last Wampanoag on Nantucket died in 1855. The last full-blooded Wampanoag in the Fairhaven area, Martha Simon, was visited by Henry David Thoreau in 1859 or 1860, shortly before she died. Thoreau wrote that she had "half an acre" of Native American features in her face, including tawny skin and high cheekbones. In Mashpee, the last full-blooded Wampanoag passed away in 1903, and the last from Gay Head probably died around the same time or shortly thereafter.

GLENN MARSHALL, the president of the Mashpee Tribal Council, is a bear of a man, with hands like baseball mitts. He wears two thick wampum bracelets on his right wrist. Glenn looks like a man you would not want to have to fight. No doubt this thought crossed the minds of the unfortunate souls tasked with removing him from a beach in Bourne in 1997, where Glenn was exercising his right as a Native American to shellfish without a permit, even though the area had been closed for conservation purposes. He was arrested, handcuffed, and—two years later—acquitted of all charges.

Glenn's office sits under slanting eaves on the top floor of the tribal council building. Back under the rough steps leading up to his office lie two brown deer legs, tied together with a thin white cord. A dream catcher hangs on the wall beside his desk—a real one, tied with brown and gray grouse feathers instead of the fluffy, synthetic purple feathers you'd find on the roadside convenience store version. Behind his desk is tacked a white tribal flag, which portrays a howling coyote seated on the back of a floating sea turtle and framed by the rays of the sun.

When I first met Glenn, he explained that because he is Mashpee Wampanoag on both sides of his family, he is related to just about every Native American in town. When I quite tentatively offered the details of my genealogy to him—namely, that I was descended from John Alden, who incidentally had been appointed by the Massachusetts General Court of 1658 to negotiate disputes between the Wampanoags and the colonists of Barnstable—his response was unexpected. Without a trace of irony, he smiled and said, "My wife is a direct descendant of John and Pricilla Alden." Glenn's take on Alden was new to me: that Alden was a respected man because he knew the sachems, but he wasn't the one doing the real dirty work. And Glenn's explanation for the friendly rivalry between the Mashpees and the Aquinnahs is that the islanders are still pissed off about a baseball game that took place in 1932, when they came to Mashpee and had their asses handed to them. His personal philosophy about the four races of man—black, yellow, red, and white—envisions the ultimate destiny of the red man as the conservator of the natural world. Predictably, his theory for the destiny of the white man is somewhat less noble. It involves something along the lines of going where no man has gone before, mucking things up, and then beating a retreat back to everybody else.

THE WAMPANOAGS TRAVELED around Buzzards Bay using a complex series of footpaths that were part of a network crisscrossing New England. Some of these paths were so old they were worn down two feet into the earth. Others were so faint that whites could not see them. In 1600, a major footpath that ran directly around Buzzards Bay was recorded. Present-day Route 44 is built on an old Native American path that led from Plymouth to the head of Narragansett Bay. The Megansett Way was one of the main Native American pathways flanking the east side of the Bay, with many secondary trails leading from it. It ran from Herring Pond in Plymouth to the east of Telegraph Hill in Bournedale, across the Monument River via a log crossing, and down through Bourne and Falmouth. The Monument River (*Manamet* in Wampanoag) ran where the western end of the Cape Cod Canal flows today. Route 28, which leads down Cape from the Bourne Bridge, closely follows the Megansett Way from just east of Monument Beach to the Falmouth town line. Route 18, which runs from New Bedford to Middleboro, is built on what was the main Native American pathway in the New Bedford area. Many of the Bay's current roads are similarly built over native paths. King Philip used this network of footpaths with great success during the 1675 war to surprise towns and then quickly fade back into the forest.

The other mode of travel used by the Native Americans on the Bay was the canoe. Because they had no draft animals or wheeled vehicles, the Wampanoags depended heavily on rivers and harbors for transporting goods. They built dugouts from single trees such as white pine or hickory, using fire, stone chisels, and clam and oyster shells to hollow them out. These canoes ranged from two-seaters to vessels that were fifty or sixty feet long.

The Wampanoags lived in villages, either directly on the water or farther inland, depending on the season. During the warm months, when they could fish and farm, they settled close to the ocean or rivers, or preferably a place where rivers and ocean meet. During the winter, they moved inland to hunt. Their favorite village sites had high ground, easy access to firewood, and a nearby source of drinking water. They lived in wigwams called *weetos*, which were round huts of pole frames covered by woven cattail mats. Weetos in summer encampments were small and temporary and housed small family groups. Weetos in winter settlements were large and semi-permanent and housed extended families. The natives would strip the mats from winter huts when they left for the coast, leaving the frames intact in anticipation of their return.

To the Wampanoags, all land was common property, owned by a tribe rather than by individuals. A tribe would defend its territory, defined by features of the landscape such as hills or streams, against other tribes. Each tribe on Buzzards Bay would have laid claim to at least one good fishing spot, although some places, such as rich shellfish beds, would have been available to all tribes.

Many coastal New England cities, including those situated on Buzzards Bay, echo the placement of Native American encampments. At the time of the Pilgrims' arrival, the Wampanoags occupied about thirty villages. Some familiar Bay towns located on the site of, and deriving their names from, Wampanoag settlements include Quisset (*Cooxisset*), near Woods Hole; Megansett (*Mahagansett*); Cataumet (*Kitteaumut*); Pocasset (*Pokessit*, meaning "the place where the waters widen"); Mattapoisett; and Acushnet (*Acooshnet*, meaning "at the place we get to the other side," or alternatively, "place at the head of the tide"). Other Wampanoag villages scattered around the Bay included Agawam ("low land close by the river"), near the Agawam River in Wareham; *Wawayontat*, in the western part of Wareham on the Weweantic River; Sconticut ("place stayed at for the summer"), at Fairhaven; Coaxet ("the place, or hill, near conquered land"), at Westport and believed to have been land wrested from a neighboring tribe, possibly the Narragansetts; and Apponagansett ("at the place the little waters enter the big waters," or alternatively, "place of the still waters"), at Dartmouth. At least five Wampanoag tribes lived on Martha's Vineyard (*Nope*), including the Aquinnahs. Collectively, they were known as the *Capowacks*.

The Wampanoags were primarily farmers. They supplemented their diet by fishing, hunting, and gathering. Their basic diet comprised corn, beans, squash, pumpkins, artichokes, fish, meat, fowl, roots, nuts, fruits, and berries. The Gulf Stream's stabilizing effect on local climate extended their growing season and allowed them to grow crops susceptible to frost, such as corn, beans, and squash. After the corn harvest, the Wampanoags would separate the kernels from the husk, dry them in the sun, and store them underground in mat-lined pits for the winter. Their beans were pole beans, and they grew many kinds of squash, including zucchini, summer, and acorn squash. Their favorite method of cooking was boiling, in either birch bark or clay pots. One of their staple foods was *samp*, which was boiled corn, either whole or pounded up, mixed with other vegetables, meat, or fish. Much of their protein was obtained from succotash, a mixture of corn and beans boiled together. Before the whites arrived, the Wampanoags ate no salt or sugar. They understood that their diet was their medicine and feared, rightly, that if they adopted the white man's diet, they would also acquire his diseases. Besides their diet, the Wampanoags' other main preventive health treatment was the sweat bath. They would place hot stones in an airtight hut and sprinkle water over them to create steam—just like in a sauna. Once they were perspiring freely, bathers would run out of the hut and plunge into a cold stream.

Shellfish were also an important part of the native diet. The Wampanoags are well known for their clambakes on the shore, which involved cooking clams, oysters, scallops, quahogs, and other shellfish in covered pits lined with rocks and seaweed. They set clams on edge around a campfire until the shells opened. The natives also gathered in large groups to dry lobsters, crabs, oysters, and clams, either in the sun or over smoky fires, to provide food for the coming year. Shellfish were dug mostly by the women. Of all the creatures brought by the English, the Wampanoags despised pigs the most, because the colonists let them loose to forage on the shoreline, where they would root about in the shellfish beds.

The Wampanoags fished year-round, pursuing mainly ice fishing in fresh water in the winter. Favorite fish included striped bass, cod, mackerel, and herring, which they took in large numbers when the fish ran up the rivers to spawn. They used fish weirs (fencelike traps built across streams) and nets that were made by the women. They also used plant-fiber lines and bone hooks made from the wishbones of fowl, with small fish for bait. Seals were harpooned from canoes. Lobsters, used mostly for bait, were stabbed behind the head with a long barbed stick in the shallows.

The hunting season started shortly after crops were harvested in the fall. The Wampanoags hunted large game, such as deer, bear, and the occasional moose that wandered down from the north. They also hunted small game, including beaver, raccoon, rabbit, and muskrat. Deer, an important resource, were trapped in hemp leg snares attached to spring poles and baited with felled shrubbery. Each hunter would set thirty to fifty of these snares within a two- to four-mile range. Deer were also taken in "hedge drives," in which deer were herded down a funnel of fences or hedges toward hunters stationed at the narrow end with spears or bows and arrows. The Wampanoags viewed fishing and hunting not as recreational activities, but instead as difficult manual labor undertaken for survival.

A LITTLE BOY was watching a fishing show on television. Watching the anglers catching and releasing their fish, the boy turned to his father and asked, "Daddy, why do they let all the fish go?" The man's amused expression grew serious as he regarded his son. His mind drifted back to a time not so long ago when he was a boy and he and a friend had gone out fishing. Having no luck, they relaxed in the summer sun, watched an osprey beating time in the wind high above them, and tried to imagine what it must be like to see a fish from two hundred yards above the surface of the ocean. Then the rarest of things happened. The fish hawk raked in its wings, plunged, and erupted unsteadily from the water with labored wing beats, trying simultaneously to shake off the weight of the water and position a fish head-forward in its talons. Beaming, he had turned to his friend. "What d'ya think?" he'd asked. His friend, also smiling, said, "Let's go home." They had witnessed perfection, and you can't top that. To the Wamps, as the boys' people are familiarly known, fishing and hunting have never been about the sport, never about the money. They keep what they catch and take what they need to live—no more, no less. To them, it's all about what you see when you're out there.

The man hesitated as he met his son's direct, innocent gaze. The boy was too young to understand. "They're different," he said. Then he flipped the channel.

WE CAN DO LITTLE MORE than speculate about Wampanoag society before 1600. Most likely, for several hundred years before the whites arrived, they gathered in small federations around one sachem, like Massasoit, to whom they paid tribute. They would have had a weak political structure, preferring to divide into small bands that probably fought among themselves. (The English thoroughly exploited this characteristic, using the divide-and-conquer strategy to subjugate the Wampanoags.) Their local lands and waters would have provided them with everything they needed. Hence, there was probably little trade with the exception of luxury items, such as wampum, copper, tobacco pipes, or pottery. They did not strive for wealth or fear poverty; they were content in their relative equality in society.

The extended family was the basis of Wampanoag culture. Men could have multiple wives. One colonial record suggested that men were accorded this privilege because it was Wampanoag custom for women to abstain from sex through pregnancy until a child was weaned. Either partner could file for divorce, in which case a woman's greatest sin was considered to be adultery and a man's mistreatment of his wife or the inability to provide for his family.

European explorers consistently described the Wampanoags as tall, handsome, smart, and healthy. One colonial record refers to them as "tall and well-formed, skin olive or copper color, hair black and straight." The dark skin color may have been as much a result of the effects of weather and the grease they used to protect themselves from cold and insects as it was genetic. They frequently tattooed their bodies, especially their cheeks, with the images of animals.

The Wampanoags were known for their hospitality, especially to travelers. In daily life, they practiced a philosophy of reciprocity: when they accepted a gift from someone, they always gave something back. Above all, they prized their freedom, as demonstrated by the colonists' inability to turn them into servants or slaves. They were a warrior race, who would fight to protect their hunting grounds, and also great lovers of sports. Their favorite game was lacrosse, which they played on the beach. The games sometimes lasted for days and were accompanied by feasting. Goals were set up to a mile apart. They also played a game similar to basketball and enjoyed tug-of-war.

Historically, the Wampanoags were great gamblers. Next to lacrosse, their favorite game was a form of gambling called dice. They also played a game in which they tossed painted stones about in a tray and a game with straws that involved rapid mathematical computations. At times, hundreds or even thousands of natives were present during gambling events. These games were sometimes played for very high stakes, including possessions and terms of personal servitude.

The Wampanoags had a strong spiritual bond with their fellow creatures. They believed that every living creature had an equal right to life, satisfaction, and food, and that it was a sin to harm any creature needlessly. They believed animals shared with them the same consciousness of their existence. They treated the spirits of hunted animals with respect. For example, they returned all fish bones to the sea. They hung up animal bones, especially skulls, in special huts and made offerings to them. They considered it a sin to waste the flesh of animals. If hunters killed more than they could eat, they were expected to give the surplus away for a feast. The Wampanoags showed trees the same respect. If they felled a tree to make a canoe, they offered it an apology, thanks, and possibly tobacco. The natives believed that if they did not do these things they would be haunted by the spirits of the creatures they had killed.

In contrast to the Wampanoags, modern man often goes into the natural world spiritually unprepared. My own religion teaches that the creatures of this world are here for the exclusive use of human beings. This teaching provides little spiritual consolation to a person if and when he or she becomes an active participant in the food chain. Thus it seems obvious to me that assuming pagan spiritual values in this area is the only decent recourse. My hope is that this failing is one not of the church's teaching but rather our interpretation of it; perhaps one day Western religions can begin to embrace not only the sacredness of human beings but also all the living things with which we share this world.

The taking of a creature's life, particularly the life of a large animal of obvious consciousness, is a momentous act, one that transfigures an individual's soul whether or not he or she is aware of it. Human beings, as a rule, are not invited into the universal cycle of death and renewal without the necessary spiritual currency. To go there without it makes us no more than criminals of the cosmos, and the consequences of doing so are real. Whether we refer to these consequences as a haunting, as the Wampanoags did, or guilt, as our psychologists might, is only a matter of semantics.

A GREAT STRIPED BASS lay quietly, sides heaving, across the bow compartment of my gray rubber inflatable. Alive, still in possession of its colors, its stripes were not stripes at all, but chocolate checks interspersed with radiant flecks of emerald and purple. The large dark pupil of its eye was aware, watchful, yet somehow resigned. All at once, it gathered its energy and flopped heavily against the wet plywood flooring in a last, fruitless attempt at escape.

I gunned the old Johnson outboard and headed the inflatable in the direction of the shoreline, just emerging from the darkness. The Bay was restless, charged with energy from the thunderstorms that had raged throughout the night. To the east, thunderheads mushroomed, the last of the passing front. Silver lightning played soundlessly on the horizon. I had motored around the point before dawn, as soon as the lightning let up, reasoning that after the storm, in the predawn light, stripers would be hungrily feeding in the rocks. On my first cast, the white jig was struck hard when it found the bottom, informing me that my theory had been correct.

Reaching the beach in the light of dawn, I lipped the bass by inserting my thumb into its huge mouth and grabbing its lower jaw firmly with my fingers. Walking a few feet up on the hard-packed sand, I swung the three-foot fish onto a shelf of clean wet gravel left by the falling tide. Quiet now, the black eye of the bass rolled back in its socket, watching me as I crouched over it. We were alone on the thin crescent of beach, the great silver bass and myself, and the universe turned to watch. Reflexively, almost compulsively, I began to pray. I asked the spirit of the fish for forgiveness, thanked it, and assured it that I took its life only for food. Then I raised a large, oblong stone above my head with both hands and threw it down hard on the wide, olive-green head of the bass. It struck with a deep thud and slid off, leaving a slight indentation in the skull. The gills of the fish flared widely as it gasped, and crimson blood began to trickle down through the clean altar of small stones. It still lived. I lifted the stone again, this time throwing it down harder, faster, again producing the hollow thud. I felt at once the primitive thrill of the kill and a strong need for the thing to be over. Finally, after one more throw, a horrible, rolling shudder shook the bass from head to tail, and it lay still. To kill a large living creature with a primitive implement such as a stone is not easy. Life clings to torn flesh with surprising tenacity.

I filleted the fish. Then I picked it up by its tail and pitched its body, still heavy with the weight of the head, underhand, end-under-end, into the Bay. It felt like a two-liter bottle of soda tied to a rope. The carcass sank slowly through a rose-colored cloud, all the while watched by the patient eyes of two black-backed gulls on the shore. The gulls might later retrieve it from the shallows, or it might drift with the tide up into the mouth of the salt pond, to be consumed by crabs. Either way, it would be recycled back into the Bay. My family would eat the fillets later that afternoon, at a ninety-third birthday celebration, within sight of the waters where the bass had swum.

THE WAMPANOAGS BELIEVED in one primary god, Kiehtan, who held the power of life and death. They did not believe in one consummate source of evil, like the Devil, but many. They did not believe that death was absolute, but rather that the body returns to the Earth, and that the human spirit is capable of coming back in another form. The Wampanoags also worshipped lesser gods, perhaps thirty-seven of them, who were responsible for all successes and failures in life. These lesser gods were embodied in the forces of the natural world and were invested with portions of Kiehtan's power. Respect and ceremony could be used to influence, but not control, these gods. They included the sun, the moon, thunder, rain, the four winds, fire, and woman. A favorite lesser god of the Wampanoags was the southwest wind, for it brought them warmth. They believed that the southwest wind blew directly from the dwelling place of the gods. They also believed that when they died, their souls traveled to the Southwest, where they would meet with their ancestors for feasting. In anticipation of this event, the Wampanoags often buried their dead, along with their favorite possessions, facing southwest in their graves.

The Wampanoags practiced a form of religion known as shamanism, in which medicine men, known as powwows, were all-powerful priests. (The term *powwow* later came to mean a cultural gathering.) Using elaborate rites, and aided by a practical knowledge of roots and herbs, the powwows could reportedly "make water burn, trees dance, and rocks move." They could also inflict physical ailments on tribal members, such as blindness and lameness. The power of these medicine men, whether supernatural, psychological, medicinal, or some combination of the three, was very real, even in the estimation of reputable English colonists. The English feared the pow-wows even more than the great sachems because they held complete power over their people. The colonists strongly distrusted shamanism because they equated it with witchcraft and devil-worship.

Spiritually, the Wampanoags considered their relationship with the Earth to be of central importance. For everything taken from the Earth, something had to be returned. It was the task of medicine men to teach the concept of the Medicine Circle, which the Wampanoags believed explained the essence of existence. According to the late Russell M. Peters, the great modern leader of the Mashpees, the lesson of the Medicine Circle is that "everything rises from the earth, and returns to it in a timeless cycle. Everything in creation is part of this circle, and it is continuous from birth until death." It was from this belief that the Wampanoags drew their strength. Interestingly, present-day Mashpees believe that the idea of the Medicine Circle is com-patible with Christianity, and they sometimes practice dual ceremonies at events such as funerals.

THE WAMPANOAGS OF TODAY continue to face many challenges. The Mashpees are embroiled in a political battle for federal recognition as a tribe, a status they have been seeking since 1974, which would allow them to fully exercise their rights as Native Americans. The Aquinnahs, although federally recognized as a tribe in 1987, still struggle economically, as they try to make a go of island business ventures, including a general store and a shellfish hatchery. The Aquinnahs are also very involved in a political bid for a gambling casino, which they have been hoping to build somewhere in southeastern Massachusetts since the early 1990s.

In *Indian New England Before the Mayflower*, Howard S. Russell concludes, "The promise for an Indian future has so far remained unfulfilled." Today, it would appear that the Native American future—for better or for worse—may be partly fueled by gambling casinos. Ultimately, however, there may be another, more spiritual means available to them to help fulfill this future.

There is a place that, though far across the world from the land of the Wampanoags, nonetheless occupies a parallel universe. Tibet, a narrow place on the map, is an infinitely deep well of spirituality. Like the Wampanoags, the Tibetans have been overrun by a larger and more technologically advanced race—the Chinese. Much of Tibetan cultural and spiritual knowledge has been destroyed in the burning of countless temples. Their leaders have been imprisoned and murdered. The fourteenth Dalai Lama, their spiritual leader, is currently living in exile. Tibetan scholars, including the late, eminent mythologist Joseph Campbell, have suggested that the ultimate destiny of the Tibetan people may depend on their spiritual learning, which, like the Wampanoags', emphasizes the kinship of all life. This valuable knowledge, they suggest, could be communicated by traveling teachers, or through the establishment of Tibetan retreats, where world leaders of all backgrounds could go to study. Could it be that the Wampanoags have their own sustaining wells of spirituality, hidden deep in the pitch pines of Mashpee and out on the clay cliffs of Aquinnah?

In his 1932 book *Thomas Mayhew, Patriarch to the Indians,* Lloyd Hare concluded, "Much has been written about what the white man may learn from the Indians. But sober investigation renders it doubtful if there are many attributes found in the better class of redskins that the better class of Caucasians do not possess." In hindsight, with the environmental future of much of our country poised at a crossroads, it does not take even a sober investigation to reveal that a sustainable land ethic is one attribute that the Caucasian settlers did not, in fact, possess.

In recent years American society has made some progress in this area. In his book *Sand County Almanac*, Aldo Leopold suggested that the current environmental movement is the precursor to the development of a third stage of human ethics. Ethics exist to counter our instinctual competitiveness that, if left unchecked, results in the unwanted destruction of other segments of our community to which we have assigned value. The first stage of ethics, says Leopold, established our code of behavior between individuals. The second, which includes the Golden Rule and democracy, defined rules of behavior between individuals and our society. The third will establish an ethical relationship between us and the land. According to Leopold, our success in evolving to this next stage of ethics depends on our willingness to expand our present definition of community to include the land and all the creatures on it.

If Leopold is right, in the years to come, as we struggle with questions of how best to preserve natural places such as Buzzards Bay, we could do worse than plumb the deep spiritual wells of Mashpee and Aquinnah for answers. After all, the Wampanoags of the seventeenth century taught our forefathers how to farm, to fish, to stay warm—how to survive on the land. Today, in the twenty-first century, might we finally be ready for the next, equally important part of the lesson: how to ensure that the land survives us?

Birds

Here we had cranes, stearnes, shoulers, geese, and divers other

beards which there at that time upon the cliffs being sandy and

with some rocky stones, did breed and had young.

—ARCHER, ON THE NESTING SEABIRDS THAT PROVIDED GOSNOLD'S PARTY
WITH FOOD AS THEY SAILED INTO BUZZARDS BAY

A COMMON TERN hovered about twenty feet above me, riding the southwest wind. The bird was working a seventy-five-foot-long area of shallow water parallel to the beach; its black-capped head and orange beak pointed sharply at the surface, its eyes scanned the water. The tern's wings beat extremely rapidly, perhaps four times a second, and it faced the strong southwest wind at all times. Every few seconds the bird flicked its head up briefly toward the southwest as if it were watching for something. It glanced up into the wind just as you would glance at the highway while changing a compact disc in your car. I realized that the tern was not only fishing, it was also flying. Occasionally, the bird gave a curious, nervous shake, or vibration, of all its body feathers. Although the hungry tern seemed frantic to capture a baitfish from the flashing school below, it exhibited the typical restraint of a predator. It refused to dive, although obviously tempted, until it was absolutely sure of success. At last, the bird rose suddenly on the wind, briefly hovered once more, folded its body into a jagged angle, and plunged beak first into the water, smashing the surface with remarkable force. It emerged several seconds later with a small, wide-bodied silver fish, possibly a juvenile herring or menhaden, draped in its orange beak. The tern, without talons to aid it, struggled to handle the fish with its beak alone. After an uncharacteristically awkward aerial display, the successful outcome of which seemed in no way assured, the bird gained control over its meal and immediately flew inland. On pulsing wings, it swiftly crossed the barrier beach to a rocky islet, moated by a salt pond, that hosted the colony. The lasting impressions I took from this creature were of boundless energy, the unceasing beating of wings, the supreme strength in those wings, and above all, a fierce, consuming hunger.

OF THE MANY SPECIES of birds that grace Buzzards Bay in the summer months, perhaps terns best embody the spirit of the season. They are consummate navigators of the prevailing southwest wind. With their dazzling plumage and sprightly manner, they are like the children of the tropical sun they follow. The three most abundant species of terns that call the Bay home during the summer months—their breeding season—are the common, the least, and the roseate.

Common terns are the birds you see most often. They are large (pigeon-sized), with white undersides, gray backs, black caps, and orangey-red beaks with black tips. Roseate terns, fewer in number and seldom seen inshore, are similar to common terns in size, but are much paler overall, with longer forked tails and black beaks. The white plumage of a roseate tern's breast carries the faintest blush of pink, like the rosy coloring of my baby son's cheeks. Least terns are significantly smaller than the other two species (robin-sized), beat their wings much faster, and have yellow beaks with black tips. Least terns are scarce in the upper parts of Buzzards Bay but nest on sandy beaches near its entrance. They are the terns you see wheeling about in dense numbers over sandy, isolated points, such as at the mouths of tidal rivers or the entrances to remote harbors such as Cuttyhunk Pond.

The islands of Buzzards Bay are home to nearly half of the entire North American breeding population of roseate terns. This is a very big deal in scientific circles because roseate terns are on the federal list of endangered species. This singular, remarkable fact is what distinguishes the Bay, ornithologically speaking, from similar, neighboring avian habitats such as Nantucket Sound. That such a high percentage of roseate terns choose to nest in Buzzards Bay is so unique and so important that some consider it to be the Bay's defining biological characteristic.

The history of terns on the Bay is a story of persecution, first by men, later by gulls. In the late 1800s, local populations of all tern species were reduced by the plume trade, which reached its height between 1880 and 1890. Terns were shot for their feathers and wings, which were used to decorate ladies' hats the world over. Roseate terns were the hardest hit, and they actually disappeared temporarily from the Bay. In the early twentieth century, thanks to the advocacy efforts of Minna Hall and Harriet Hemenway, the founding mothers of the Massachusetts Audubon Society, legislation was passed to protect birds from plume hunters. Tern populations on the Bay immediately rebounded and recovered to saturation point. Unfortunately, the terns had little time to enjoy their regained peace before they encountered the next deadly challenge—gulls.

Historically, the largest nesting populations of both common and roseate terns, the two species for which Buzzards Bay is best known, were on Penikese Island, one of a string of islands that divide Buzzards Bay and Vineyard Sound, collectively known as the Elizabeth Islands. From the 1930s through the 1960s, an exploding gull population, fueled by garbage from town dumps and fish waste discarded in New Bedford Harbor, drove all the nesting terns off Penikese. Gulls threaten terns chiefly by displacing them from nesting areas, although some species, notably the great black-backed gull, will prey on tern eggs and chicks. Common and roseate terns prefer to nest far up on the beach where there is some vegetation, and so do gulls. Gulls tend to spread out while nesting, covering relatively large areas, while common and roseate terns form dense nesting colonies that occupy small amounts of space. Least terns do not compete as much with gulls for nesting areas because they prefer the open beach, as do piping plovers.

The bullied terns of Penikese fled to Bird Island, off Marion, and to Ram Island, off Mattapoisett. Gulls pursued them. By the early 1970s, hordes of gulls had pushed the terns off Ram and were doing the same on Bird. In 1970, Mass Audubon decided it was time to act, before the terns were gone for good.

AS I APPROACHED the front door of Ian Nisbet's home in North Falmouth, I was immediately accosted by two inquisitive dogs that appeared to be small collies. I winced. His first impression of me is going to be that I'm not a dog person, I thought. I have never been able to shake one side effect of having had a paper route as a child: I view dogs as the enemy. Suddenly, the front door cracked open, an arm reached out and handed me two dog biscuits, and a voice with a strong British accent announced: "Here you are. Feed them each one of these, and they will be your friends for life."

Ian is one of those people who describe themselves as retired, then go on to discuss their latest professional project. His home flanks the Wild Harbor River marsh—the same marsh that was fouled in 1968 by the *Florida* oil spill. His bathroom has a large, sunny bow window that looks out on the lovely winding tidal creek and surrounding salt marsh. Two exotic flowering plants with large magenta blossoms frame the window. A carved wooden tern, gray and white, sits on the sill. This arrangement captures the mental organization of the man. Ian Nisbet, a native Scot, views the natural world—perhaps the entire world—through the filter of terns. He is one of the people responsible for bringing the terns of Buzzards Bay back from the edge of biological twilight.

Ian is passionate about birds. He has a reputation locally as a bit of an eccentric. He has a large head, plastered with messy white hair, and big, slightly droopy ears, all set on a rather smallish body. He is exceedingly polite and generally has a bright twinkle in his eyes that escalates into a wildfire when he starts talking about birds. David Allen Sibley bird guides are scattered about his house like thrown confetti. While he was still a student, Ian wrote the definitive history of terns in Massachusetts. He also served as the scientific director of the Massachusetts Audubon Society.

We chatted in his kitchen. The conversation turned, as it inevitably does in discussions about terns on Buzzards Bay, to Ram and Bird Islands. "Where is Ram, anyway?" I asked him. "Aren't there a couple of Ram Islands in the Bay?"

"Yes," Ian replied. "It's the Ram off Mattapoisett, not the one off Marion, that hosts the breeding terns. Bird Island is in Sippican Harbor, which is the outer harbor of Marion." Then, sensing my confusion, he said tentatively, "Bird isn't near the Ram off Marion." With a chuckle, he added, "There are Rams up and down the coast of Maine as well. Do you know why they are all named Ram?" I had no idea. "In the summer, the farmers would put all the horny male sheep out on the coastal islands to keep them from the ewes. Then, in the fall, they'd bring them back in to impregnate the ewes."

After sharing this bit of lore, Ian went on to explain that islands are a favorite nesting spot for terns because typically they are free of the predators found on the mainland.

When Mass Audubon decided enough was enough in 1970, they chose Ian Nisbet, along with a colleague, Bill Drury, as their knights to battle the gulls. They sent the men out to Bird Island to push back the bickering hordes. "Ah, yes," Ian recalled, "we shot them with rifles, from the window of the lighthouse."

"Of course," I said, picturing the Scotsman taking pot shots at gulls on the remote island, his hoots of jubilation ringing across the wide expanse of the Bay. "Got him!" And "Brilliant shot, Bill!"

"You must have shot a lot of gulls," I said.

"Actually, no—gulls are quite smart. If you shoot one, fifty leave," he replied.

Mass Audubon's strategy worked. By 1990, with the gulls gone, the tern population on Bird Island had rebounded to thirty-five hundred pairs—two thousand pairs of commons and fifteen hundred pairs of roseates—and has remained constant to this day. That same year, encouraged by Nisbet and Drury's success on Bird, the Massachusetts Division of Fisheries and Wildlife launched an effort to poison the nesting gulls on Ram. By 1991, the gulls were gone. The terns moved back immediately, and their numbers have been increasing ever since. Today, Ram Island is home to about two thousand pairs of nesting commons and five hundred pairs of roseates. Ram is owned by the state—MassWildlife—and is operated as a bird sanctuary with restricted access. Bird is owned by the town of Marion and is informally managed by MassWildlife staff, who direct visitors to see the nesting birds.

When I asked Ian where he thought the terns will nest in the future, he offered his hope that they will move on to Penikese Island. He explained that Ram and Bird are both threatened by erosion. Penikese is eroding as well, but the island is approximately seventy-five acres in size, so it will last significantly longer than its smaller cousins. Depending on the height of the tide, Bird Island measures only one and a half to two and a half acres. Ram is slightly larger, at two and a half to three acres. When I asked if hurricanes were eroding the islands, he noted that winter storms cause even more damage. The terns have already lost one historic nesting place in the Bay to erosion, the Little Weepeckett Islands. "It took only about sixty years for the Little Weepecketts to be reduced to a pile of rocks," Ian told me. "Bird and Ram will be similarly whittled away in a few hundred."

In 1819, a lighthouse was constructed on Bird Island, and a wall was built around the island's perimeter to protect the lighthouse from erosion. During the Hurricane of 1938, eight feet of water swept over the island. Everything went but the lighthouse. The wall was moderately damaged. Today, waves driven by the southwest wind crash over the wall and wash back against its landward side, eroding the land within it. A restoration project is currently underway to rebuild and reshape the wall and to add backfill that will return the land within the wall to the level it was in 1819. When the project is completed, suitable nesting area for the terns will be doubled. The island used to be a popular destination for boaters, who sunned themselves on a sand spit on the northwest end of the island. Over the past thirty years, the sand spit has eroded away. Today, people visit Bird only to fish or see the nesting birds.

Ian left Mass Audubon in 1980, but he chose to stay involved in the tern restoration project on the Bay. "I haven't been paid for my work with the birds since 1980," he confessed. By 1998, he and the other tern warriors had focused their sights on Penikese, the first and most entrenched stronghold of the bickering gulls. "By that time, people didn't take to shooting or poisoning, so we used dogs against the gulls. *Those dogs*," he said pointedly, nodding at the two canines sprawled across my feet under the kitchen table.

"Those dogs?" I repeated incredulously, peeking under the tablecloth at the collies with new interest.

"Yes, Lochin and Tressa," Ian replied. "Lochin is short for Lochinvar, the hero of the Walter Scott poem. He was a handsome young man when we got him, so we called him Lochinvar."

Not knowing much about the nineteenth-century poet and novelist Scott, I later looked up his poem "Lochinvar." The first verse goes like this:

> O, Young Lochinvar is come out of the west
> Through all the wide border his steed was the best

And save his good broad-sword he weapon had none
He rode all unarmed, and he rode all alone
So faithful in love, and so dauntless in war
There never was a knight like the young Lochinvar.

"They're basically sheepdogs," Ian explained. "So when nothing else is moving, they chase the gulls." The animals I had mistaken for collies were actually Shetland sheepdogs, commonly known as Shelties.

"They look kind of big for Shelties," I commented.

"That's because they bred them down to toys that weigh twelve pounds," Ian said. "The first thing they bred out of them, you know," he continued with a sly wink, "was the brains."

He took Lochin and Tressa to Penikese Island in the spring of 1998 to wage war on the gulls. In just two seasons they successfully chased the gulls from the isthmus, the sandy land bridge connecting the two main parts of the island, and Tubbs, the smaller half of the island beyond the isthmus. "The idea was to stop the gulls from nesting in April and get the dogs out of there by mid-May, when the terns arrive," explained the scientist.

"Another reason we are trying to get the nesting terns to build up on Penikese is that it is more secure for them there," Ian said. "There are fewer predators there than on the other islands."

Because of their proximity to the mainland, Bird and Ram Islands are prone to raids by a truly fearsome predator, the great horned owl. When an owl discovers a tern colony, it will return to it relentlessly, night after night, to snatch and devour the chicks. The terns are completely defenseless against the owls after nightfall.

All the while, I had been enjoying Ian's slightly eccentric demeanor. He looks at you intently and speaks politely and precisely, while his eyes sparkle and flare with mad glee. I recognized that characteristically British trait of exhibiting to the world impeccable reserve while just managing to mask profound delight in that same world's inherent absurdity.

"Except for the owls, islands are a pretty safe place for terns," he continued.

Then came a curious, dark look. "But it's dangerous, you know, for the owls to travel to the islands. They'll travel only about one mile to reach them."

"Why's that?" I asked.

"Well, you see, owls' feathers are soft, designed for silent flight. The cost is that they don't shed water like regular feathers." Ian held his hands in front of his face, fingers nearly touching, and fanned them to imitate silent flight. His burning eyes locked on mine, conjuring for me the shadowy form of a great horned owl silently whizzing over the midnight-blue Bay, bent on bloodshed. "If the owl gets caught in the rain out on the islands," he continued ominously, "it will get waterlogged and become incapable of flying back to the mainland. If the gulls find it in the morning, they will drive it into the water and drown it." As he described the evil bird's death, I could see that, too: the sodden brown owl, flopping hopelessly in the water, harassed by the plunging gulls, its horrid bill snapping and tearing white breasts red, dying like a vampire in the cheerless gray predawn light.

"Owls," the scientist concluded, laughing, "do better on the mainland, eating cats."

"Cats?"

"Yes, cats. It's amazing how many house cats owls kill. Coyotes typically get blamed. I have a friend who studies great horned owls, and he told me that he once found eight cat collars scattered below a nest."

I wondered what other predators eat terns.

"A coyote got to Penikese one year, but luckily, it wasn't there when the terns were nesting. It eventually swam back to Nashawena. And rats can cause huge problems. One year a rat got onto Ram and did a lot of damage."

"Only one?" I asked.

"Yes, we were lucky it was only one. And sometimes a night heron will discover terns and start preying on them heavily. That's about it. But, wait— we do have an ant problem on Penikese. We haven't studied it much yet, but little red ants are getting into the tern eggs when they are hatching. And of course, let's not forget humans. We protect the terns from people, too."

IN THE PAST THIRTY YEARS, Ian Nisbet and the rest of the tern warriors have restored the terns on the Bay from a remnant population on just half of Bird Island to a thriving presence on all of Bird, Ram, and much of Penikese. "We've got the gulls completely off Ram and Bird," Ian told me. "They're still a problem only on parts of Penikese."

Ian, Lochin, and Tressa are now focusing their efforts on Muskeget, an island that lies between Martha's Vineyard and Nantucket. Like Penikese, Muskeget historically served as one of the terns' local breeding strongholds. The scientists hope eventually to restore the tern population to former levels there as well.

FROM THE TERNS' ANIMAL PREDATORS, we moved on to human threats. I wanted to know how a recent oil spill had affected nesting terns. In April 2003, the *Bouchard 120* spilled nearly 100,000 gallons of oil into Buzzards Bay.

"Ram got heavily oiled, Bird was lightly oiled," Ian told me. "That project is run by Carolyn Mostello. Ram had the largest nesting colony of roseates the previous year, so it was a real crisis. For about a month, in May, Carolyn's team tried to scare the returning terns away by flashing lights and shooting cannons at night."

I asked how the terns made out.

"Many of the birds returned to Bird Island to nest, where they were originally from. Some went to Penikese. The ones that stayed on Ram made out relatively okay."

According to the Oil Pollution Act, a parallel piece of legislation to the Superfund Act that specifically covers oil pollution, if oil is spilled, the responsible party needs to both clean it up *and* restore any natural resources that were damaged as a result of the spill. This could mean, for example, that the responsible party must fund programs to bring back tern populations or restore damaged beaches. To get the responsible party to pay up, however, there must be solid evidence of damage, and that can be produced only through scientific studies. Ian and his colleagues are completing the study of the damage that the *Bouchard 120* caused to Bay tern populations.

Other scientists are conducting similar studies to gauge the damage to other species impacted by the spill.

Ian Nisbet's tern study is being conducted for a group of trustees that includes two federal government officials—one from the National Oceanic and Atmospheric Association (NOAA), one from the United States Fish and Wildlife Service—and one state official from the Massachusetts Executive Office of Environmental Affairs. The trustees will use the results of Ian's study to justify damage claims against Bouchard Transportation Company. The scientific evidence will be evaluated by a joint assessment team consisting of the trustees and a consulting company, Entrix, Inc. Entrix represents Bouchard and its insurers, a British consortium of insurance underwriters, in the negotiation.

When I spoke with Ian, the main problems he faced were bureaucratic delays in issuing a contract. Bouchard's insurance company had to grant approval for the study, and Bouchard had to provide funding for it before Ian's team could move forward. Both the approval and the funding for the study were delayed until after most of the oil had disappeared and after the terns had finished breeding. Whether Bouchard and their insurers did this intentionally is unknown.

Whatever the reason for the delay, when Ian realized that the funding would not be made available for his team until it was too late, he put up the cash for it himself. He hired three veterinary medicine students from Tufts University to sample blood from and otherwise test the health of the terns. When we spoke, six months after the oil spill, five months after he proposed the tern study to the trustees, and three months after the students had completed the necessary fieldwork, a contract was finally being signed between Tufts Veterinary School and Entrix to fund the work. Personally, Ian was still eight thousand dollars in the hole.

I asked about the forthcoming study. I knew I was overstepping my bounds, but I couldn't control my curiosity.

"I can't yet disclose our findings," Ian replied cautiously. "What I can tell you, however, is that the birds we saw between fifteen and thirty-nine days after the oil spill were not physically affected but were physiologically affected."

I must have looked confused. "The oil suppressed their red blood cells," he quickly explained. "The birds were anemic. They experienced reasonably good breeding success, but probably not as much success as they would have had they not been exposed to the oil. The exposure may have resulted in all kinds of negative effects, including decreased vigor when raising their chicks. If you have anemia, you get fatigued very quickly. I suspect the parent birds may not have worked as hard to raise their chicks as they might have. Another possible effect we are studying is whether the oil exposure affected the adult terns' ability to survive over the winter."

"If you find that the oil impacted the roseates," I asked, "will their classification as an Endangered Species come into play?"

"If we discover there was damage to the roseates," he replied carefully, "the consequences will be more serious than if only the commons were impacted. That's all. I simply can't reveal any more information."

In March 2004, the U.S. Attorney's Office found Bouchard Transportation guilty of criminal negligence for the *Bouchard 120* oil spill in Buzzards Bay and levied a fine of approximately ten million dollars, the largest oil-spill fine in New England history. They ruled that the company had violated the Clean Water Act and the Migratory Bird Treaty Act by killing more than 450 birds, including at least sixteen protected species. The fine was in addition to the roughly forty million dollars Bouchard had already spent on cleanup and insurance. Nevertheless, the environmental community's reaction was mixed because the settlement failed to impose major new safety regulations on Bouchard, such as a ban on single-hulled barges, that would help prevent future oil spills. At the time of this writing, civil cases against Bouchard, which take into account the destruction of natural resources, and which could result in significant additional fines to the company, were pending. Ian Nisbet's team's tern study was not factored into the criminal settlement but will weigh heavily in the coming civil case brought against Bouchard by the federal government.

As I took leave of Ian Nisbet's sun-filled home on the marsh, I asked whether he considered the tern restoration project on Buzzards Bay to be a success. "One thing I must emphasize," he said, with a scientist's typical caution, "is that it takes a long time to get anything done around here." He nodded out the window at the Bay. "Twenty or thirty years to accomplish anything. When you work with tern populations, you need to take into account that the average age of a tern is ten years, while some live to twenty-five. But in general, the numbers of terns are up from when we started—twice the number of roseates, four or five times as many commons. The combination of getting rid of the gulls and controlling predators has been the key."

"It seems to me," I offered tentatively, "that there is an effort by the scientific community on the Bay to restore the environment here to its original state."

Ian laughed and his eyes twinkled. "That's what it's all about, isn't it? Return things to the way they were." Then, as the Scotsman retreated behind the closing door, he added, half in jest, "Just take the humans away and we'll be there."

THE BIRDS THAT YOU are most likely to see on Buzzards Bay in the winter months are sea ducks. Representatives of this group that are common to the area include common eider, bufflehead, common goldeneye, red-breasted merganser, and three species of scoters: black, surf, and white-winged. The red-breasted merganser, which, unique among its peers, is strictly a fish-eater, is especially plentiful.

In addition to sea ducks, other species of waterfowl commonly seen on Buzzards Bay in the winter months include two species of geese, Canada and brant; two species of loon, common and red-throated; two species of grebe, horned and red-necked; and two species of cormorant, great and double-crested. Both species of loons tend to stay offshore, diving for fish. Great cormorants replace the double-crested in the winter until about March, when the double-crested species reappears. Northern gannets might occasionally visit the Bay from more open waters nearby.

Common winter gull species include ring-billed, herring, and great black-backed, and an occasional Bonaparte's gull. Bonaparte's gulls lose their familiar black head in the winter, with only a black spot behind the eye remaining.

Although most shorebird species on the Bay migrate south for the winter, the sanderling and the dunlin remain. Sanderlings, the birds that skitter up and down the beach chasing waves, lose much of their coloring in winter and appear mostly white. Winter dunlins look similar to sanderlings, but they have a droopy bill and their plumage is darker on top.

In our marshes, the great blue heron can often be seen fishing quietly in ditches and saltwater creeks.

ON THE DAY I MADE my annual visit to the pond, the blinding glare of the low January sun was overwhelming. It blotted out the sky over the pond, exploded from the shimmering water on its surface, and radiated toward me in shafts through the bare, upright branches of a highbush blueberry. Out of that glare, like a mirage, emerged one thousand bobbing black heads, attached to a floating, rippling blanket of lesser scaup. The males of this species of duck display a dark head and tail that sandwich a body of elegant pin-striped gray, and a surprising powder-blue bill. The females are chestnut-brown with the white face blaze of a pony. This unexpected immensity of life was asleep, peacefully cocooned on a pond only a hundred yards—across the barrier beach—from the Atlantic surf and less than a mile from the busy center of Falmouth. Somehow, these avian winter visitors were able to enjoy warmth and slumber while floating in an icy bath blasted by noonday sunlight.

Each winter, like the ducks, I migrate to this salt pond in the heart of Falmouth to rest. I know that I will have little company besides the winter birds. The hush of the pond calms me, and the brilliant, crisp colors of the winter birds act as a powerful antidote to the sensory deprivation that marks the season.

Now an unseen signal had been passed, and the scaup were awake. Awakened scaup do a very unbirdlike thing—they purr and mew, like cats! And they splash wildly, like bluefish savaging a beachfront of bait. Eight buf-flehead ducks scudded around the raft of scaup—five black-and-white drakes and three drab gray hens with white cheek spots. The plump males, inviting a poke in the belly, pumped their heads and moved among the scat-tering females with the improbable speed of table-hockey figures. They seemed animated purely by pride, these roosters on the pond—indeed, they are water cocks. Their formal black-and-white heads looked inflated, rigid yet flexible, like plastic toys blown up with a bicycle pump. The white of their hoods and bodies is shocking, and decidedly not of New England. It belongs, rather, to the far north where the birds nest. It is the dazzling hue of the arctic fox and the snowshoe hare.

Away from the glare, in the damp tangle beside the pond, a furtive scratching in the shadows led my eye to the dusky silhouette of a white-throated sparrow. This short bird with deep patrician body boasts a white throat patch, a dab of yellow in front of its eye, and a black-and-white-striped cap. Focused, unaware of my presence, it tossed leaf litter riotously into the air with a seesawing motion of head and tail in its search for food.

Above the pond, the shoreline vegetation of yellow grass, bare blueberry, and lordly tupelo was replaced by scrub oaks draped with sea-green moss, leaning black cherries, rusted-green cedars, purple jack pines, and bouncing green arcs of insatiable briar. Everywhere, trunks and branches were broken, smashed, and jammed, and through it all wove the binding thread of countless hanging vines. Here lay the hunting grounds of the chickadee nation. At close range, these familiar, black-capped acrobats reveal a subtle olive back and chestnut belly. Hunting the tangle with mechanical precision, they hopped, twisted, and seemingly defied equilibrium by ratcheting around branches at will. They moved quietly and hurriedly with jerky motions, like actors in an old silent film.

Descending to the marsh that flanks the pond, my eye was drawn once again to the pond's surface as a belted kingfisher plunged precipitously down toward the scaup, still dominating the waterscape with sheer mass. Clothed in a dapper, slate-blue jacket and vest, the kingfisher is a flying, crested head—a true "jug head." A fisherman, it uses this apparent deformity to smash the surface of the water when it dives to spear a fish with its bill.

On a raised platform at the center of the pond, an ignoble herring gull slouched in the squalor of sticks that had been the throne of a noble osprey. Below, twelve more of its kind stood on a sandbar, motionless, expectant, as if anticipating the end of the world. Closer to the shoreline, a red-breasted merganser, a long, low canoe of a duck, lowered its head to preen its rusty breast and pierced the blue winter sky with its glossy green, spiked crest.

On the far shore of the pond, framed against the distant ocean surf, a northern harrier, or marsh hawk, circled, raked in its wings, and dropped like an anchor into the golden grass. Erupting upward momentarily, it fluttered and tilted only inches above the ground, struggling to maintain its balance as it tracked the movements of its escaped prey. The display begged the question: Would this creature be more efficient wingless, hounding its lunch like a weasel through the dense, rotting tunnels of the marsh?

Over the entire panorama of the salt pond hung a comforting shroud of peace and well-being. Watching the birds' behavior, I sensed an unspoken acceptance in them, a quiet resolve, a "biding of time." Maybe the quietly routine behavior of the birds was in keeping with the subdued character of the season. Or perhaps, like me, on this particular afternoon these birds were just content to relax and enjoy the silence and sunlight of a mild winter's day.

TODAY, BIRD HABITATS on Buzzards Bay are threatened by development, pesticides, and oil spills. In addition, wind turbines—a technology that Mass Audubon is currently focused on—might pose a threat to Nantucket Sound bird populations and, someday, Bay populations as well. Cape Wind, a private developer, has proposed the Sound as the site of a massive wind farm. Buzzards Bay, off Gunning Point in Falmouth, was also proposed as a site, but Winergy LLC, the developer, withdrew its proposal. Winergy cited local opposition as their reason, but more likely their decision was related to the difficulties of getting such a project approved anywhere in state coastal waters. All of Buzzards Bay is considered state waters, and the state has conferred many usage rights to the coastal towns, so any such project requires compliance with extensive state and local permitting. In contrast, the wind farm proposed for Nantucket Sound would be built in federal waters, so it would require only a federal wetland-filling permit to move forward. According to the Coalition for Buzzards Bay, a volunteer advocacy group, the fact that the Bay lies in state waters may make it difficult for an offshore wind farm to be sited here under today's laws.

Simon Perkins, of Mass Audubon and head of the Christmas Bird Count in the state, told me that nobody really knows the extent to which wind turbines threaten birds. "All we know is that tall structures pose a threat to birds, and the taller the structure, the greater the threat."

Perkins is concerned that no one has carefully studied the relationship between turbines and birds, even in Europe, where large wind farms have been in use for some time. We do know that birds can avoid the turbines in the daytime under clear weather conditions and that they hit them at night and during inclement weather conditions, such as fog or storms. Researchers find it difficult to study this phenomenon because during storms nobody is around to see what's going on, and by the time the storms pass, the evidence—bird carcasses—has washed away.

Another obstacle to studying the impact of wind turbines, or any threat, on bird populations is that there is seldom good baseline population data available. The numbers of birds residing on Buzzards Bay during any given year are largely a mystery. This is important, because if we don't know how many individuals of each bird species are present in a given area, it is impossible to determine how many might have succumbed to a particular environmental event, such as an oil spill. Mass Audubon hopes to improve this situation, at least for Nantucket Sound, where the group is currently assessing winter waterfowl populations. Although Mass Audubon has no immediate plans to do the same for Buzzards Bay, it might someday be able to extrapolate the population data generated from the Sound to the Bay.

The reason that Mass Audubon has no plans to conduct similar population studies on Buzzards Bay has to do with the nature of the primary environmental threat to bird populations here—oil spills. The incredibly depressing fact is that people expect spills. As Simon Perkins put it, "Oil and the whole industry around it is nothing new. People are used to hearing about oil spills. They're jaded." And that makes getting yet another baseline population study funded a tough proposition. In contrast, wind energy is new to our area, it's controversial, and people are currently seeking to learn all they can about its energy-producing potential and its possible effects on the environment. Funding dollars for research studies follow. It's also difficult to generate support for research connected to oil spills because they are unpredictable. Nobody knows when another oil spill will occur, what its size will be, or the extent of the damage it will cause. In contrast, proposed wind farms have a known construction date and scope.

Mass Audubon was very involved in the cleanup after the *Bouchard 120* oil spill because it owns land around Allens Pond and holds a conservation easement on Barney's Joy Beach in South Dartmouth, two areas that were plastered with oil. I asked Perkins how the *Bouchard 120* spill affected birds wintering on the Bay.

"Basically, all the winter bird species that had yet to leave by April were impacted," he replied. "The common and red-throated loons took the brunt of it. But individuals from virtually every wintering species were affected. Many eiders, scoters, red-necked grebes, and horned grebes present at the time were oiled. Unfortunately, we don't know the percentage of the birds oiled from each species because of the lack of precise baseline data."

I personally witnessed two oiled birds after the spill. One, a blackened female common eider near Salter's Point, wobbled on the rocks of the shoreline and paddled unsteadily away as I tried to approach her. The other was a tar-black cormorant carcass slumped in the marsh on Bassets Island, a blood-filled socket remaining where its head had been gnawed away by an opportunistic predator.

"Does cleaning the oiled birds work?"

"We got out of the business," Perkins explained carefully, "because the survival rate of oiled birds is very low. Cleaning is intended more for the mental health of humans than it is for birds. The process is very labor-intensive, and it makes little sense to allocate resources after the fact. Organizations are better off focusing on things such as sponsoring legislation. If you're cleaning birds, it's too late. The horse is out of the barn by then."

THE HORSE IS OUT of the barn by then." After I hung up the phone with Simon Perkins, I got depressed. In my mind's eye, the blue expanse of the Bay sparkled. I watched an endless procession of hazy, towering oil barges, their scrappy tugs laboring far out in front of them, ghosting up the shoreline of the Elizabeths towards the Canal. Each year, according to the Army Corps of Engineers, two billion gallons of oil are transported through Buzzards Bay. Most of it is shipped in single-hulled barges like the *Bouchard 120*, ships that are notoriously unable to prevent spills when damaged. For example, over two-thirds of the barges that Bouchard Transportation routinely uses to ship huge quantities of oil through the Bay have single hulls. Ironically, there is a federal law that requires double hulls, but it was watered down to protect the profits of the shipping companies. They were given until 2015 to fully comply with the legislation. That is, they have until then unless somebody can find a way to shorten that time frame. Combine this lack of double-hulled vessels with the fact that Buzzards

Bay is a relatively shallow body of water, and you're looking at a major environmental disaster in the making. It appears that our barn door is very poorly secured.

Out of the torn belly of the *Bouchard 120* bucked and twisted one spooked horse—approximately 100,000 gallons. The spill had a significant impact on the ecology and economy of the Bay. Seabirds died. Beaches closed. Shellfish were contaminated, and shellfishermen were put out of work. Now consider that when the *Argo Merchant* broke apart on the Nantucket shoals in 1976, it gushed 7.6 million gallons of oil into the surrounding waters. That's *seven million, six hundred thousand gallons.* There are fleets of *Argo Merchants*—entire herds of horses—in our barn. How long until they get out? And what will happen to our "stately sound" when they do? For the sake of the Bay, we must demand the use of double hulls now. Let's secure our barn door before it's too late.

Wildlife

So the rest of the day we spent in trading with them for Furres,

which are Beavers, Luzernes, marterns, Otters, Wild-cat skinnes

very large and deepe Furre, blacke Foxes, Conie skinnes, of the

color of our Hares, but somewhat lesse, Deere skins very large,

Seale skinnes, and other beasts skinnes to us unknowen.

—BRERETON, ON THE ANIMAL SKINS THE NATIVE AMERICANS ON THE BAY
BROUGHT TO TRADE WITH THE ENGLISHMEN

THE WILDLIFE FOUND around Buzzards Bay today, although obviously not as plentiful or varied as in Gosnold's day, is still remarkably abundant. Some animal species that were uncommon, such as harbor seals, have now increased to such an extent that some people consider them to be nuisances, raising concerns over how—or even if—we can coexist with them. Species that were either purposefully or accidentally introduced, such as rainbow trout, today spur lively debates among local biologists about the rights of alien versus native species. Still other creatures, such as the diamondback terrapin, are so uncommon or secretive that they remain, in Brereton's words, "beasts unknowen" to most of us.

THE LLOYD CENTER for Environmental Studies is housed in a contemporary, Southwestern-style building that caps a bluff over the mouth of the Slocums River in South Dartmouth. It was originally built as a private home. When I first saw it, I thought, Why would anyone build this house here, on Buzzards Bay? But by the time I left, I was thinking, Why would anyone ever move out? The Lloyd Center offers one of the best views of the Bay you will ever experience.

It was a chilly morning in late March, and I had come to the center to talk with the research director, Marc Mello, about harbor seals. Marc hangs out in a sun-filled observatory on the third floor. He's got a telescope that he uses to watch seals hauled out, or lying, on rocks off Mishaum Point. On the day I met him, if Marc Mello had been any mellower, I would have had to crank him up with one handle of his handlebar moustache, like an old prop plane. His sedate appearance was deceptive, however; I found his mind to be as vigorous as any other scientist's. It might be that Marc's demeanor reflects the practical realities of his vocation. He likes to hunt insects in the pine barrens at night. His e-mail name is Mothman.

The center's staff keep fish that were captured nearby in tanks in their basement for public viewing. In addition to familiar local representatives such as scup, their collection also boasts a remarkable selection of tropical fish. The explanation for this pleasant surprise is that during hot summers warm water eddies spin off the broad oceanic river of the Gulf Stream and carry these southern treasures into Buzzards Bay. Places like Horseneck Beach can be covered by man-of-wars—stinging tropical jellyfish—and the Westport River often teems with exotic fish species.

The center's tropical fish collection includes several species of groupers: striking blacks, pretty white snowies, and the nags, dull, cream-colored, and peppered with red dots. Other tanks are animated by spotted, green coronet fish, spotfin butterfly fish, jack crevalle, sergeant major fish, lizard fish with reptilian snouts and teeth, big eye, and last but not least, the magical seahorses that sometimes show up in the Westport River in surprising numbers, clinging to beds of eelgrass. The staff also keep some freaks down in the basement, including a hermaphroditic lobster. Hermaphrodites boast both male and female sex organs. "It's rarer than even a blue lobster," Marc told me proudly. "We used to have a blue lobster. Actually, it was half blue—split lengthwise down the middle, blue on one side, normal on the other."

Suspended from the ceiling beside the main staircase is the splendid skeleton of a seventeen-foot pilot whale, the remains of a female found washed up on Mishaum Point. She was so old when she died that she had only one tooth left. Restored by students to a gleaming white masterpiece, the skeleton was not always such a pleasure to behold. "The whale got cut up into pieces and left in a pile of manure out back," Marc explained.

"That must have smelled great," I commented.

"Actually, it wasn't that bad—things left in manure don't smell," he replied.

The tide was dropping, and the seals off Mishaum were just becoming visible from Marc's observatory. I could see two animals cresting offshore boulders. I knew I had to get closer.

HARBOR SEALS ARE of the order Carnivora, a scientific classification that groups them with bears, raccoons, dogs, weasels, and otters. Their Latin name, *Phoca vitulina*, means "sea calf" or "sea dog." They are of the suborder Pinnipedia, which means "fin foot," a group that includes seals, sea lions, and walruses.

Modern harbor seals appeared in the North Pacific two to three million years ago when the Bering Strait formed. Today, harbor seals are widely distributed throughout the North Pacific and North Atlantic Oceans. Scientists estimate their worldwide population at about half a million animals, with fifty thousand to one hundred thousand inhabiting the western Atlantic from Greenland to the central United States.

Research suggests that harbor seals can live up to thirty years in the wild. Males grow to six and a half feet and weigh up to 375 pounds. Females reach about five and a half feet and weigh up to 330 pounds. Although harbor seals range in coloring from light gray to black, the animals found on Buzzards Bay generally appear gray-brown. They have webbed limbs; the front ones carry blunt claws, the rear, used to propel the animal through the water, look like fans when spread. They have large eyes that can see in dark, murky water. They use their long whiskers, which grow from their upper lip, to sense vibrations under water, particularly at night or in deep, dark waters. Harbor seals can dive to three hundred feet deep and swim twelve miles per hour. They can stay underwater for half an hour but generally do so for less than ten minutes. They sleep on land or in the water. Their method of sleeping in water is called bottling, with just their head visible, like a drifting bottle. They generally don't make any noise, except when they feel threatened, when they may growl, hiss, snort, or sneeze.

Harbor seals have a highly variable diet, depending on what is available in a particular season and location. On Buzzards Bay, this means prey species commonly found from fall until spring around the Elizabeth Islands, the seals' main haunt. Mainly, they eat squid, shellfish, crustaceans, and a wide variety of fish species. They consume, on average, ten to eighteen pounds of food each day.

Each year harbor seals return to the same breeding grounds. Pups are born well developed and fully capable of swimming and following their mothers. They first learn to catch shrimp and crabs, then graduate to fish. Although pups tend to stick close to adults, their mortality can reach 30 percent in the first year. Pups may be abandoned, starve, wash away in storms, or die of disease or injury.

Locally, harbor seals have no natural predators. With the exception of coyotes, which may occasionally take a sick animal, their population on the Bay is affected only by minor outbreaks of disease. They are most notably susceptible to the flu virus and a virus similar to canine distemper. Sometimes they become entangled in fishing nets and drown or fall victim to marine debris, such as packaging materials. Plastic can block their digestive tract or cause a "full" signal to be sent to their brains, causing them to stop eating.

In the 1900s, harbor seals were hunted by fur traders who prized the fur of pups less than one month old. Commercial fishermen, who often view seals as competitors, killed them at their haul-out sites (gathering places where the seals typically rested). In the late 1800s, there was a bounty placed on their heads by both Maine and Massachusetts. Maine lifted its bounty in 1905. In Massachusetts, you got five dollars for every seal nose you brought in until 1962.

Today, harbor seals are protected from most human predation. The big break for the species came with the passage of the Marine Mammal Protection Act (MMPA) of 1972, which was reauthorized and amended in 1994. According to the MMPA, it is illegal to hunt or harass any marine mammal in United States waters. Basically, you aren't allowed to interact with the animals unless you have a good reason to and carry a permit. The National Oceanic and Atmospheric Association (NOAA) adheres to the following policy regarding human interactions with wild marine mammals:

"Interacting with wild marine mammals should not be attempted and viewing marine mammals must be conducted in a manner that does not harass the animals. NOAA Fisheries cannot support . . . activities that involve closely approaching, interacting or attempting to interact with whales, dolphins, porpoises, seals or sea lions in the wild. This includes attempting to swim with, pet, touch, or elicit a reaction from the animals." It is fortunate for us that these restrictions exist, particularly for harbor seals. If harassed, the seals can deliver a very nasty bite. And, because their mouths have a high bacteria count, the bite of a harbor seal can result in a bad infection. As Marc Mello puts it, "I tell people that harbor seals look cute until they are locked onto your arm."

Thanks to the Marine Mammal Protection Act, the harbor seal is now the most abundant marine mammal in New England and the only one commonly found in Buzzards Bay. Forty or fifty years ago, a seal was a rarity on the Bay. Now there are hundreds. The Buzzards Bay Project (part of the Massachusetts Executive Office of Environmental Affairs) counted three to four hundred in the late 1980s, and their population has increased steadily since then. Many of the seals in the Bay are younger animals, as mature seals are less migratory, and tend to stay in established territories to the north. You can find harbor seals in Buzzards Bay from mid-October until early May, when they leave for the coasts of Maine and Canada to breed. Breeding season runs from mid-May to early July. If you see a seal here in the summer, it is probably injured or a gray seal. Gray seals occasionally visit from breeding colonies on Monomoy and Nantucket.

Harbor seals are scattered around the Bay, at Seal Rocks in Cataumet, at the mouth of the Westport River, and at Round Hill in South Dartmouth. About fourteen live in the vicinity of the Lloyd Center. The largest concentrations in the Bay, however, are found around the Elizabeth Islands. There, the most popular haul-out spots are Gull Island, off Penikese, where several hundred seals can typically be found basking in the sun, and Pease Ledge, off Cuttyhunk. Both of these areas essentially disappear at high tide.

In general, you will find seals hauled out on low-lying ledges, rocks, or deserted beaches. They choose low rocks because, unlike sea lions, they are uncoordinated on land and have trouble clambering up onto high ones. Seals typically haul out during the afternoon but may do so at any time of day or night. From a distance, a hauled-out seal looks exactly like a rotten banana, curved up smilelike, balanced on the surface of the Bay. While haul-out sites at northern breeding grounds are used as rookeries, the seals you see hauled out on the Bay are generally resting. They tend to use one or two sites regularly. Gathering at a haul-out site is about the only social behavior seals exhibit; typically they are solitary creatures. They keep their distance from one another even when hauled out, preferring a few feet or more of personal space. They often respond with aggression if another seal touches them and they become less and less tolerant of physical contact as they mature. It's important not to disturb seals at haul-out sites. Studies show that human disturbances can have a major effect on haul-out numbers, and if disturbances are severe the seals may abandon a site altogether.

I WAS CROUCHED on a boulder on Mishaum Point, watching seals. On the walk out, I had been hurried along by a freezing, twenty-mile-per-hour wind at my back. The Bay was churning with aqua-green waves and whitecaps. As I dropped into the lee on the west side of the point, conditions changed instantly. The wind quieted, it was warm, and the Bay stretched away, a placid sheet of azure blue.

For my part, I was burned out, numb with stress. The country was on the verge of war with Iraq. The headline of the *New Bedford Standard Times* I had picked up that morning announced, "Hussein Rejects Ultimatum." In response to George W. Bush's demand that Saddam Hussein get out or face being run out of his country, the dictator had flatly refused to back down. A day earlier, Saddam had predicted, "The mothers and wives of American servicemen would cry tears of blood." That morning, the man entering the convenience store in front of me had held the door, a rare gesture—but one of many that would become commonplace as the nation became galvanized by the onset of war. I went to Mishaum because I knew that a deserted Buzzards Bay beach was the perfect antidote to the tension that gripped the land.

In front of me, a crescent of fifteen rocks swept away from the point toward the mouth of the Little River. The first rock of this mini-archipelago lay about a hundred yards offshore, making meaningful observation possible only through my field glasses, and placing me—I hoped—well within the stringent boundaries of the Marine Mammal Protection Act. I could see twenty-one seals congregated on ten of the rocks, which had emerged above the ebbing tide. Seven of the animals rested singly. Two of the rocks held three seals, and one large boulder held seven. The animals were gray-brown, with whitish undersides. They all appeared to be adults, with the exception of one baby—a small, fuzzy brown lump, only a couple of feet long—that was part of the group of three. The big rock holding the largest group of seals stood far out in the basin, in the middle of the crescent. Tapering into the water at one end, and rising to nearly three feet above the waterline at the other, the boulder looked as if it had a stringer of trout casually draped over it. On the high square end, two large, sleeping seals lay on their sides facing me, whitish underbellies exposed, four flippers jutting out. From underneath, they looked remarkably like woodchucks or fat gray squirrels struck dead on the roadside. The singles were all resting in the classic upturned-banana pose. One of them, occupying a rock that was flush with the waterline, appeared to be lying on top of the water. Many of the seals were sleeping on their sides. Others were alert, sitting up with their heads raised, like dogs. The lone individual on the rock closest to the shore appeared to be nervous; it kept turning its head toward land.

The seals were primarily motionless. Occasionally, one would slowly raise or lower a fore flipper. Once or twice, an animal lurched its way up a rock on its belly, jerking first its head up, then its tail flippers. Sometimes one would separate its back flippers and raise them aloft, stretching. About the place and the languid forms there hung a comforting weightedness of peace and solitude. Above me the sky was a distant, very pale blue. The entire archipelago and the seals it harbored were awash in shimmering, dancing diamonds of sunlight. A few wet seals reflected the light as if they had mirrors strapped to their backs.

Beyond the archipelago, on the other side of the basin, sprawled the creamy beaches of Demarest Lloyd State Park and Barney's Joy Beach. To the north, a solitary, massive cedar-shingled barn sat on countless empty acres of tan, undulating grassland. To the southwest lay the entrance to the Bay and, beyond that, the Atlantic. With the exception of the snoozing seals, a few wheeling herring gulls, and a small flock of goldeneyes putting around near the rocks, the entire basin was empty. The quiet was intense, interrupted only by the subdued pounding of the surf against the other side of the point and the occasional ringing of a tradesman's hammer readying a summer property for the coming season. No ugly oil politics can find me here, I thought to myself. There are no frightening foreign dictators, no sand-storms, no poison gas, no tears of blood. This was the best of Buzzards Bay: pristine, remote, timeless, untouchable.

I was surprised to find no seals lying on the beach. The fifty-foot swath of shoreline was covered with rocks. And these weren't just rocks: they were the kind of boulders that you build jetties from. It was as if God's own dump truck had unloaded on this half-mile of coastline. But other than the seals safely ensconced on the water-bound rocks offshore, no seals were in sight.

I began to realize that I was developing a bond with the seals. They're like Yankees, I theorized. They're playful when young, but they often end up curmudgeons. They treasure their personal space. They hate to be touched, even by their own. (I don't even like for my family members to hug me.) Like me, they feel most comfortable on a deserted stretch of beach. I envied their lifestyle. By the middle of May, when the crowds of human tourists start to arrive, the seals are well on their way to some remote northern coastline. Maybe I could go with them, I thought. I'm a good swimmer. But how would I cut across all the boat traffic at the mouth of Boston Harbor? The tiny cove next to the seals' archipelago would fill up with boats soon. For now, though, the seals owned this basin. They were unmolested by humans. They were safe.

Reluctantly, I conceded that it was time to go. I picked my way back along a modest ribbon of beach above the boulders. The thin strip was an exquisite sea carpet, woven of tiny stones and pink slipper shells in equal measure. I paused to examine lobster buoys and Canada geese feathers that lay scattered about. I trudged along more and more slowly. In the end, I too surrendered to the spell that the warm spring sunshine cast. Like my new marine friends, I draped my body over a warm, low boulder. My energy and my stress slipped away, and I too dozed for awhile. Later that evening, as I sat in my living room, my memories of those shimmering diamonds of sunlight morphed into the silver snowfall of a static-filled news broadcast. White flashes exploded in the city of Baghdad. The black smoke of oil-well fires rose into the air.

As it turned out, the seemingly impenetrable sanctity of the basin—what seemed a perfect refuge from the problems of the modern world—proved to be an illusion. If I could have divined the future that day, I would have told the seals to migrate early. For just a few weeks later, the Devil came to Mishaum Point. He arrived in the guise of oil spilled from Bouchard Transportation Company's *Bouchard 120*. On that April night, the waters off Mishaum began to bubble and hiss. The Dark One, lithe, muscled, glowing faintly crimson in the moonlight, waded ashore unseen. He rushed from the Bay, laboring, his arms and torso swinging, like a bather struggling to reach the beach through waist-deep water. Between belches of salt water, his laughter came in high-pitched, cackling bursts. Reaching the cobbled shore, he lurched forward onto all fours and retched a revolting vomit, as black as sin, down a full mile and a half of shoreline. Panting and drooling black saliva, he rotated his horned head and cast a menacing look at the houses on the point. Then he rose and, with a triumphant snarl, bounded back into the Bay. Next stop, Barney's Joy Beach.

The haul-out area of Mishaum Point's seal colony was at the epicenter of the *Bouchard 120* oil spill. Afterward, I couldn't bring myself to go back. I did see photos of the effects of the tragedy, though, on the Buzzard Bay Project's Web site. Areas of my rocky point were now drenched in oil: several gallons per linear foot. According to local reports, the seals on the tiny archipelago were blackened with oil. Later, I heard that some seals in other parts of the Bay had migrated before the *Bouchard 120* spill. I only hope that some of the seals I had seen that day at Mishaum had already gone, too.

I HAVE NEVER SEEN a diamondback terrapin. That is, I was sure I had never seen one until I talked to Bob Prescott at the Mass Audubon Wellfleet Bay Wildlife Sanctuary, after which I realized I surely had. A diamondback in the Bay looks like a swimming thumb. If you extend your arm in front of you and make the thumbs-up sign, then swing your arm to one side, your thumb closely resembles what you would have seen moving across the surface of the Bay if you had unknowingly spotted the turtle.

I realized that I'd seen a diamondback a few years back, while fishing with my young nieces near the outflow of a salt pond on the west side of the Bay. I saw—for just a few seconds, out of the corner of my eye—a swimming thumb. It had the wobbly, paddling motion that characterizes a swimming turtle. It was moving quickly away from me, out into the gentle swells. For an instant I was sure that a tiny, dime store turtle had been watching me—

but no, that was clearly impossible. I dismissed the incident and went back to watching my little nieces cast their lines. It wasn't until years later, after talking to Bob Prescott, that I realized what I had seen. Prescott explained that diamondbacks are very secretive and have learned to avoid human beings. He also told me that the swimming-thumb behavior I had witnessed is called snorkeling.

The diamondback terrapin is named for the diamond patterns on its shell. The word *terrapin* is derived from the Algonquin word *torope*, which is what Native Americans called several different kinds of aquatic turtles. The diamondback is an exceedingly handsome turtle. On young turtles, the diamond-shaped plates, called scutes, are inscribed with deep growth rings. As the turtles age, the scutes become smoother. The scutes, complete with growth rings, look like this:

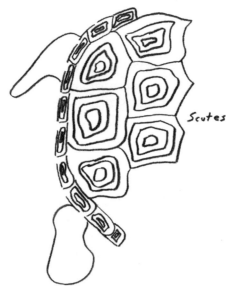

Scutes

The terrapin's top shell, or carapace, ranges in color from light brown to greenish-gray to black. Its shorter bottom shell, the plastron, is more color-ful, ranging from yellow to olive or orange. The turtle's body is an ash gray or buff color and prominently marked with black spots or dashes. The diamondback is considered a moderate-sized turtle, with the carapace of females reaching around eight or nine inches and the carapace of males, five or six. The larger females also tend to be lighter-skinned and more richly patterned.

Diamondbacks often grow much darker as they age and lose their skin patterns. Females in our area reach sexual maturity at about eight years and males at about three. Biologists believe that terrapins typically live up to twenty years in the wild. A few individuals in the Wellfleet population are known to be at least forty years old. Diamondbacks have large heads, strong, armored jaws, and large, webbed hind feet. Their large heads and strong jaws enable them to eat hard-shelled prey, including clams, mussels, snails, and crabs. They also eat dead fish, some plants, and probably anything else they can get hold of.

Diamondbacks live mostly in salt marshes. They also like other quiet salt-water environments, such as shallow bays and estuaries, although they are quite capable of negotiating the open waters of the Bay. Diamondback terrapins are the only turtles in the United States that live in the brackish water zone between fresh water and salt. Their natural range extends along the Atlantic and Gulf coasts from Cape Cod to Texas, with Cape Cod being the northern extreme. Our terrapins tend to be smaller than their southern cousins because their active season—less than six months—is very short.

Diamondbacks spend their days feeding in marshes or baking in the sun on the banks of tidal creeks. At night they bury themselves in the mud. They are active on Buzzards Bay from March through November. In the winter they brumate—that is, hibernate—either resting on the creek bottom or burying themselves in the mud near the high-tide mark of creek banks or under the banks. The only other time the turtles leave the water is to nest, in June and again in July. They nest mostly during the day and sometimes at night, in sandy areas above the high-tide mark, laying twelve to twenty pinkish-white eggs in a six-inch-deep hole. About three months later, the quarter-sized hatchlings scramble and tumble down the beach into the marsh. Diamondbacks spend their first few years of life buried under mats of tidal wrack and debris.

An aura of mystery rivaling that of Bigfoot attends the diamondbacks on Buzzards Bay. They are not a plentiful species; in many of their habitats, nobody even knows they're there. And there is good reason for their scarcity and secretiveness. The diamondback has the unenviable distinction of being the turtle of turtle soup fame. In the late 1800s and early 1900s, the terrapins were considered a culinary delicacy and were regularly served in turtle soup in the finest restaurants on the East Coast. The terrapin trade reached its peak here just before World War II. The turtles were considered such a gourmet item that they were sold wholesale for a dollar a piece. Many diamondback populations near coastal cities were all but wiped out. Around 1910, from Pleasant Bay in Chatham alone, thousands of turtles were barreled annually and sent to New York and Boston. In addition, while the restaurant trade is generally blamed for the decimation of the species in Massachusetts, the pet trade, which still traffics in diamondbacks, and the destruction of salt marshes have also contributed to their decline. Once hunted to the verge of biological twilight, the diamondback terrapin is now protected by inclusion on the Massachusetts List of Endangered, Threatened, and Special Concern Species (the state version of the federal Endangered Species list).

Diamondbacks are perhaps best known in the South. In Maryland, the species is the state reptile and also the mascot for the state university. They are still harvested for food on Chesapeake Bay. It appears that diamondback terrapins existed on Buzzards Bay historically, although probably always in fewer numbers than in the South. After studying the turtles for many years, Dr. James D. Lazell wrote in *This Broken Archipelago: Cape Cod and the Islands, Amphibians, and Reptiles*: "One thing I will guarantee . . . diamondback terrapins are native to Massachusetts."

Diamondback populations are scattered around Cape Cod in isolated colonies, from the entrance of the Bay all the way out to Wellfleet. This sporadic occurrence of the species might reflect a slow recovery from the restaurant trade, but evidence also suggests that it has always been this way. In his book, Lazell notes that populations of the terrapins were scattered inextricably about the Bay and Cape Cod. Today, scientists still don't know all the factors that limit local diamondback populations. Food, which is generally abundant, doesn't appear to influence colony distribution. Neither does climate. Wellfleet Bay, located at the northernmost boundary of the terrapins' range, paradoxically boasts Massachusetts' largest population, estimated at roughly five thousand individuals.

The largest populations of diamondbacks on Buzzards Bay live on the west side. There are colonies in the Slocums River, Allens Pond, Mattapoisett, Marion, and Wareham. Curiously, the species has never colonized the islands. If you ask people on the Elizabeth Islands, Martha's Vineyard, or Nantucket about the turtles, no one's ever heard of their presence on the islands. On the Cape, significant populations of diamondbacks have flourished in Barnstable Harbor, the Great Marsh, and Pleasant Bay in Chatham. Lazell's book mentions several reports of sightings in Falmouth marshes, Sandwich, Bourne, and Mashpee. He records that a diamondback was presented to the Woods Hole aquarium in 1974, but it was released without being photographed. Lazell is skeptical of these reports, equating them with sightings of the Loch Ness Monster. The naturalist expresses frustration and confusion in regard to the gaps in his species' distribution maps, noting that many seemingly ideal habitats go turtleless. In the end, Lazell attributes some of these absences to people simply overlooking the secretive reptiles.

Lazell's hunch may be right. Today, Don Lewis, a local expert on the reptiles, claims that whenever he has found suitable habitat on Buzzards Bay or Cape Cod, he has found terrapins. You simply need to be an expert to find them. Even the terrapins around the Lloyd Center—where they make a habit of noticing such things—went unnoticed until a couple of years ago. The turtles were discovered, happily, by kids. Students at a natural history day camp, the kids were participating in a standard exercise at the mouth of the Slocums River called "What I Found in Two Meters of Marshland." At the conclusion of the activity, the budding naturalists called out their findings: "I found two fiddler crabs, a quahog shell, and a mussel." "I've got two fiddler crabs, a quahog shell, and a minnow." "I have two fiddler crabs, a quahog shell, a turtle, an oyster shell. . . . " "*What?*" shrieked the counselor. "Back up—a *turtle?!*" And that was the beginning. Today, the Buttonwood Zoo in New Bedford, other conservation groups, and the students at Tabor Academy are actively monitoring the threatened diamondback populations around the Bay. They are always happy to hear about new sightings.

A dark secret haunts the diamondback terrapins that make their home on Buzzards Bay. It would appear that they are, most horribly, mongrels. Our turtles simply look different from the purebloods out in Wellfleet, and they're smaller than the Wellfleet specimens, which can grow to a foot long. Bob Prescott speculates that Buzzards Bay diamondbacks are smaller because they are younger. But the true story, which can still incense certain members of the local biological community, is this. One warm spring morning in 1968, James G. Hoff, a scientist at Southeastern Massachusetts

University in North Dartmouth (now the University of Massachusetts Dartmouth), rose from his bed and decided this was the day. He got in his car and headed down to southern New Jersey. When he got there, he loaded up his trunk with a hundred diamondback terrapins. Then he took the turtles back to Buzzards Bay and released them. When, four years later, he proudly announced what he had done, he received a deluge of criticism from the local scientific community. Lazell himself brands the act "one of the great biological travesties of our region." The concern was, and apparently still is, that the introduced turtles would interbreed with local populations, disturb natural patterns of genetic variation, and produce offspring poorly adapted to the Bay environment. As justification for his act, Hoff insisted that diamondbacks were never native to the Bay, and that any previously introduced populations had been rendered extinct by the turtle soup craze. Local biologists didn't want to hear it, and they hung him out to dry. Incredibly, today there are plans in the works to use DNA testing to determine once and for all if our terrapins are pure-bloods or, as suspected, only lowly mongrels.

The handsome, reclusive diamondback, rescued from the soup pot, faces new challenges today. Pollution in our estuaries is one. Some scientists use the turtle as an indicator species to gauge environmental quality because it doesn't appear to tolerate polluted water. An indicator species is the canary in the coal mine; it's the first to disappear when an environment is degraded. The terrapins also get run over by cars when they cross roads to look for suitable nesting areas. They get minced up by boat propellers. Nationally, the biggest threat to the species might be the crab pots used to catch blue crabs, which drown the turtles. Lobster pots can kill them, too, but generally only if the pots are set in shallow waters. In the Chesapeake Bay blue crab fishery, crabbers successfully avoid trapping the turtles by using a "terrapin excluder," a device attached to the entrance of a crab pot that blocks the passage of a turtle's shell.

Recently, a massive die-off of local terrapins occurred at the Fox Island Wildlife Management Area at Blackfish Creek in Wellfleet. In the winter of 1999 – 2000, and again in the winter of 2000 – 2001, more than one hundred turtles died. They were ensnared and drowned in several nets that became lodged in the channels leading into the marshes. The nets—plastic, lightweight, similar to garden netting—were castoffs from local aquaculture operations. The nets proved especially deadly in Wellfleet; because of the high tidal range there, the turtles are swept in and out of the marshes, through the channels, with each tide. The nets were there to intercept them. A cooperative cleanup effort by environmentalists and shellfishermen put an end to the problem. In all areas throughout the terrapin's range, however, lost or discarded netting remains a major threat.

Lawns near the water also doom the diamondback. According to Bob Prescott, "The turtles don't mind digging through bark mulch or peat moss to nest, but they won't dig through grass." If you live near the Bay and want to help the turtles, Prescott recommends digging a small sandy pit in your lawn. "They're terrapin magnets," he claims. The turtles will scurry up to half a mile from the beach to take advantage of your patch. You can even land-scape it with dune-loving, herbaceous plants—anything but beach grass. If you see a diamondback digging a nest, in your patch or anywhere else, you can help protect the baby turtles from predators such as raccoons, muskrats, skunks, and crows by surrounding it with temporary fencing. If you don't have fencing, you can make do with a milk crate or a quahog basket.

If you are lucky, you may one day spot a diamondback terrapin on the shore of the Bay. You'll have a much better chance if you are doing something quiet, such as paddling along in a kayak. If you do catch sight of one, the terrapin will most likely have spotted you first and will be swimming rapid-ly in the opposite direction. Remember the swimming thumb and believe what you see. And don't forget to congratulate yourself, for you've just spotted one of the rarest, most secretive, and mysterious creatures found on Buzzards Bay.

THE RAINBOW TROUT'S scientific name, *Oncorhynchus mykiss*, comes from the Greek *Oncorhynchos*, which means "hook snout," and the fish's Kamchatkan (Native Alaskan people) name, *mykiss*. The rainbow trout has a salmonlike shape, and like the salmon, the male develops an out-thrust jaw during breeding season. The record size for a rainbow trout caught in fresh water is 31.27 pounds. Those fish that spend time at sea—known as sea-runs—can exceed 42 pounds.

The rainbow trout is a beautiful fish. You can distinguish it from other trout by its numerous dark spots set against a pale background. Other trout have a pale-on-dark spot pattern. The rainbow's back is olive green, its belly pale white. Its most striking feature is the shimmering pink, red, or purple stripe that runs along its side, giving the fish its name.

Rainbows are native to western North America. Their natural range extends from Alaska to Mexico. Because of their qualities as game fish—fast growth, hardiness, the ease with which they are caught, and fighting ability—they have been introduced to many other parts of the country. Although they are not native to Massachusetts, rainbows have been stocked here for so long (since the late 1800s) that they have nearly been accepted as natives. They prefer to live in cool to cold, highly oxygenated water. Rainbow trout feed on a wide variety of native prey, including insects, crustaceans, mollusks, and other fish.

MassWildlife stocks 110,000 trout annually in about forty ponds and forty-one streams in southeastern Massachusetts. The program is funded by fees from fishing and hunting licenses. The trout are raised in one of five state hatcheries, the closest one to Buzzards Bay being the Sandwich Hatchery on Cape Cod. Most of these stocked trout—around 57,000 of them—are rainbows. On average, the rainbows are twelve to fourteen inches long and weigh about one and a half pounds when they are released. The state also stocks roughly 25,000 brook trout, the only trout native to Massachusetts; 15,000 brown trout, like the rainbow, an introduced species; and 1,000 tiger trout, a cross between the native brook and the brown. In general, anglers find the native brook trout and the hybrid tigers easy to catch. Rainbows are a little more challenging and provide great sport, often leaping clear of the water when hooked. Of all the stocked trout, the browns are the hardest to catch and often attain the largest size.

Individual ponds are typically stocked with between 500 and 10,000 trout, and streams with 200 to 2,000. Factors determining the number of fish include the size and quality of the body of water, accessibility to anglers, and fishing pressure. Most of the trout are stocked from mid-March to early May, with a significantly smaller stocking done in late September to early October. Trout fishing in Massachusetts is open year round.

Bodies of water around Buzzards Bay that are stocked include Ashumet Pond, the Coonamessett (sea-run browns), the Acushnet River (brook trout), the Agawam River (brown trout), the Mattapoisett River (brook, brown, and rainbows), Marys Pond (rainbows and brook), Shingle Island River (brook and brown), Bread and Cheese Brook (brook), and the east branch of the Westport River (brook and brown).

ON THE DAY I WENT with Steve Hurley, of MassWildlife, to stock rainbow trout, I heard the pulsing, trilling call of the spring peepers for the first time that year. On a sunny spring day, Marys Pond in Rochester is about the prettiest place you've ever seen. It's a deep blue kettle pond, walled by dusky green stands of mature white pine. Two-hundred-foot native giants, some five feet in circumference, towered over the pond, shading out undergrowth and leaving only an open, parklike understory. Low-angling spring sunlight played on the purple pillars of the scaled trunks creating dappled patterns of light and shadow. The slopes beneath the trees were softened by orange-gold pine needles. Scattered around the sandy shoreline of the pond were bright red cranberries, imported from a massive, abutting bog. The woodland was a great cathedral, with the pond itself a sepulchre of holy water at its heart.

The rainbows were lovely, too—foot-long specimens with mottled green backs and a paintbrush swipe of purple down their sides. The streaks were a richly pigmented purple, full of sparkles similar to the ones that my nieces smear on their faces. The fish were all glitter.

Steve had backed the old green Chevy flatbed squarely into the pond. Nose in the air, the truck looked as if it were clinging to the shore with its big worn tires. Steve's helper Jeff, who had a ponytail that reached nearly to his beltline, stood on the back of the truck ladling trout, a dozen at a time, out of the tanks with a square, long-handled dip net. In the bright sunlight, the payload was a squirming mass of flashing, vivid purples and greens. The net was tied off at the bottom, with an extra foot of untrimmed mesh extending below the knot. Instead of ejecting the trout carelessly into the water by flipping the net inside-out, Jeff carefully lowered each load onto the back edge of the truck bed and stepped on the dangling mesh, thereby anchoring the net. Then, using his foot as a fulcrum, he slowly pushed the handle of the net up so the rainbows could slide out onto the surface of the water.

The tank unit was about twelve feet long and five feet high and was divided into six compartments, each with a lid that opened like a commercial ice cream cooler. Each tank was filled with churning white water. The water is kept at 50 degrees Fahrenheit and is saturated with oxygen. At that temperature, "saturated" translates into ten parts oxygen per million parts water. Steve explained that rainbows take five to ten parts oxygen in their water. That doesn't sound like much, but like five to ten creamers in a cup of coffee, it's actually a high ratio; when you look into the tanks, all you see are air bubbles. The fish tanks on the old Chevy rely on water recirculation to oxygenate the water. Some newer tanks pump oxygen directly into the water, like recreational fish tanks. In all, the fish tanks on the Chevy hold approximately 950 gallons of water, and, of course, the trout, which on this day numbered about 600.

Hoping to get a closer look at the fish, I asked Jeff to ladle out a netful of rainbows for me. I jammed my hand into the writhing mass, but the flashing trout were remarkably energized and proved impossible to catch bare-handed. Jeff pointed out a native brook trout, or "brookie," mixed in with the rainbows. It was just six inches long—half the size of the rainbows— even though it was the same age, one and a half years. Here was a clear illustration of a major reason that the rainbow is the star of the stocking show. The brookie had large, creamy dapples on its brown back (contrasting with the dark-on-light spot pattern of the rainbows) and a pretty pale-orange belly. All these fish had been raised at the Sandwich Hatchery. The brook trout were hatched from eggs produced by brood stock maintained at the hatchery; the rainbows came from eggs purchased out of state. In the raceways at the hatchery, clear water from springs is shot over the trout. The fish are fed several times a day with commercial fish pellets, the same food fed to the farmed rainbows you buy in the supermarket. Unlike commercial fish farms, however, the hatcheries don't use hormones to stimulate growth, or antibiotics to control disease encouraged by overcrowding, which is not an issue. Steve thinks the hatchery trout are actually healthier to eat than our native game fish, many of which are saturated with mercury.

As Jeff continued to carefully ladle rainbows off the back of the Chevy, I saw what looked to be the first osprey pair of the season appear, spiraling high in the sky. They drew closer as more rainbows entered the water, until they were definitely not gulls. In the placid blue water of the pond behind the truck, I could see numerous swirls. Some of the trout were jumping, a behavior biologists call porpoising. "They do that a lot when we release them," remarked Steve. "They're just saying, 'Where am I?'"

The ospreys weren't the only predators congregating near us. Fishermen came too. They drifted down through the columns of pine, moving soundlessly, quickly, like fog. You turned around and someone was standing right next to you. Steve was unfazed. "Sometimes they'll catch them right off the back of the truck." After all, that's the only reason these fish were being stocked—to be caught by fishermen.

Steve calls the trout fishery a "put and take" operation, and that's exactly what it is. About 80 percent of the fish stocked that day would be caught within a few months. About 10 percent would make it to the following spring, when they too would be caught. According to Steve, the rainbows have a tough time here in the summer; they are forced to survive in only a few oxygenated layers of water. Sometimes they will hang around near a spring, where the water is cooler and more oxygen-rich. Even if they survive the fishermen, Steve explained, the rainbows won't breed in our local ponds because the water is too acidic. As the only good trout pond in the New Bedford area, Marys Pond gets a lot of fishing pressure. It's prime-time fishing. And that's okay with Steve; he views the trout, at least for the record, strictly as a resource that provides food and recreation for citizens.

I began to get edgy as the crowd around us grew. The fishermen didn't appreciate the special attention I was getting from the biologists and kept elbowing in on our discussion. Two guys in hooded sweatshirts set up folding chairs, plunked down a cooler, and spiked their rods in the sand as if they were fishing for stripers on Nauset Beach. Another with a cigar and a three-foot rod, similar to the ones my nieces use, caught and released a trout while the truck was still in the water. The fish looked small and fragile hanging from the guy's big mitt. The fishermen all used small gold spinner lures and power bait, a mysterious pink mixture that they globbed on their hooks like silly putty. I caught snippets of conversations that revolved largely around 100-proof whiskey, the challenges of staying sober for fourteen years, and the merits of pit bulls as pets. Out behind the Chevy, up to his chest in water, a well-dressed fly fisherman in waders grinned as he flogged the surface around him in a circular pattern. "Boy, do I light up when I hear this truck coming," I heard him tell Steve.

Steve knows that some environmentalists don't like the stocking of non-native rainbow trout. One environmentalist told me flat out that, unlike the native sea-run brook trout, "the rainbows don't belong here." Although much of our ecosystem has adapted to the presence of the rainbows over time, environmentalists believe that the introduced fish are still hard on local invertebrates. Steve's attitude is that there were never any fish around here anyway. He described the deep-river fisheries of places such as Ohio with comparative awe. I heard this same story from a surprising number of people, fisheries managers and environmentalists alike. Apparently, the shallow streams and ponds in southeastern Massachusetts never supported a large, diverse population of freshwater fish. Typically, our ponds held chain pickerel (the top predator), yellow perch, and a few other species. That's it. This began to make more sense to me when I thought back to my days as a young boy fishing locally in fresh, unstocked water. All I ever caught was yellow perch. Steve, a self-described environmentalist, makes a sharp distinction between MassWildlife's views and those held by the kind of environmentalists who take issue with their rainbow program. "We're conservationists—out for the best use of the resource, as opposed to preservationists, who simply want to keep whatever species are there, there."

Steve and Jeff also spoke to me about a disturbing trend they see taking place today on the ponds of southeastern Massachusetts. Shorelines are getting built out, and no trespassing signs are multiplying. Typically, one of the first things new owners of waterfront property do is make a beach by raking out all the vegetation along the shoreline. This practice causes sand to migrate, which results in myriad ecological problems in the pond. One is that the migrating sand tends to block up any herring runs leading into the pond.

In between fielding questions from the ever-growing crowd of fishermen, Steve gave me the *Reader's Digest* version of the advent of what he calls "fish culture" in Massachusetts. During the era after the Civil War, which was characterized by scientific advances, people hit on the concept of producing fish in hatcheries. The citizens of Massachusetts decided they wanted more fish in their ponds and streams. One of the first hatcheries in the country was started right down the street from Marys Pond, in Wareham. They brought in smallmouth and largemouth bass from New York, salmon, and then later, in the 1880s, rainbow trout from the Pacific Coast. They tried carp before deciding that the fish muddied up the bottom too much.

From the 1950s through the 1970s, Marys Pond was part of a fisheries management movement called pond reclamation. Biologists treated the pond with rotenone, a pesticide that was discovered in South America when someone noticed aborigines pounding sticks, throwing them into streams, and subsequently harvesting dead fish. The biologists used rotenone to kill off all the warm-water fish species in Marys Pond. Afterward, they stocked it with trout.

By the time the Chevy lurched out of the water onto the beach, after a total unloading period measured only in minutes, seven fishermen were congregated around us, four of whom were fishing. It was a tranquil scene.

That tranquillity stayed with me as I drove up the expressway that evening toward home. The sun was a flashing gold orb, the visual equivalent of cymbals crashing at the finale of Beethoven's Fifth Symphony. Folk music was playing on my radio, and my soul was singing along. I tried not to think about the fact that I would again watch the Battle of Baghdad on the evening news. It was inescapable. That morning, Saddam Hussein had said, "The enemy must enter Baghdad, and Baghdad will be his grave." I felt like turning around and going back. I wished I had stayed, on that hope-filled blue spring day, to see the golden sun drop down between the columns of majestic pines in the holy peace that is Marys Pond.

THE BLUE CRAB'S scientific name, *Callinectes sapidus*, means "beautiful savory swimmer." Blue crabs are members of the Portunid family, or the swimming crabs. They use their flattened, paddlelike rear limbs to swim, mostly sideways, as a means of locomotion and escape. The crabs thrive in brackish water, which is found in estuaries, where fresh water from rivers mixes with the salt water of the ocean. Juvenile blue crabs favor lower-salinity water, meaning water with a lower salt content. The adults are more randomly distributed across habitats, but in general, larger crabs and male crabs dominate areas of low salinity, while females prefer higher-salinity areas.

Blue crabs are the crab of Maryland crab house fame, the kind you smash with a hammer on picnic tables while on vacation down South. Many people are unaware that Buzzards Bay also provides a favorable environment for blue crabs. Factors that make the Bay conducive to blue crabs include large areas of marsh edge created by a curving coastline, low coastal-wave activity, and a low tidal range. One major difference between our blue crabs and those found in the waters of the South is that down there they grow faster. Southern waters are more productive because the time it takes a blue crab to reach reproductive maturity is determined by water temperature and the length of the growing season.

Cape Cod is considered to be the northern extreme of the blue crab's range, although in warm years the species sometimes reaches Nova Scotia. The southern boundary of its range is northern Argentina, Bermuda, and the Antilles. Through ship ballast water, the crabs have been accidentally introduced into far-flung places that include Europe, North Africa, Southeast Asia, and Japan.

IN BUZZARDS BAY, blue crabs achieve their natural splendor in the sun-blasted, waning days of summer, when the air hangs thick and still, the muddy back flats are warm and putrid, and no-see-ums attack like locusts when the wind dies. You know it's a good morning for crabbing when you wake early from the heat. On these still, sweltering mornings, at low tide, the colorful blue crabs—olive, blue, and cream—prowl the estuaries under a foot of clear water. They stand on the bottom with their glorious, sky-blue-tinged claws raised to battle intruders. On these mornings, I raise the engine on my tin boat to reduce drag and let the southwest wind shuttle me gently across the flats. Row to the southwest, drift to the northeast, repeat. As long as the tide holds.

Crouching in the bow of the skiff with a long-handled dip net, I scrutinize the carpet of bottom rolling toward me. I am careful not to lean too far forward and add my silhouette to the boat's. There! The unmistakable sight of a big male blue crab, a splash of energy and color set against a featureless canvas of brown muck. Claws raised, prepared for battle, the crab's feet are ever so slowly beginning to scuttle sideways as the gladiator assesses the threat. Depending on the strength of the breeze, you generally have only about five seconds to strike with the net before the boat drifts over him and he is gone. (I have very rarely caught an alarmed blue crab by striking from the trailing side of the boat after it has passed over him.) That is, you have that amount of time if he doesn't spook, rise magically off the bottom, and swim out of your limited field of vision into the murky distance. When you see a blue crab begin to swim, it's startling; I get the same feeling I got when I was a kid and watched one of those amphibious cars—the antique ones with the twin propellers—drive right off the boat ramp and churn out to the dock. The transition between methods of locomotion is slightly awkward, but then things operate amazingly well. Sometimes, you'll see a crab paddling furiously along on the surface of the Bay, completely exposed to predators and seemingly oblivious.

After you spot the crab, you start to dip your net into the water in slow motion, from the direction in which the crab is sidling, then quickly plunge the net down, making sure you hit bottom. Then you pull the net back into the boat, give it a hard, fast flip to vomit its contents inside out, and *bang!*— The displaced warrior is ricocheted against the tin bottom of the boat, along with a quart of black, fast-drying mud. (The cardinal rule of crabbing is never, ever to attempt it without a good sponge in your boat.) If you're fast, you can eject the crab into a ten-gallon plastic bucket, but speed is of the essence. If the crab is not freed from the netting immediately, it will latch onto it with its powerful claws, leaving you with the nearly impossible task of separating the two. When this happens, at best the crab will lose a claw; at worst you stand to lose the remainder of your drift. The number of drifts is critical to your success. Once the rising tide attains a level of more than two or three feet, visibility fades, it becomes too difficult to strike quickly with the net, and the game is over. In times of good hunting, you will encounter a crab every six or seven feet of your drift.

Occasionally, you will be fortunate enough to stumble upon two crabs in the midst of a ferocious territorial melee. Generally, at these times the contestants are so absorbed in their battle that both can be taken with one scoop of the net, providing you with a bonus. When a blue crab joins you in the boat, he gathers his wits instantly. He unfailingly lands with his claws up, watching you, perpetually prepared to defend himself. A loose crab will usually try to get his back into a corner. Then you must try to grab him from behind, carefully avoiding the outstretched claws, which seem to be able to rotate nearly backward, a definite advantage.

THE BLUE CRAB'S reproductive strategy is characterized by a high rate of reproduction, fast growth leading to early sexual maturity, a short life span, and a high death rate. Animal species that use this strategy are highly vulnerable to seasonal, environmental, and biological conditions, which can result in wild fluctuations in population. Thus, the local blue crab population can rise and fall dramatically from year to year. The population is also naturally cyclical, with cycles running in periods of five years or more.

Blue crabs are opportunistic feeders, consuming almost anything they come across, including each other. Much of their diet consists of shellfish, fish, crustaceans, carrion, and plants. They themselves provide food for many kinds of vertebrates—including humans—and at least sixty kinds of fish. On Buzzards Bay, blue crabs must be at least four inches wide across the shell from point to point to be legally harvested.

Blue crabs live a maximum of four to eight years in the wild. They grow by molting, or shedding their shells. Between molts, their growth is suppressed; after molting, they grow rapidly. Adults typically grow by around 30 percent after each molt. The crabs molt roughly twenty times in their lives. Molting frequency slows down as the crabs age: small crabs around five millimeters wide molt every three to five days, while crabs seldom molt at all after reaching sexual maturity. There are several factors that influence how often the crabs molt, and thus how quickly they grow, including the availability and quality of food and water temperature.

It's easy to determine the sex of blue crabs. Males have brilliant blue shading on their shells and claws. When you flip them over, they have a distinct, T-shaped abdomen. Females have orange-tipped claws and their abdomens are either triangular (immature crabs) or broad and rounded (mature crabs). Blue crabs mate in shallow, low-salinity waters, near marsh banks or aquatic plants, in areas chosen by the females. Females mate only once in their lives. In contrast, the spawning, which occurs later, takes place in areas of higher salinity, such as those found in lower estuaries. Females produce up to three million eggs, with bigger crabs producing the most. Blue crab larvae develop floating in salt water. Unlike the adults that can tolerate a wide range of water temperatures and salinities, the larvae are highly vulnerable to changing environmental conditions. As plankton, blue crab larvae are fed on by other plankton, jellyfish, and fish. Later, the larvae settle to the bottom, and begin to migrate up into the estuaries. As they pass through the successive stages of their life cycle on their way to becoming adults, blue crabs alternately move into and out of various inshore habitats.

WHEN YOU GO toe-to-toe with a blue crab, you sense that if these creatures were man-sized, our evolving species never would have made it. As it is, a five-inch-wide blue crab—about the right size for good eating—is quite capable of intimidating a six-foot-tall man. Once, when I was crabbing a back flat in Bourne that I have worked since I was a child, I was accosted at the mouth of the estuary by an environmental police officer, who snuck up on me from behind a nearby mooring area with a sudden roar of engines and a massive wake.

"Whatcha doing back there, shellfishing?" he demanded.

"Nope, just crabbing." (I knew full well the area was closed to shellfishing.)

"How big are those crabs?"

"They're all about five inches across."

Eyeing my ten-gallon pail with distrust, the officer turned to his mate, obviously a trainee. "Take a look at those," he muttered.

"Here you are," I offered cheerfully and passed the lurching white pail, full of jet-black low-tide water and crabs, across the gunwales. If you have never peered into a bucket of writhing, combative blue crabs, locked onto each other like a barrelful of monkeys, it is like looking into the jaws of hell. The rookie gasped, stumbled backward, and tersely bid me on my way. I grinned and motored off.

I was bitten by a blue crab once when I was a boy, and it hurt badly. Some people claim that you can get blood poisoning from their bite. Blue crabs have excellent vision both in and out of the water, and they are extremely fast and accurate with their claws. Sometimes, in my tin boat, I will spar with a blue crab, marveling at its speed, testing its resolve. Both qualities are consistently unimpeachable. I find the exercise to be an easy means of exposing myself to the chilling, violent predatory force of Animal. It awakens the same sleeping force that exists in me, in all of us, locked away, stifled by the yoke of civilization. Blue crabs are absolutely devoid of anything akin to fear. It is rather unsettling to realize that this small, fierce crustacean is in no way intimidated by us. It has crossed my mind that if the crab I was sparring with were larger, it would undoubtedly, without the least hesitation, kill me. Then, after I was dead, it would probably eat me.

Happily, we eat them, and with great delight. After a humid morning crabbing on the still flats of Buzzards Bay, splattered with pungent black mud, your scalp tingling from no-see-ums, you face the unpleasant task of boiling your catch in a pot of steaming water. Then you scorch your fingertips as you painstakingly pick them clean, popping their shells off, concentrating on the twin lumps of white meat by the rear legs. But afterward, there is the unmatched refreshment of a cool outdoor shower to look forward to and the reward of a fresh crab salad sandwich for lunch, served with light mayonnaise and a slice of garden-fresh tomato in the shade of the porch. Crab is a heavy food, a celebration of the season in which it is taken. To eat blue crab on a sultry August afternoon on the Bay is to have more than just a meal; it is a rite, a ritual. It is a means of putting your body and soul in cadence with the natural rhythms of the place. To eat blue crab in such a way is to make yourself part of the great, smothering blanket of heat and humidity that is Buzzards Bay in late summer.

Hurricanes

The eleventh, he came not, neither sent, whereupon I commanded four of my company to seek out for crabs, lobsters, turtles, &c. for sustaining us till the ships returned, which was gone clear out of sight, and had the wind chopped up at south-west, with much difficulty would she have been able in short time to have made return.

—ARCHER, ON GOSNOLD'S OVERDUE TRIP TO NEIGHBORING PENIKESE
ISLAND TO HARVEST CEDARS AND THE STRONG WINDS THE EXPLORERS
EXPERIENCED ON BUZZARDS BAY

OUR ABILITY TO COEXIST with the natural world is perhaps most severely tested by hurricanes. The shores of Buzzards Bay can be an extremely dangerous place during a hurricane if storm track, wind speed, and tide all happen to combine in a certain way. The upper reaches of the Bay, facing southwest and shaped like the narrow end of a funnel, are particularly vulnerable to storm surges, those massive waves pushed inland by hurricane winds. Throughout the world, residents of coastal areas fear storm surges. The deadliest storm surge in history occurred during the Bangladesh cyclone of 1970. That giant wave swept over low-lying coastal areas and killed at least 300,000 people. The biggest storm surge ever recorded was the forty-two-foot-high wall of water driven into Australia's Bathhurst Bay by a hurricane in 1899. Historically, major hurricanes have driven storm surges of ten to fifteen feet into the upper portions of Buzzards Bay. I went to Providence, Rhode Island, to interview John Ghiorse, chief meteorologist at NBC10, about hurricanes. I chose to speak with John not only for his meteorological expertise, but also because he spent a dozen years sailing on Buzzards Bay and has firsthand experience with the weather here, including bad weather.

According to John, the biggest change in meteorology in recent years is that weathermen used to try to predict the weather one or two days in advance, and now they are working on five to six. John, who in addition to his duties at the station also lectures in schools, told me that certain kids get excited about weather around the age of nine or ten. He sees them light up in classrooms when he starts talking hurricanes. Most of these kids begin studying weather as amateurs, only to have their hopes of a professional career dashed when they realize they have to master high-level math and science courses, such as physics. As John explained, "The everyday language we use at the station to discuss meteorology is the language of math." Many of these kids go on to become amateur weather buffs who are quite capable of making significant contributions to the science.

WHEN I WAS A CHILD, I felt the energy of hurricanes deep down. I just had to be out of doors when a tropical storm approached, feel its great energy roll in over the treetops on hot swells of wind, wondering all the while why there was no rain. I would let the storm's power fill me and run about wildly as only a child can do. In a young boy's mind, there is nothing that can possibly be faster than himself when he is running at top speed. During a mighty storm, however, it never took long for me to concede that the wind was faster. I would unfailingly end up running in diminishing circles until I fell flat on my back, arms outspread, yielding to the storm's awesome power. Now, when I remember big storms, in my mind's eye I see them from upside down. I remember looking up in awe at the great, stately oak in front of the house as it heaved down and raked the earth with its uppermost branches, like a woman bending at the waist and whipping the ground with her long hair. I remember how impossible and undignified that sight appeared. I can still see my mother's small white face peering out at me anxiously from the bow window, the front door opening a crack, and the soundless motion of her lips as her call was spirited away by the roaring wind. Burdened with adult cares, she was unable to free her spirit and truly feel the storm. Today, as an adult, I am similarly unable to free my own.

THE WORD HURRICANE is derived from the Spanish word *hurican*, which most likely was derived from *Hunraken*, the name of the Mayan storm god, and a similar word, *huraken* ("evil spirits"), used by the native peoples of the Caribbean. Those who have experienced the awful power of a major hurricane firsthand would certainly agree that evil spirits were involved.

A hurricane forms in the summer or early fall when a large mass of air somewhere south of the Florida coast, heavy with moisture, begins to spin. This air mass sucks the heat energy from the warm waters of the Caribbean and converts it into wind. The more heat energy the mass of air consumes, the faster it spins. Once the spinning mass reaches a speed of seventy-four miles per hour, it becomes a hurricane and begins to move. *Where* the hurricane moves is largely dictated by the temperature and pressure of adjacent air masses. In general, the storm will always take the path of least resistance.

Hurricanes are characterized by a twenty- to forty-mile-wide eye at their core that is composed of warm, relatively calm air. Around the core, winds revolve at seventy to two hundred miles per hour. Hurricanes contain an unfathomable amount of energy. In fact, if we could capture just *one* percent of the energy of just *one* hurricane, we could meet all the power requirements of the United States for an entire year.

There are ways other than weather reports to learn if a hurricane is on its way. Nature provides its own signs, if you know how to read them. Sometimes green appears in the sky, particularly at sunset. The moon displays intense halos, or rings of light. Stars dance. Out on the Bay, low pressure and wave action cause weeds and scum to cover the surface, and the water smells bad.

According to the National Weather Service Forecast Office in Taunton, Massachusetts, forty-one tropical storms and hurricanes have affected southern New England since 1900. Twelve of them hit land with significant impact, bringing high winds, coastal flooding, and heavy rainfall. A major storm has hit land here every decade of the 1900s, with the exception of the 1920s. Ten of these twelve storms made landfall in August or September, the other two in July. The period from 1938 to 1955 was a particularly active one, with five storms, four of which were major hurricanes. The fifteen-year period from 1985 to 1999 was also quite active, with four major storms in the area. The three worst hurricanes to hit Buzzards Bay in recent history are generally considered to be the Great New England Hurricane of 1938, Hurricane Carol (1954), and Hurricane Bob (1991).

About 85 percent of the Atlantic's major hurricanes come from Cape Verde, and those storms in turn are born in Africa. Since the 1930s, scientists have recognized that these storms are "seeded" by what are called African easterly waves. These waves, which come from the east and travel west, are a product of the extremely hot air masses that reside over the Sahara Desert in northern Africa. These hot air masses butt up against the cooler air along the African coast, an action that causes instability, which in turn creates a wave that rolls westward with the trade winds. The instability created in the normal air circulation over the ocean by these easterly waves starts the chain of atmospheric activity that results in a hurricane.

An important factor in determining whether a hurricane from the tropics reaches Buzzards Bay is something called a Bermuda high. A Bermuda high is a stationary air mass of cold, high-pressure air that often squats over the middle of the North Atlantic Ocean. The presence of a Bermuda high can prevent a hurricane from tracking toward the Bay by deflecting the storm to our west, or the east, and safely out to sea. If a high is not in place, a hurricane will steam up the East Coast using the Gulf Stream as a highway, gathering heat energy from its warm waters and gaining speed as it comes. Bermuda highs also have other important effects on Bay weather; for instance, they trap masses of warm air over the Bay and prevent them from moving out to sea, which creates fog and rainy weather.

FACTORS THAT DETERMINE the effects a hurricane will have include the track of the storm, its speed, and the level of the tide when it strikes. To appreciate the importance of the storm's track, or path, you need to understand how a hurricane works. The major movement associated with hurricanes is spinning winds. In the Northern Hemisphere, the winds in a hurricane spin counterclockwise. In the Southern Hemisphere, they circulate in a clockwise direction. This pattern is the result of what is known as the Coriolis force, which is caused by the Earth's rotation.

The other movement that occurs in a hurricane is the forward motion of the storm itself, which is typically slower than the speed of its revolving winds. Hurricanes that come here are generally moving northward. These two movements—the spinning winds and the forward motion of the storm—join forces in such a way to create an area of exceptionally high winds within the hurricane. The strongest winds in any hurricane, regardless of the hemisphere in which it is found or the direction in which it moves, are in the area of the storm where the circulating winds are moving in the same direction as the storm. This is because the winds moving in the direction of the storm are accelerated by the storm's advance. The diagram here illustrates this concept.

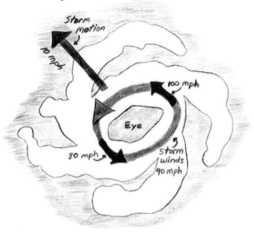

Based on a drawing from the Atlantic Oceanographic
and Meteorological Laboratory

Here's another way to think about it: You step onto the moving sidewalk at the airport with your baggage, heading for the terminal. You continue to walk on the revolving belt. As you whip past people walking on the main concourse, your arms sore from holding your heavy bags, you secretly rejoice in the fact that your total forward speed has been accelerated by the speed of the belt. In this example, the speed of the belt corresponds to the forward motion of a hurricane and your walking speed to the portion of the revolving winds within the hurricane that are traveling in the same direction as the storm.

Because the winds of hurricanes in Buzzards Bay spin in a counterclockwise direction, and because these storms are moving northward, the strongest winds are on the right side, or to the east, of the storm. (For example, if a hurricane with 95 mile-per-hour winds moves into the Bay from the south at a speed of 30 miles per hour, the winds on the east side of the storm, aided by the storm's advance to the north, will attain speeds of well over 100 miles per hour.) According to John Ghiorse, the latest meteorological research indicates that this phenomenon does not reflect a hard-and-fast rule, as was formerly believed. It is more likely to apply to accelerating hurricanes than to hurricanes moving at a slow pace. For the most part, however, meteorologists still consider the general rule—in a northward-moving hurricane, strongest winds are on the east—to be valid.

So what does all this technical information about storm track mean to you when a hurricane is approaching Buzzards Bay? Simply this: *If the storm tracks to the west of the Bay, watch out*. Areas to the east of the hurricane's track will be struck by the highest winds and will sustain the most damage. In the twelve major storms Buzzards Bay has experienced since 1900, the core of strongest winds, and also the largest storm surges, have always been found to the *east* of the storm track. All three storms considered to have been hardest on Buzzards Bay—1938, Carol, and Bob—tracked to the west of the Bay. In contrast, the heaviest, often torrential, rainfall dealt by these hurricanes was always found *along* and to the *west* of the storm track. As a result of this trend, today local weathermen like John Ghiorse focus mainly on trying to predict where the center of an approaching hurricane is going to be, especially in relation to coastal areas.

The speed of a hurricane—both of its winds and of the forward motion of the storm itself—is the second major factor that determines the severity of its impact. In the United States we use the Saffir-Simpson scale, which is based on wind speed, to rank the intensity of hurricanes. Category 1 is defined as a mild storm; category 2 as moderate; category 3 as extensive; category 4, extreme; category 5, catastrophic. Categories 3 through 5 are collectively referred to as major hurricanes. Major hurricanes reach maximum sustained surface winds of at least 111 miles per hour for at least one minute. Although major hurricanes account for only 21 percent of all storms that make landfall in the United States, they account for 83 percent of all damage.

The speed at which a hurricane moves toward us, and whether that speed increases as it moves in, is also very important in determining the severity of the storm's impact. All twelve major storms that Buzzards Bay experienced in the 1900s accelerated significantly as they moved northward into the region. Because major hurricanes tend to accelerate through this geographic area, we typically experience a relatively short period of high winds, compared to other places in the western Atlantic that experience slower-moving storms.

Tide is the third major factor to consider when attempting to predict the effects a hurricane will have on a coastal area such as Buzzards Bay. If it is high tide when the hurricane strikes a shoreline community, the winds and the accompanying storm surge will cause far greater flood damage than if the arrival of the storm had coincided with any other point in the tide cycle. Of the three worst storms to hit the Bay, '38 hit at high tide, Carol slightly after, and Bob before. The worst possible time for a hurricane to arrive is during a high spring tide. Spring tides are tides of greater-than-average range (higher highs, lower lows) that occur twice a month, coinciding with the new and the full moons.

BEARING IN MIND the factors that influence the severity of a hurricane—track, speed, and tide—let's take a closer look at the three big storms that took the heaviest toll on Buzzards Bay. Most people who have spent any time in the area know that the Great New England Hurricane of 1938 was one of the most devastating hurricanes ever to hit the area. Classified as a category 3 storm, it killed 564 people, destroyed almost nine thousand homes, and emerged as the costliest storm in all of U.S. history.

The hurricane blew in late in the day on Wednesday, September 21, 1938. Nobody knew it was coming because it wasn't forecast: weather satellites didn't exist yet, and there weren't many weather stations. And there was absolutely no reason to expect it because a storm of that magnitude hadn't hit New England in almost a hundred years. While the hurricane was racing up the coast from Long Island and Connecticut, blissfully ignorant Buzzards Bay residents were going about their business—some of them even taking pictures of the restless Bay on the beaches.

The hurricane made landfall at Milford, Connecticut, and sped northward at 60 miles per hour. Unlike most hurricanes, which peter out as they reach our area, '38 didn't slow down. Blue Hill Observatory measured the peak wind speed at 121 miles per hour—a record measurement. The storm coincided with high tide and sent twelve- to fifteen-foot storm surges (known at that time only as tidal waves) crashing into communities all around the Bay. Downtown Providence was submerged under twenty feet of salt water, and parts of Falmouth and New Bedford were under eight feet. New Bedford's fishing fleet was totally destroyed.

When '38 hit, the world was just stepping into the abyss of the Second World War. In the Saturday, September 24, edition of the *Cape Cod Standard-Times* (forerunner to today's *Cape Cod Times*), the articles that accompanied

the hurricane coverage were all about impending war: "Americans warned
to flee [Czech] Republic"; "France Mobilizes Part of Reserves"; "War
Tension Hurts Stocks." A few days later, the headlines read, "Peace Appeal
Sent to Hitler"; "Roosevelt Appeals to Hitler and Benes." Clearly, for the
residents of Buzzards Bay, September 1938 was a time of uncertainty and
fear, with great tempests loose in both the natural world and the civilized
world.

One of the most tragic incidents of '38 happened at Gray Gables Point in
Bourne. On the night of the storm, a two-story summer house owned by
Mrs. James Lane was swept completely off the point into the Cape Cod
Canal. It ended up floating in the water, banging against the north abutment
of the Bourne Bridge. All five occupants—including three older women
from New York and one of their grandsons, age 11—died. Ironically, one of
the victims—Hayward Wilson, 54, of Buzzards Bay—had gone to the house
to warn the occupants of the tidal wave that was approaching.

In Cataumet, Bay waters rose so high that they came over the dunes into
Squeteague Harbor and flooded the first floors of houses there. Sand dredging equipment from a dredge in Megansett Harbor crashed into the boathouse of Paul Dudley Dean. The causeway leading out to Scraggy Neck was
submerged under twelve feet of water, and Seabury Gibbs, the caretaker
of the neck, was marooned there for the night, along with several summer
residents.

Across the Bay in New Bedford, the wind-driven tide rose steadily higher all
afternoon. With darkness came a flood that submerged beaches, highways,
and factories. Workers were marooned. Utilities abruptly lost power. At
high tide, the water at the head of the Acushnet River rose twelve feet
higher than normal.

Woods Hole, in Falmouth, was a wreck due to its location between the
Bay and Vineyard Sound. As the *Falmouth Enterprise* put it, "A tide seven feet
higher than normal on the Sound side and a corresponding high tide two or
three feet higher still on the Buzzards Bay side combined to bring what
resembled a tidal wave to Woods Hole on Wednesday evening." Storm plus
tide equaled destruction. Columbus O. Iselin, a scientist at the Woods Hole
Oceanographic Institution, said at the time, "If the high tide had been at any

other time of day there would have been no flood. . . . At 7 P.M. the water was rushing like a mill race through the Eel Pond Channel into the harbor." The worst damage occurred at Penzance Point and behind Eel Pond, on Millfield Street, which was described as "a torrent of rushing water." Two men in a rowboat rescued residents on the street until "their rowboat was flung against a pole by a treacherous turn of current and they were thrown into the water. Both by good fortune were brought up against trees, which they proceeded to climb." On Penzance Point in Woods Hole, the body of William T. Briggs, the caretaker of the A. Parks estate, was found, one of eight Falmouth storm victims. As the storm waters rose, Hartley L. Cassidy Jr., a high school student, pushed a large Buick convertible to safety from the Naushon Island landing parking lot. The car was owned by H. D. Wells, an American author and historian from New Mexico who was visiting the Forbes family on Naushon. Wells rewarded the enterprising boy with a ten dollar bill.

JOHN GHIORSE'S TAKE on the Hurricane of 1938 is that without the benefits of a weather forecast and ongoing local news coverage, most people didn't even know they'd had a hurricane until it was over. His perception is borne out by one of the first headlines I saw about the storm, in the Friday, September 23, edition of the *Standard-Times*: "Missing Man Found." "It seems that Cornelius Forhan of Buzzards Bay, missing since Wednesday afternoon, was found late yesterday in Sandwich. . . . He was rowing a skiff in Sandwich Pond, seemingly oblivious to the hurricane's aftermath." Cornelius was one of the lucky ones. In Wareham, which sustained some of the heaviest damage of any community on the Bay, newspapers proclaimed: "Wareham in Desperate way—9 Dead, 18 Missing; Loss is $1,500,000." Two days after the storm, Wareham was declared a "village in despair." Three days later, officials were still hunting for bodies along Swifts Beach and Swifts Neck. The death toll in the town eventually reached thirteen, and damages were estimated at $2.5 million.

Wareham selectmen, after surveying their town, announced that more than three hundred cottages and other dwellings had been completely demolished, and that six hundred more were badly damaged. Ten of the large summer homes on the shoreline between Wareham and Onset were practically destroyed. The selectmen went so far as to issue a resolution: "That all children be kept at home. . . . That all persons without official business or other sufficient reason be in their homes after dark. . . . That no liqueur be sold in the town until further notice."

Flooded septic systems and the health risks they pose are one of the things we have learned to expect when coastal areas are hit by major hurricanes. But in 1938, these health risks were poorly understood. Dr. T. L. Swift, the Falmouth health inspector, issued a notice to people living in flooded areas, cautioning that "all flooded places should be thoroughly cleaned and disinfected before being reoccupied. Particular care should be taken where there is any overflow from cesspool or septic tank."

Looting, another major problem that has come to be associated with hurricanes, also occurred in the wake of the storm. Despite the deployment of two hundred National Guardsmen, looting in Wareham continued unabated. After the storm, witnesses reported seeing at least three trucks loaded with merchandise rolling out of town in the dark of night. Looting was so widespread in Bourne that the town adopted martial law, and the police chief warned sightseers to stay away. A detail of fifty National Guardsmen was deployed throughout the community. The Saturday after the storm, a *Standard-Times* headline reported that in the past day more than 3,000 permits had been issued to residents allowing access to sections of Bourne that had been closed to everyone but property owners. Looters there had been blatantly hauling away unsecured property, using whatever means available, and had even used boats to plunder Tobys Island. Wholesale looting of damaged summer homes took place along the waterfront in Patuisset, Monument Beach, and other places.

One of the National Guardsmen sent to Woods Hole to control looting was told to halt everyone except Woods Hole residents from proceeding along the road to Nobska—"not that there's anything to guard down there," he told the *Falmouth Enterprise*. "But, heck, from what I've seen of some of these pirates they'd swipe the gold outa your teeth. Some of our boys saw men in boats lugging away all sorts of things as dawn broke Sunday."

One positive result of the Hurricane of '38 was the boost it gave to the local economy. A news story about Bourne reported, "At least a dozen wealthy summer home owners have placed orders with contractors to view their demolished property and start plans for completing new construction. . . . Scores of unemployed have been given jobs by property owners, anxious to start repairs."

Perhaps the most important long-term consequence of the Great New England Hurricane of 1938 was that it taught people to respect hurricanes. For the most part, owners of shoreline summer homes that were destroyed did not rebuild. Others moved their damaged homes farther inland. After '38, Bay residents—indeed, people throughout New England—also started paying attention to modern storm warnings. That paid off sixteen years later in 1954, when Hurricane Carol arrived.

HURRICANE CAROL snuck up on us. It was August 1954, and a storm moving at a mere five to ten miles per hour began to meander up from the Bahamas. On the evening of August 30, people in New England went to bed with no idea they would be battling a major hurricane the following day. That night, east of Cape Hatteras, North Carolina, all hell erupted. The storm accelerated to more than 35 miles per hour. It swept into Old Saybrook, Connecticut, the next morning and took the lives of sixty-five people. Carol's winds gusted so high on the Rhode Island coast that they blew the roofs off houses. It was this rapid, overnight acceleration that caught many Buzzards Bay residents by surprise.

The upper reaches of Buzzards Bay suffered the most in Carol, as they had in 1938. According to *Hurricane 1954*, a special publication of the *New Bedford Standard Times* put out on September 11 of that year, the storm's "effects on the long narrow harbors of New Bedford, Padanaram, and Wareham were what you would expect if you turned a fire hose into a bathtub filled with toy boats."

Onset and Wareham were flooded again. The bluffs on the beachfront at Onset and Point Independence were cut away, and the Onset Yacht Yard at Point Independence was wrecked. According to a September 2 *Cape Cod Times* article, three thousand to four thousand evacuees from local beaches were sheltered at Memorial Town Hall. Toby Hospital admitted forty patients, several suffering from heart attacks. After the storm blew through, residents in the area carried all their furniture and carpets out to their front yards to dry.

In Bourne, residents were evacuated from areas of Monument Beach, Pocasset, Wings Neck, and Nyes Neck. Sixty-nine evacuees stayed overnight at Otis Air Force Base. On Patuisset, the storm pushed one house off its foundation, which hit another, pushing it off its foundation into another, which likewise ended up off its foundation. At the Massachusetts Maritime Academy, in the town of Buzzards Bay, the cars of officers and midshipmen were washed into the Canal. At Monument Beach, the Bigelow Boat Yard collapsed, and the Bay rose almost to the railroad tracks. The storm washed out the road to Mashnee Island and Shore Road at Back River, delaying the fall school opening by a week. Just as in '38, another house ended up in the Canal. This time it was Elmer Clapp's cottage on Taylors Point, which was reduced to rubble by the storm. Railway workers found Elmer inside his floating home, drowned. In his pocket they found a hearing aid and two valuable diamond rings stashed for safekeeping.

Once again, the National Guard was deployed to assist the police against looters. The entire 685th Battalion was activated, and parts of it were sent to Bourne, Wareham, and Marion. Casual visitors were banned in Bourne, and resident passes were again required to enter the various villages. In *Cape Cod Times* photos of Monument Beach taken after the storm, the town looks as if it is populated by GI Joe dolls.

Carol tore into Cataumet and swept away one wing of the Robinson's Boat Yard building. Many of the summer homes on Hospital Cove Beach were washed completely away. At Megansett, the yacht club was swept away for the third time since 1938. Only the foundation was left intact. Many of the boats in the harbor were smashed up against the breakwall or were floated over the point into Squeteague. Over at Wild Harbor, rising water flooded waterfront homes, and only one sailboat held its mooring. Several catboats blew out to sea and were never recovered. The *Falmouth Enterprise* reported that at Quisset Harbor, "Oakes Spalding's *Peterman II,* which is for sale, was picked up and placed neatly on top of a car parked on the pier." The car was crushed; Oakes's boat survived the incident unscathed.

In Falmouth, people remembered '38 all too well and began to fight Carol as the storm intensified. Repairs began even before the winds died out. There were striking similarities between the two storms there, especially in Woods Hole. Carol hit Falmouth hard because her winds nearly coincided with high tide, which was at 1:38 P.M. in Falmouth Harbor. Also, the town was at the far eastern edge of the storm, which was centered over Providence and Boston. According to the *Enterprise*, "Waves surged across Main Street to pour into Eel Pond, which overflowed across School Street and Millfield Street." Poor Millfield Street got it again. This time, however, almost everyone stayed in their homes. A fuel oil tank burst in the Millfield Apartments, spreading oil through the flood waters and into people's houses. Incredibly, a pamphlet found floating down the middle of the street offered this counsel: "Be cheerful in the face of adversity." Penzance Point residents also chose to stay in their homes or those of their neighbors, while water raced across the point, washed out the road, and jettisoned first-floor furniture into Buzzards Bay. Over at the Oceanographic Institution, Captain John F. Pike was quoted as saying, "Another foot of tide and we would have lost everything." Buildings on the institution docks were pushed back three feet by Carol's storm surge, and the vacuum caused by her winds imploded the huge front window of its brand-new building.

Carol caused serious damage to water, gas, and electric utilities. In Falmouth, the water pressure dropped drastically as flood waters poured over roads and smashed water mains. At the height of the storm, five thousand gallons of water a minute flowed uncontrollably from broken house pipes and a broken main on Surf Drive. In the town of Buzzards Bay, residents were warned not to light any gas facilities. In areas of Pocasset and Wings Neck, where beach houses had been pushed completely off their foundations, gas service was shut down because of snapped pipes.

Once the electricity went out, it wasn't easy to get service restored. After the storm, the Cape and Vineyard Electric Company notified its customers that any wiring that was submerged in salt water would have to be replaced. Company officials explained that because salt conducts electricity, deposits on wires would cause short circuits. Before service could be restored, homeowners had to get the repairs done themselves, and then the town's one wiring inspector had to inspect the work. This last requirement was the real holdup.

Carol was nearly as hard on the western shores of the Bay as she was to the east. At Sconticut Neck and West Island, 130 summer homes and 35 year-round ones were completely destroyed. According to *Hurricane 1954*,

Horseneck Beach in Westport was swept clean, "with only the sand left." New Bedford sustained $50 million in damage, $10 million of it to waterfront industry. The hurricane sank six fishing boats there and beached thirty-one more. During the storm, the *Redstart*, a local scalloper, struggled unsuccessfully to make port against the raging waters of the Bay. She went down with eleven fishermen on board; all were lost. To the south, Padanaram was the scene of shattered yachts and swamped waterfront buildings.

WHEN BRADFORD TRIPP saw the sky in the East turn yellow the morning of August 31, 1954, he finished his breakfast, set his fork down, and said quietly, "Mother, I'm going down to check on the boat." The boat was the *Olad II*, a fifty-foot schooner docked at Concordia Yacht boatyard in Padanaram Harbor, where Brad, a student, was working for the summer.

As Brad began to relate this story, he closed his eyes and placed a hand across his brow. Blessed with a fine memory, he saw again the disastrous events of that tumultuous morning in '54. . . . When he arrived at the boatyard, the wind was hauling out of the east, and the water was rising, fast. He and another man started lashing the *Olad II* to the crook of Concordia's big stone wharf with fourteen lines, one of which was made of one-and-a-half-inch-thick nylon. By the time they finished securing the *Olad II* and stepped down onto the wharf, the tide had risen so high they couldn't get back on. They stood and watched Padanaram Harbor as the wind escalated to hurricane force. Carol had arrived.

The first boats to go were three sixty-foot wooden sailing yachts, moored two-thirds of the way down the harbor on the west side. They parted from their moorings and were swept up onto the rocky shoreline, where all three broke their backs and were demasted. Brad remembers how the falling masts took out the power lines, creating vivid sprays of sparks. As Carol's winds shifted to the south, the sailing masters at New Bedford Yacht Club next door labored to secure their day sailors and get their kids off the docks. The men at Concordia watched with concern as the screaming wind snapped the lines and broke the floats free, sending one float carrying half a dozen children spiraling toward the stone wharf at Concordia. It was a perilous situation. If the float escaped past the wharf, it would be blown into the Padanaram Bridge, now nearly submerged by rising storm waters, where the children faced certain death by drowning. The men at Concordia knew they were the kids' only chance. Brad and two others hurriedly sloshed their way through rising water to the spar shed, a building where masts are stored that stands flush with the waterline. They smashed the windows from the inside, jammed their arms through, and with outstretched fingers frantically tried to grab the kids as they rocketed past. They missed. Sprinting after the float, they were able to grab it when it banged into the wharf once more, and they helped the children to shore. Then they all stood by and watched the rest of the club's floats careen to ruin against the bridge. I asked Brad how the kids looked. "They looked scared!" he said, eyeing me with obvious surprise. He doesn't remember anyone crying, though.

Turning his attention to the *Olad II*, Brad noticed that the boat, which normally sat five and a half feet below the dock at high tide, was now floating six feet above it. With floodwaters above his knees, he decided to head back to Concordia's Red Brick Building, which sits on the shoreline at the base of the wharf, and perch on its steps. Around 11 A.M., the winds hit their peak, and the devil began to dance in the harbor. Brad couldn't see much, even though it wasn't raining. "In a hurricane," he explained, "the wind cuts the tops off the waves and hurls them through the air." What he could see, to his horror, was the spar shed collapsing across the wharf like a house of cards and falling right into the *Olad II*. "It cleared those lines right out." The thirteen lesser lines, made of hemp, snapped like threads. The massive nylon line, anchored to the great chain that ran underwater the entire length of Concordia's wharf, held. The schooner swung slowly outward 180 degrees, coming to hang stern-to in the south wind. That one big line chafed through one and a half inches of the vessel's mahogany railcap, but by God it held. After the storm, the company that made the line paid the *Olad II*'s owner several hundred dollars for photographs of the vessel's stern. The pictures appeared in an ad campaign promoting the newfangled nylon lines.

Meanwhile, out in the harbor, sailboats that drew six feet of water were being washed smoothly over the bridge. They came dragging their big mushroom moorings, which caught like grappling hooks on the south side of the bridge and left the boats dangling, hung up and wrecked, on the north side. The unfortunate captain of one of these boats went overboard, and his body was discovered a few days later in the marsh on the east side of the harbor. Carol had escalated to full force so quickly—within ten minutes—that captains who had rowed out to check on their boats were trapped on them, unable to reboard their bucking dinghies. Ironically, for the most part, these manned vessels were the only ones that had any chance of surviving the storm. Two captains, one on a Concordia yawl, the other on a sloop, ran their engines on their moorings, wrenching their wheels back and forth like madmen, in a successful bid to outmaneuver an entire fleet of boats unleashed and drifting up the harbor past them. Two New York Yacht Club boats, too big to clear the bridge, met their fate stove in against it. The captain of a fifty-eight-foot ketch that was dragging two anchors and a mooring up the harbor was somehow able to maneuver his vessel to safety by grounding it on the sand spit at the corner of the bridge.

By this time, the harbor had risen a good twelve to fifteen feet above the normal high-tide mark. From his perch on the steps, Brad peered into the whipping spray and watched a PT boat anchored on the far side of the dock that the kids had broken loose from. The captain was trying to ride out the storm by running the boat's engines and facing the bow into the wind. It was no use. The boat was frighteningly underpowered. When the new owners had converted the heavy military craft to a yacht, they had pulled the huge gas engines designed to power it and replaced them with twin diesels. They were about to discover just how serious an error in judgment they had made. Unable to hold its own against the south wind, the boat was pushed stern-first all the way around the submerged wharf into Concordia Basin, an area of open water now divided by slips. As Carol's unrelenting winds shifted at last into the west, the doomed craft was propelled into a fence on Elm Street, where it finally came to rest.

If anyone hung around long enough to see the PT boat meet its fate, it wasn't Brad. He was long gone, having seen enough of Carol's fury for one morning. With the Bay rising all around him, he had sprung from his seat and fled, up into the village, up to the safety of high ground.

In the end, Carol destroyed about four thousand homes in southern New England and more than three thousand boats. Many parts of eastern Massachusetts lost electric power and phone service. Miles of power lines and countless trees were blown down. Forty percent of the region's crops, including apples, peaches, corn, and tomatoes, were destroyed by strong winds.

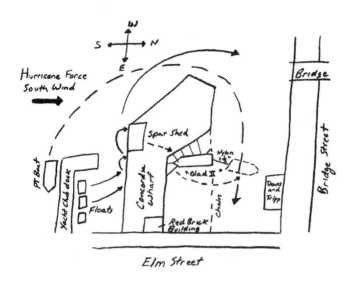

For Buzzards Bay, Hurricane Carol and the Hurricane of '38 shared many characteristics. Like '38, Carol was rated as a category 3 (extensive) hurricane. Although Carol's sustained winds were not as fierce as those in '38—registering only 80 to 100 miles per hour—her gusts reached 135. Carol also tracked to the west of the Bay, over Providence and Boston, leaving the Bay on the dreaded east side of the storm. Like '38, Carol was moving rapidly as it hit us, about 60 miles per hour.

An important difference between the two storms was that '38 hit at high tide and Carol struck slightly after it. This was fortunate, because in many places Carol actually delivered a stronger storm surge than her predecessor had. In New Bedford Harbor, the storm surge reached fourteen feet. But because Carol struck after high tide, the overall storm tide, or flood, was smaller than in '38.

Perhaps the most important difference between '38 and Carol was that people were better prepared to deal with a hurricane in 1954. Although there were still no satellites, coastal weather forecasts had improved. And thanks to the lessons learned in 1938, many fewer people lost their lives; with the great majority of deaths occurring at the storm's savage landfall in

Connecticut. Much of Carol's devastation resulted not from inadequate forecasting but rather from the storm's peculiar method of arrival.

An ad run by Potter Electric Company of Falmouth in the September 2, 1954, edition of the *Cape Cod Times* summed up Hurricane Carol the best: "Potter says—'It could have been worse. With all the damage, we have much to be thankful for. But we never want to see Carol again.'" Thankfully, we haven't. Carol was the last category 3 hurricane Buzzards Bay has experienced to this day.

HURRICANE BOB MADE LANDFALL over Newport, Rhode Island, on August 19, 1991. He came ashore escorted by tornadoes. At 11 A.M., Lieutenant Governor Paul Cellucci declared a state of emergency. By 2:30 P.M., the bridges to the Cape were shut down. Like Carol's, Bob's winds came first from the east, then the south, and finally, the west. They blew steadily for about two hours at 85 to 100 miles per hour, with gusts of 125. At 3 P.M., the two main power lines to the Cape, each carrying 115,000 volts, went down, and Com Electric's 155,000 Cape customers lost power. It was so windy on the Cape that in Provincetown Joe George sailed down Ryder Street on roller blades using his raincoat as a sail. The hurricane drove a storm surge of ten to fifteen feet into the communities of the upper Bay, causing major destruction to property, boats, crops, trees, and power lines.

Hurricane Bob, like the Hurricane of '38, struck at a time of political unrest in the world. Soviet president Mikhail Gorbachev was deposed by a military coup on the same day as the storm. The day after, a *Cape Cod Times* article read: "Moscow—Backed by fearsome military might, the chiefs of the Soviet Army, KGB, police, and fellow right-wingers yesterday sequestered Mikhail S. Gorbachev, clamped a state of emergency on Moscow and swiftly moved to freeze or gut many of the deposed Soviet President's reforms." Unrest seethed elsewhere in the world as well. A headline in the same edition of the *Cape Cod Times* read: "Iranian group seeks to delay hostage deals." The text: "Tehran, Iran—A government faction opposed to the West is seeking to delay hostage release until the 1992 U.S. presidential elections, saying the Islamic Republic can wring concessions out of the United States." Five Americans who had endured six hard years in captivity still had a year to go before they were freed.

In New Bedford, most of the damage was to trees and power lines. Over 300,000 people lost power and suffered for days after the storm with food spoilage and no telephone or water service. At the entrance to the harbor, they slammed shut the massive steel doors of the hurricane barrier, which fulfilled its purpose by successfully preventing the storm surge from reaching the inner harbor. Three hundred fishing vessels, shouldered up against the pier, were saved. The bad news was that when the gates snapped shut at 1:00 P.M., five boats that were trying desperately to make port were locked outside. They survived, riding out the storm in the outer harbor, but as you can imagine, the captains weren't happy about it.

Padanaram was one of the hardest hit communities on the Bay. Tides in the harbor rose dramatically at the height of the storm and washed over the Padanaram Bridge, collapsing it. One hundred and thirty boats, mostly sailing vessels, broke off their moorings. Twenty ended up on their sides on the bridge, and another fourteen disappeared and were presumed sunk. After the storm, the Dartmouth Police Department was strained to capacity fending off looters and sightseers.

In Fairhaven, many properties on Sconticut Neck were badly damaged by flood waters. On the shoreline of Mattapoisett, sixty-five homes and thirty boats were wrecked. Out on Angelica Point, homes were torn off their foundations. In Marion, which resembled one big tangle of fallen trees and power lines, sixty-five boats were damaged, and homes and businesses on the shore were flooded. At Tabor Academy, two large sailboats were beached on the lawn of Lillard Hall.

Bob hit Wareham about two and a half hours before high tide. Even so, the community once again suffered some of the worst damage on the Bay, with heavy flooding and widespread devastation. Twenty-five homes were destroyed, and businesses along Main Street were flooded. Hardest hit was Swifts Beach, which was so littered with debris that the National Guard was still cleaning it up five days after the storm passed.

Bourne fared nearly as poorly. The town suffered severe flood damage, with five homes destroyed and the railway damaged. The Toby Island Bridge was washed out, and the Bourne causeway was partially destroyed. There were so many fallen trees in Bourne that County and Shore Roads were closed,

and it was nearly impossible for rescue workers to reach two victims who
were trapped in their car and injured by a falling tree. Taylors Point got
flooded from both sides; the point was wrecked yet again. As he watched
his front steps floating away, John Perrone told reporters, "I thought I'd seen
everything in my 69 years, but nothing like this. I could cry, but I'm too old
to cry." In the town of Buzzards Bay, Beth Weston, age twenty-one, decided
to go for a swim down Tower Lane.

Falmouth experienced extensive damage to property and the town's fourteen harbors and beaches. Approximately three hundred boats were damaged by the storm. The staff at Falmouth Hospital had to learn to work
with paper and pencil again when the computer system was taken down.
Falmouth police log entry, 3:38 P.M. (Selectman John S. Elliot reporting):
"The eye is now near Boston. In Falmouth, we've had gusts to 85 miles
per hour and they're expecting a 15 to17 foot tidal surge in Buzzards Bay."
After the storm, in the August 27 edition of the *Falmouth Enterprise*, Hugh R.
McCarthy of Falmouth made the following comparison between Bob and
Carol: "As far as winds go, Bob was every bit as impressive as Carol. The only
difference between the two was that we caught Carol at the worst time—
high tide—and water damage here was considerably more from that storm
thirty-seven years ago. Bob dislodged big houses from their foundations.
Carol picked them up and tossed them inland or destroyed them outright."

Woods Hole took another beating, largely because high tide occurred at
4:40 P.M. there, just after Bob hit. Luckily, as David G. Aubrey of the
Oceanographic Institution noted at the time, the high tide was a relatively
small one. Nonetheless, the Landfall Restaurant, near the Vineyard ferry
terminal, flooded. The anemometer—an instrument used to measure wind
speed—broke in the Hole when winds hit ninety-six miles per hour. Local
firefighters emerged as the heroes of the storm. One of them, Gary E.
Sebens, made the following comments regarding their work to clear Woods
Hole Road: "It was pretty scary working under the big trees because large
limbs kept falling off them."

After the storm, cleanup efforts were slow, for one reason because President
Bush opted to provide federal cleanup funds for public but not private properties. Also, residents were not allowed to pump out their cellars themselves because of widespread contamination by heating oil; instead, they had

to wait for special tank trucks to arrive. Because Bob hit in August, the vital summer tourism industry took a heavy hit. Many vacationers evacuated in the hours before the storm arrived. Some power outages lasted for more than a week, which didn't help the situation. Neither did the fact that the state of emergency issued by Lieutenant Governor Cellucci was not lifted until Friday, August 23, four days after the storm. The beaches also closed. Falmouth health officials elected to close their beaches indefinitely, citing as justification flooded septic systems and animal waste from street runoff. David B. Carignan, the Falmouth health agent at the time, reported, "I've heard on the radio that New Bedford is dumping large volumes of virtually untreated sewage into Buzzards Bay." One Cape Cod motel owner, who estimated her financial losses from the storm to be $10,000, offered this insight: "In terms of the storm, it's bad for business. But if you have a gas station, a grocery store or a hardware store, it's gold."

The lasting memory shared by many is of fallen trees and downed power lines. The day after the storm, the typical Bay resident woke up, stepped outside, saw their car or fence crushed by a fallen tree, and went back in to call their insurance agent. Everywhere, you heard the sound of chainsaws clearing fallen trees. (Cape Cod Hospital later admitted twenty-five to thirty victims of chainsaw injuries.) Residents were also out power-washing away the sand, grit, and tattered leaves that covered their homes.

One of the more curious consequences of the storm was that the bees went crazy. Yellow jackets and hornets swarmed the fallen trees and stung everyone in sight, presumably because their nests had been destroyed. But no one knows precisely what caused the behavior. Cape entomologist David Simier threw up his hands and said, "Definitely their whole behavior changed. . . . Something went haywire, something got screwed up. They were actively being aggressive." Perhaps the bees were simply possessed by hurricane madness, the same madness that grips otherwise sane people during a hurricane and makes them abscond with other people's furniture in the night.

IF YOU WERE WATCHING the weather report on the morning of August 19, 1991, you would have seen a broad arrow with a sharp tip inscribed on the map, charting Hurricane Bob's trajectory as it cruised into Massachusetts. At the very tip of that arrow, on the Onset bluffs, sits the home of Alice and Frank Miller. Up in Attleboro, where Alice had taken her husband for a hospital visit, the Millers and their doctor saw that arrow. "I can check you in for one more night if you want," the physician told Frank as he turned away from the TV. "No, thanks," said the Millers in unison, and they headed back home to the Cape. Hurrying south down Route 25, theirs was the only car on the road. They passed a traffic jam headed north that extended all the way down to the Bourne Bridge. When they got to Onset, Frank said, "Why don't you go down to the hardware store and get some batteries for the radio, just in case." So Alice picked up their little buff-colored dog, Sam, and walked down the road fronting the harbor the short distance to the store. When she emerged, it was exactly noon, and all the light had gone out of the world. That's how fast a hurricane comes up: in the amount of time it takes to buy batteries. A pelting rain slashed at her face. Out in front of the bluffs the Bay was churning. Alice was frightened. She knew she had to get back up the steep hill to the house, and there was no shelter between here and there. Sam was trembling, more scared than she was, so she tucked him under her raincoat and bravely set off. She struggled to walk against the high winds and through the water flowing around her ankles.

By the time she reached the house, Alice was soaked to the bone beneath her raingear and covered in debris. She wouldn't want you to know this, but she stripped down right in the hallway and changed. It was raining so hard that Alice and Frank could barely see out their windows. The house started taking on water through the second-floor sliders that faced the Bay. If you sit on the Millers' couch today and look up at the dropped ceiling, you can still see water stains, compliments of Bob. To prevent the house from flooding, Alice took a half-dozen bath towels and started soaking up the water that was pooling on the floor. She'd wring them out into buckets, then quickly open the sliders and throw the water out. Sometimes, between filling buckets, she would glance hurriedly outside to see what was going on in the harbor. She saw boats being thrown right up onto the Point Independence Yacht Club building. Half a dozen more were stacked up under the Point Independence Bridge. Out in front of the house, the Bay had come over the beach and surged ten feet up the twenty-foot bluff. That afternoon, after Bob passed, lots of people went down on the beach to gawk at the remains of wrecked boats. Several hundred had broken off their moorings. Some of them landed on the main beach, others in front of the old Holland Inn, a few on Wickets Island out in the middle of the harbor.

One of these casualties, a cabin cruiser, lay with its FOR SALE sign clearly visible. Some locals called up the owner and told him, "You had better get down here and get the For Sale sign off your boat," which he promptly did. Frank figures the owner made out much better from his insurance reimbursement than he would have if he had sold that boat.

The basements of the homes on Independence Point were all flooded, with water reaching up to their porches. Onset Mobile Park, full of trailers, was swamped. The Stone Bridge Marina was totally destroyed. For a week afterward, the streets in Onset were blocked off, and giant flatbed trucks and cranes rolled in. It was great entertainment for the Millers, watching the big boats being disassembled and hauled away. Not so entertaining was waiting five days for the electricity to come back on.

The demented yellow jackets were everywhere, and all the residents of Onset were talking about them. Alice, shaking her head in wonder, told me, "We never, *ever* had bees here." The bees were particularly active up around the second floor of the Miller's home, which was the declared territory of Sam the dog. According to Frank, the tiny hunter chased them around like the proverbial chicken with its head cut off. In the end, Sam got what he wished for and ran under the bed yelping, stung hard in the mouth.

Up on the bluff, overlooking the tranquil Bay, a Japanese cherry that had been stripped of its leaves bloomed, much to the astonishment of the Millers and the throngs of milling tourists. Alice thinks the phenomenon was a result of the warm air the hurricane brought. All around Onset, azaleas followed suit, putting on stunning shows of pink and coral-red blossoms.

Because of several important differences between Bob and its predecessors, '38 and Carol, the storm caused less destruction to Buzzards Bay than either of the other two. Chief among the differences, both the arrival and the track of Bob were forecasted. Also, though Bob was rated a category 3 hurricane over Cape Hatteras, by the time it reached the Bay it had diminished to a relatively weak category 2 storm. Bob was moving at around thirty miles per hour as it approached the Bay, but it slowed down. In contrast, '38 raced through at sixty miles per hour. It also helped that Bob struck most areas before high tide. It was very fortunate for the communities around Buzzards Bay that Bob's winds diminished and its forward motion slowed, because historically an accelerating category 3 hurricane results in deaths. The hurricane did kill six people in Connecticut.

Nevertheless, compared to other parts of the state, Hurricane Bob was particularly hard on Buzzards Bay and Cape Cod, largely because of its track, which lay just to the west of the Cape Cod Canal. This left the Bay on the east side of the storm, and the storm's strongest winds hit towns such as Wareham and Falmouth. Final damage estimates by the governor's office approached $1 billion for coastal Massachusetts, with most of the damage sustained on Cape Cod.

When all was said and done, Robert Thomson, chief meteorologist at the National Weather Service in Taunton, characterized Bob best: "Bob was in a year with a minimum amount of hurricane activity. All it takes is one."

SO WHAT KIND of hurricane activity can we expect on Buzzards Bay in the future? Dr. William Gray, of Colorado State University, known to meteorologists as the granddaddy of hurricane forecasters, might be the individual best suited to answer that question. Gray has forty years of experience in meteorology and has specialized in predicting hurricanes since 1984. He notes that, globally, there has been no increase in the number or intensity of hurricanes in recent years. Since 1995, however, there has been an increase in both the number and intensity of hurricanes in the Atlantic Basin. According to Gray, we shouldn't think about hurricanes as having active or quiet years, nor as having long-term, gradually rising and falling cycles. Instead, he points out that major Atlantic hurricane activity appears to alternate between active and quiet phases that span twenty-five to forty years. Quiet periods appear to correspond with cooler-than-normal water temperatures in the North Atlantic. This was the case from the 1970s to the early 1990s. In the active hurricane period from the late 1920s through the 1960s, the North Atlantic was warmer than usual. Water temperatures have begun to heat up there since 1995. On his Web site, Gray states, "It is quite possible that the extreme [hurricane] activity since 1995 marks the start of another active period that may last a total of twenty-five to forty years."

Gray's Web site also provides a chart labeled "Atlantic Basin—Individual years with the numbers in each category." In the column that lists the number of major hurricanes for each year, there is no total greater than three in the years from 1965 to 1994. Once you get to 1995, however, the numbers look like this:

YEAR	N° OF MAJOR STORMS
1995	5
1996	6
1997	1
1998	3
1999	5

Gray's charts also indicate that the total number of hurricanes (as opposed to only major ones) for each of these years has risen drastically, which points to a sharp rise in overall storm activity. This is important because as storm activity picks up, the odds that we will be dealt a major hurricane increase.

JOHN GHIORSE WARNS that it is difficult to generalize when predicting the effects of hurricanes because each one arrives with its own unique twist. That said, a historical analysis of the hurricanes that have wrought the heaviest damage on Buzzards Bay furnishes an equation that nearly always adds up to massive destruction of coastline, property, and potentially, human life. The equation: A hurricane of at least category 2 (moderate) winds tracks northward up the East Coast unimpeded by a Bermuda high, accelerates as it enters our area, tracks to the west of the Bay, and strikes at or near high tide. This deadly set of circumstances has remained unrealized since Hurricane Carol in 1954. History tells us that it's only a matter of time until it happens again.

As nature's way of regulating the heat and energy of the planet, hurricanes are a vital part of our ecosystem. John, who is intimately familiar with their destructive effects, told me: "We wouldn't want to get rid of hurricanes even if we could." The trick for us, then, is to learn how to live with them and to remember the lessons we've been taught. Forgetting is a real possibility, because hurricanes that possess the deadly combination of characteristics necessary to inflict the kind of damage that 1938 did to Buzzards Bay may come along only once every hundred years.

John buys into the theory that our region is presently in a cycle of accelerated storm activity, and that as a result the odds are good that Buzzards Bay will experience a direct hit from a major hurricane in the near future. Unless you were around for Carol in 1954, you haven't lived through anything like it.

SOUTH BEACH at Salter's Point in South Dartmouth is a wild place. The summer residents don't go there much, preferring to swim at the little beach on the north side of the point that hunkers down in the lee of the incessant southwest wind. South Beach is reserved for the occasional solitary fisherman, sunbather, dog walker, or young people pitching tents on the weekend, overflow from one of the homes hosting a wedding. Mostly, though, the beach is home to wild creatures.

In the morning, if you get there in the gray half-light, before the splendid pink orb of the rising sun dominates the horizon, you may glimpse the nervous doe and her fawn clinging to the border of the marsh. She will have seen you first, and with one fluid bound and a white flash of tail she and her offspring will disappear into the tawny grass. Less often, you will see the buck in his glory, looking as if he is gathering all the light of the emerging day between the tines of his rack. The watchful osprey wheels low overhead here, *cheep-cheeping* like an overgrown songbird, and the snowy egrets hold their posts along the shallow sliding rivulet that joins the salt pond to the sea, stillness made stiller by motion. The terns beat in low over the beach with military discipline from who-knows-where out to sea, delivering their squirming silver payload of fish to waiting nestlings. Over the sliding silver stream, chestnut-and-blue barn swallows twist and turn, rise and dip, as thick as mayflies, showing the world what it means to fly. Purple-blossomed beach pea riots in sea-green tangles over the rocky upper beach, and in the wet, heavy silence of the dawn, after a warm night-time rain, the tiny whorls of garden snails, pale orange or yellow, enliven the damp sand flowing beneath the rich green foliage and perfumed magenta blossoms of the beach roses.

South Beach wasn't always this way, wasn't always wild. In the early years of the twentieth century, a row of nine cottages stood here, staring out through white-rimmed eyes at the long shadowy line of the Elizabeth Islands on the horizon. They were cottages only in the most liberal sense of the word; no beach shanties these, but fine homes, built of good timber, cedar shingle, and red brick. In the daytime, throngs of smiling, tanned young people lay on the smooth white beach, sucking up the comforting heat into their grateful bodies. In the evening, young children were bathed in claw-foot tubs and put to bed early between clean white sheets upstairs, where they could hear the voices of laughing men and women, the tinkling of ice into cocktail glasses, and the strains of jazz music rising from below. The warm southwest wind hummed through the open windows, harassing the wispy curtains, and the children were never without the murmur and crash of the waves. With their feet they could feel the gritty sand that had reached the bottom of their beds despite their mother's best efforts, and they pulled the sheets and light cotton blankets over their heads to better see the ghostly green flashes of fireflies that they had smuggled in, trapped inside a glass mason jar with holes punched in the lid. The teenagers dribbled in later, in groups, the boys falling asleep wondering at that special sweet girl, a child-hood friend, that had bloomed just that summer into a soft, curved surprise bearing the dark mystery and irresistible attraction of woman.

On September 21, 1938, the great hurricane came and took it all. The Bay rose in a fury, and with her watery, fierce gray grip seized the fine timbers and bricks of the cottages and, along with all the gentle memories, washed them away, across the salt pond behind the beach, scattering them in bits well inland. One man's life went with them. The entry in a local history book kept by residents, captioned "HURRICANE, September 21," reads, "The tide rose 11 feet above normal high tide and the wind blew 100 miles an hour." A black-and-white photo shot after the storm, taken at a wide angle down the length of the beach, depicts a scene reminiscent of the after-math of an atomic bomb blast. The line of fine homes is gone, the view down the beach unobstructed to distant Mishaum Point. With the exception of one great timber, there is not even any wood visible, only boulders strewn over what used to be the smooth sandy beach.

Over the years, the storms and tides have softened South Beach, bringing back the sand, but clues to the tragedy remain. A singular brick-and-mortar fireplace hearth erupts oddly out of the sand. A surf-smoothed set of gray concrete steps, set at an angle, comes and goes with the drifting sand. Occasionally you stumble over a round pink brick. And perhaps most curi-ous of all, a man and his wife sit religiously on the same spot of beach each bluebird summer afternoon. They unfailingly smile and greet passers-by with the words "Nice day, isn't it?" They are descendents of those residents who lived to see that day in 1938 that was anything but nice, and what's left of their inheritance is the parcel of wild beach on which they now sit.

At least one of the homes on South Beach was later rebuilt. Its fate is told in an entry in the local history dated 1954: "Hurricane Carol—House on South Beach washed away." At some point, people with sense decided that the homes on the beach must never be rebuilt. Across the United States today, our population is flocking to the coasts, recklessly building homes on islands, on barrier beaches, in places known formerly only to the terns and the other wild creatures. Those who build them choose to ignore the lessons of the past, and are thus doomed to relive tragedies such as the one that occurred on Salter's Point in September of 1938. For hurricanes, in the end, are nature's way of warning us there are some places she holds dear, some places that are better off left wild.

The Elizabeth Islands

At length we were come amongst many faire Islands, which we

had partly discerned at our first landing; all lying within a

league or two of one another, and the outermost not above six

or seven leagues from the maine.

—BRERETON, ON GOSNOLD'S DISCOVERY OF NANTUCKET,
MARTHA'S VINEYARD, AND THE ELIZABETH ISLANDS

THE ELIZABETH ISLANDS are a chain of islands that run from
Woods Hole fourteen miles in a southwesterly direction to the mouth of
Buzzards Bay. The Elizabeths form the boundary between the Bay and
Vineyard Sound. Accordingly, the Wampanoag name for these islands,
Nashanow, means "between." The main islands in the chain are Naushon,
Pasque, Nashawena, Cuttyhunk, and Penikese. Together they form the town
of Gosnold. Cuttyhunk is the only island in the Elizabeths that is entirely
accessible to the public (generally by ferry), and the only island that has any
commercial development. Penikese is owned by the state of Massachusetts
and run by MassWildlife as a bird sanctuary. The state also leases a portion
of the island to the Penikese Island School, a rehabilitation facility for troubled teenage boys. The rest of the islands are privately owned by the Forbes
family of Boston. With very few exceptions (boaters have limited access to
beaches at Tarpaulin Cove on Naushon and Quicks Hole on Nashawena),
these islands are inaccessible to the general public.

> *In this island is a stage or pond of fresh water, in circuit two miles, on the*
> *one side not distant from the sea thirty yards, in the center whereof is a*
> *rocky islet, containing near an acre of ground full of wood, on which we*
> *began our fort and place of abode, disposing itself so fit for the same.*
> —ARCHER, ON GOSNOLD'S HISTORIC SETTLEMENT ON CUTTYHUNK

WILLIAM SHAKESPEARE CONTEMPLATED his companion in the same manner that an old man admires a beautiful young woman. It was worldly men like the one now before him that provided the playwright with the threads his literary genius spun into priceless cloth. "I must ask thee to repeat thyself, friend," he said deliberately, his features registering surprise. "Thy words struck mine ear most terribly."

Bartholomew Gosnold swirled the port in his crystal glass and stared into it thoughtfully before replying. "Thou'st heard right, Sir, 'tis true. Methinks I am going back, this time to a colony we shall establish in Virginia. Curse that Elizabeth Isle, dam of sea-storms, and those bothersome savages at Gosnold Hole. 'Tis in Virginia that Heaven will grant England permanence in the New World. If ever I return to thee again, I pray it will be with a noble fortune."

England was beginning her rise to prominence in the world, and the young lioness counted these two men among her greatest souls. The masterful writer was at the height of his power, all his plays behind him but one. The celebrated explorer had only just returned from his voyage to New England, where he had discovered and named Cape Cod and Gosnold Hole, which we know as Buzzards Bay. Unbeknownst to Gosnold, he would never again see his "stately sound." He would die of disease in Jamestown, Virginia, along with half of that fledgling colony, at the age of thirty-five.

On that congenial evening, Gosnold filled Shakespeare's hungry ears with raw tales of an island boasting storms so fierce and a reef so fearful that no ship blown to her shores could escape doom. The great mind of the bard, a force of its own, began to work. Years later, in 1611, the author would hearken back to that evening spent with the explorer when he began to spin a final, magical tale of shipwreck and the supernatural set on a remote, tempestuous island.

"*Boatswain!*"

"Here, Master; what cheer?"

"Good; speak to the mariners. Fall to 't, yarely, or we run ourselves aground. Bestir, bestir."

On the far side of the Atlantic, Shakespeare wrote *The Tempest* while dreaming of Cuttyhunk.

I ADMIT THAT THIS SCENARIO is my speculation, but some scholars have suggested that the unnamed island in *The Tempest* was Cuttyhunk. This idea is based largely on the fact that Gosnold's voyage to America was sponsored by the Earl of Southampton, who at the same time was a patron of Shakespeare's. The supposition is that because the two men had the same "employer," they must have known each other and may have discussed Gosnold's voyage. Of course, scholars have suggested other inspirations for the island; for example, my Harvard Classics edition of *The Tempest* suggests that it was "the Bermudas." But, being a Yankee, I prefer to believe that Shakespeare's island is really *my* Cuttyhunk.

Cuttyhunk is the southwestern-most island—the one on the very tip—of the Elizabeth Island chain. It marks the traditional eastern boundary of the entrance to Buzzards Bay. The island is approximately two miles long and one mile wide, or about five hundred acres in size. The name *Cuttyhunk* is derived from the island's Wampanoag name, *Poocutohhunkunnoh*, which according to one translation means "place out in the middle of the sea." Historians believe that the Wampanoags used Cuttyhunk, like Penikese, only as a temporary base for hunting and fishing.

In 1602, Gosnold discovered the island and named it Elizabeth Isle, after Queen Elizabeth I. His encampment on the island was the first English settlement in America. At the time of Gosnold's settlement, Cuttyhunk may have been attached to neighboring Nashawena Island, for the Englishman estimated its circumference to be at least sixteen miles. Gosnold's men built a fort and a storehouse on a tiny island in West End Pond. Today, Gosnold Monument, erected in 1903 by the Old Dartmouth Historical Society, marks the location. The settlement lasted only three weeks before the men decided they wanted to go home. Apparently, they didn't find much of value in the area except furs, cedar, and sassafras, which was plentiful on the island and was used medicinally in England. In addition, the men who had been chosen to stay behind, probably to maintain the settlement as a trading post, knew they would be left with inadequate provisions. Also, Gosnold's relationship with the local Native Americans might have been rapidly deteriorating. When they first arrived on Cuttyhunk, the men found the ruins of a wigwam and a fishing weir. Later, they traded with friendly Native Americans visiting from the mainland. According to Archer's account, however, the Englishmen took an abandoned canoe from Penikese Island,

and the natives later turned hostile and attacked them, an unfortunate event that may have figured in their decision to leave.

From about the mid-1600s, much of Cuttyhunk was owned by the Slocum family of Dartmouth, who used the island for farming and grazing sheep. At one point, it was actually known as Slocum's Island. Families on the island kept small gardens and owned cows and chickens. The men farmed and fished for mackerel in the spring, lobsters in the summer, cod in the fall, and quahogs in the winter. Around 1685 all the Elizabeth Islands, including Cuttyhunk, were assigned to the town of Chilmark on Martha's Vineyard. In 1864, the Cuttyhunk Fishing Club bought most of the island from the Slocums and brought prosperity to many locals by employing them as chummers, gardeners, and caretakers. The Fishing Club also brought regular ferry service from New Bedford, and boardinghouses and tourism on the island started to thrive. Also in 1864, the Elizabeths seceded from the town of Chilmark and formed their own town, Gosnold, with Cuttyhunk as its seat.

In the eighteenth and nineteenth centuries, both Buzzards Bay and Vineyard Sound were extremely busy shipping channels. In 1851 more than six thousand ships, mostly schooners, passed Cuttyhunk in three months. In the late 1800s, when whaling was king in New Bedford and clipper ships traded heavily with the Far East, many Cuttyhunkers served as pilots guiding ships through the treacherous ledges of Buzzards Bay. Pilots would sit up on Lookout Hill with their "long glasses," or telescopes, and watch for approaching sails. According to the Cuttyhunk Historical Society, Cuttyhunk pilots once guided eleven ships into New Bedford in a single day.

Exceptionally strong winds, heavy seas, and fog combined to make these routes extremely dangerous. The treacherous Sow and Pigs Reef, off Cuttyhunk's west end, is part of a marine area on the south side of the Elizabeths that sailors called "the Graveyard" because countless shipwrecks occurred there. (The last whaling ship to sail out of New Bedford, the *Wanderer*, was shipwrecked off the west end of Cuttyhunk in 1924.) First the Massachusetts Humane Society, then the U.S. Life-Saving Service, and finally the Coast Guard maintained life-saving stations on the island, which was the scene of many heroic rescues. Today the island cemetery is filled with the unmarked graves of sailors who washed ashore and the headstones of Cuttyhunkers who died in rescue attempts.

After World War II, summer people began flocking to Cuttyhunk. Power-boating grew popular, and docks and other marine facilities were built on the shoreline to accommodate visitors. By the 1950s, most Cuttyhunk men made their living as bass, swordfish, tuna, white marlin, and dorado fishermen. Some remained in the traditional occupations of lobstering, cod fishing, and shellfishing.

Today, Cuttyhunk Island is quaint and thinly populated, attracting residents who want sea views, a slow pace, and solitude. Unlike nearby Martha's Vineyard, no celebrities congregate there. There are few restaurants or other amenities. You can't even buy liquor. Most tourists rent a mooring on Cuttyhunk Pond, the main harbor, which can be reached via a narrow channel from the Bay, walk up Lookout Hill to marvel at the view, buy a souvenir, sample some seafood, and set sail after lunch. And that's exactly the way the Cuttyhunkers, who treasure their island paradise, want to keep it.

I WENT TO CUTTYHUNK in search of the supernatural. I had only just begun researching the island when I learned that it is inhabited by ghosts, known to the islanders as haunts. As recently as the summer of 2003, locals reported seeing a little girl in an old-fashioned white dress drifting along the shoreline like a wisp of fog. There are other indications, too, of the supernatural on the island. An ancient, mysterious Wampanoag phallic symbol was found on one of the beaches. And there are islanders who observe an unwritten rule that old people who are sick must never be sent there. Conversely, Cuttyhunkers who are sick believe they will recuperate faster if they remain on the island. Some islanders mail sea glass that they collect on the island to working mariners, believing it will stave off disaster.

What I was most interested in was ley lines, that is, paths that connect ancient or sacred sites and that allegedly channel supernatural energy. I had in hand a 1995 *Boston Globe* review of *The Sparrowhook Curse* by Robin Moore, author of *The French Connection* (and coauthor of *The Happy Hooker*), who spent many summers at his parent's home on Cuttyhunk. In the book review, Moore is quoted as saying that two ley lines cross on the island, on Cemetery Road near the shore. In 1980 a physicist visited the island and reportedly confirmed the existence of the ley lines by dowsing. One of the lines is said to wing right across Lookout Hill near the observation stand before soaring out over the Atlantic. And in the *Globe* article, Moore claims that Split Rock, a granite boulder on the hill that is neatly halved in two as if by a laser, owes its division to the force of this ley line.

Some islanders also believe that Cuttyhunk is inhabited by little people, mischievous leprechauns whose personalities lean heavily toward the dark side. Robin Moore claims that Split Rock is the home of the Deva, a spirit that controls the little people. He relates the Cuttyhunk legend about how, when businessman William Madison Wood started to build a mansion on Lookout Hill for his son Billy Wood in 1924, the little people went up to Andover, Massachusetts, and caused Billy to drive his brand-new Stutz Bearcat into a tree. Billy was killed, construction of the house ended, and the hill was left to the Deva.

Belief in the little people reaches farther back than current islanders and authors of thrillers. In fact, the Wampanoags believed that the Elizabeth Islands owed their very existence to little people. They believed that there were little people called Pukwudgees, about ten inches tall, who constantly annoyed and played tricks on them. According to myth, the natives asked Maushop, a giant who lived in the cliffs of Aquinnah (formerly Gay Head on Martha's Vineyard) and ate whales, to help them exterminate the troublesome tricksters. Maushop and his five sons started to pursue the little people, but the Pukwudgees discovered the plan and killed Maushop's sons with bows and arrows. Maushop carried his sons' bodies to Buzzards Bay and buried them there. Over time, as the waters of the Bay rose, the mounds of sediment under which their bodies lay were separated, forming the Elizabeth Island chain. So, when Robin Moore talks about the little people, he may unwittingly be describing the Pukwudgees, visiting the island to dance on the grave of a fallen enemy, which would be just like them.

It was with all this lore in my head that I first went to Cuttyhunk, in the winter, the very depth of the natural year. The island was gray, windswept, and empty. I stood alone near Cuttyhunk Pond and watched its sole inhabitant, a herring gull, drop a quahog on an empty dock. I gazed across the bleak water at the rise of land bordering Canapitsit Channel, that treacherous, rock-strewn passage that separates Cuttyhunk from neighboring Nashawena Island. Standing there, I got the distinct feeling that my presence was known—not exactly watched—by something brooding, something slightly unfriendly. It was a restrained force that wanted to act but could not, like a chained German shepherd. I tried to dismiss the feeling as a product of the gloomy season and my recent research into the supernatural.

Later that day, with the article about Moore in hand, I visited Split Rock on Lookout Hill. I perched on the rock, my arms draped out at right angles like spiritual antennae, and tried to detect the force of the ley line. I felt nothing. Next, I stood with one foot on either side of the crack, my body thus divided by the line. Still nothing. Glancing down between my feet, I noticed that the fissure was chock-full of discarded peanut shells, a suspicious state for the pathway of a force reputably strong enough to split granite. Desperate for a supernatural fix, I at last reclined on the rock, striking exactly Moore's pose in the *Globe* photo. I even tried taunting the Deva, but there was just nothing out of the ordinary there. I left Cuttyhunk that day feeling disappointed, thwarted in my quest for the supernatural. It was not until my next visit that I began to discern the truth about Cuttyhunk. There is magic there, but it resides in nothing more exotic than the people and the relationship they have with the land.

I RETURNED TO CUTTYHUNK the following June. I made the crossing on the *Alert II*, a ferry based out of New Bedford. The *Alert II* is long, low, lean, and blue, like the early-season bluefish that some people call racers. She was docked behind a fleet of rusted-out commercial fishing boats with names like *Georges Bank* that look as if they've been to hell and back. I watched the crew load three silver kegs of Sierra Nevada Ale, a brown box with a duct tape label that said "Full o' Beef," one washing machine, and two potted arborvitaes. A musician in a cheap blue suit wandered by carrying a battered guitar case and a music stand. On board, I shared the stern with a red-haired woman dressed all in pink, with pink blotches noticeably covering her face. Unsmiling, she stared resolutely in the direction of the island. By the time we disembarked she was laughing.

On shore, the atmosphere could not have been more different from my previous visit. It was the first day of summer. Well, not officially, but it was the first day the sun had shone in three weeks. The islanders, whose winter population of 35 swells to about 500 during the summer months, welcomed its appearance, rejoicing, everyone commenting on it with wide smiles. The day was also memorable because the gentle, golden light that characterizes the Bay in the summer hung sublimely over Cuttyhunk Pond. The island was drunk on the heated scent of beach roses. The sea was sultry and heavy as well, with that kind of quiet surf that echoes in your head like an afterthought. The trills of red-winged blackbirds and the brilliant solos of song sparrows gave voice to a general feeling of warmth and well-being.

I asked a passerby where I could find the Corner Store, where I hoped to get a cup of coffee. "Over there, on the corner," he said dryly, looking at me as if I were daft. After that, I stopped asking questions. Up the street, I passed a building with a wooden swordfish over the doorway that read MARKET. Golf carts whizzed by with assorted bumper stickers: SAVE BUZZARDS BAY; SCHOOL'S OUT DRIVE CAREFULLY; I'M NOT A TOURIST I'M AN ARMED NATIVE. On the island, golf carts and ancient pickup trucks are the chief modes of transportation.

I went down to the Fish Dock because I learned that's where everything happens on Cuttyhunk. Whenever I called a Cuttyhunker for an interview, I would be told, "You'll probably find me down on the dock." On my first visit there, I spoke with Jimmy Nunes, a charter boat captain who has lived on the island all his life. My original plan had been to meet with Charlie Tilton Jr., another renowned captain descended from an old island family, but he gave me the slip. I had read about Charlie and his family in *Cuttyhunk and the Elizabeth Islands*, a book published by the Cuttyhunk Historical Society. In the book, there is a picture of Charlie as a young man with his father, Charlie Tilton Sr., another renowned fishing guide, gaffing a great white shark. The shark swam into Cuttyhunk Harbor in August 1954, and Charlie and his father went out and harpooned it. It took them three hours to haul it in. The fish scales on the island weren't up to the task of weighing it. Locals estimated that the thirteen-foot, seven-inch shark weighed between fifteen and eighteen hundred pounds.

I approached Jimmy mistakenly thinking he was Charlie, at the pre-agreed time I was supposed to "find" Charlie Tilton on the dock.

"I just passed Charlie coming in," said Jimmy, watching my expression carefully. "He must be halfway to the Vineyard by now. I'm Jimmy Nunes."

I grinned and tried to make the best of it. "Actually, I was hoping to interview you as well."

Jimmy was disembarking from his striper boat with a tight-knit group of fishermen who clearly had no intention of speaking with a stranger. When I gave him my pitch about being a writer, they looked at him inquiringly, as much as to ask if this was a potentially ugly situation that needed resolving. Jimmy hesitated, then turned to me with a gentleman's look of defeat. "We're going up the house for lunch," he said. "We'll talk when we come back?" I nodded. When their golf cart purred back onto the dock, Jimmy dismounted from his cart like a cowboy from his horse and joined me in the doorway of his captain's shed. Beside us stood a big silent guy dressed in full black and brown camouflage. The man had caught fifteen stripers that weighed more than fifty pounds, Jimmy told me by way of an introduction. I wasn't about to argue with them.

"How's the fishing?" I ventured.

"Fishin's always great, it's the results that vary," quipped Jimmy with a sparkle in his blue eyes.

I explained that I was interested in what was happening environmentally out on the Bay. Jimmy perked up. "I'll tell you who's wrecking the Bay. Those big draggers coming out of New Bedford dump all their garbage overboard when they hit Quick's Hole." I asked whether he ever saw any of the punctured five-gallon drums of waste oil rumored to be dumped by some boats in the fleet. "I see them drums full of oil all the time." Jimmy was becoming uneasy. The silent guy in the camo looked as if he were considering methods for disposing of me. I figured I had time for just one more question.

"What's changed on Cuttyhunk since you were a kid?"

Without hesitation Jimmy replied, "Old-time Cuttyhunkers are dying out and the tourists are taking over." He nodded in the direction of the sleek sport-fishing yachts cluttering the pond. "Prices on property have skyrocketed. Things have gotten so bad out here that some people have put their homes in trusts so their kids can't sell out." About ten minutes had passed, and Jimmy looked imploringly at me. "Have we talked enough yet? I want to go fishin'." I thanked him and watched as he and his mates immediately embarked and headed back out to sea.

Up the dock a bit from Jimmy Nune's striper boat lies the *Oldsquaw*, Bruce Borge's lobster vessel. When I first met Bruce, he was pitchforking various body parts of striped bass, big striped bass, into a tub of salt to be used as bait. He was horsing around with a couple of island kids he had obviously known since birth. Bruce is the only lobsterman on Cuttyhunk, where the fishery originated. He's been lobstering there for forty years. In the winter, Bruce fishes for crabs down in Florida, using about three hundred crab pots. In addition to being the only lobsterman on Cuttyhunk, Bruce is very likely to be the last. I asked him how the lobstering was in Buzzards Bay.

"I've been fishing the Sound for fifteen years now. Bay's been sick that long. The Sound's getting to be the same way. Same thing's going on with the crabs in Florida. . . . No one knows what the problem is, too much salinity, too little salinity. . . . "

"When you're gone, will there be anyone else?" I asked.

"Nope, none of the young guys want to do this," he replied.

Bruce has some interesting theories about the crash of the local lobster fishery. According to him, technology ruined everything. Today, anybody can drop a trap and return to it with the aid of modern navigation equipment. He also believes that the wire trap contributed to the fishery's decline. "If we outlawed wire traps, two-thirds of the guys would leave the business. They wouldn't be able to carry enough traps to make it worthwhile."

Bruce told me that it's not the same out there on the water anymore, either. "Used to be, you'd set two lines of traps and not think twice. Nowadays, you come back and somebody's run a line right through 'em." From the sound of it, Bruce isn't long for the business. "There's talk of a buyout," he muttered, "and if there is, I'll be first in line."

My next challenge was to find Don Lynch, the islander who owns the Sea Tow franchise for southeastern Massachusetts, including Cape Cod. When I was trying to find him, I mistakenly approached a captain on the dock named Duane Lynch. He was sitting on a stool in his captain's shed plucking eel skins out of a ten-gallon bucket of water. He was making eel skin rigs, a traditional striped bass bait made by stretching the skin of an eel over a chain or a conventional bass plug. Noticing that I was watching him, he glanced up and said, "Not many people know how to do this anymore." "You're not Don, right?" I asked. "Nope." "Can you tell me where I can find Don?" "Go up to the corner, go left, his is the house with like four boats in the yard." Later, I told Don how I had found him. "That would be my son, Duane," he said, laughing.

If you see a Sea Tow boat on the water, it's one of Don's. He keeps a couple of his yellow boats on the water at all times, with one usually down around Falmouth. His base is a large rustic barn near the shore of Cuttyhunk Pond, with a yard full of bright yellow boats in various stages of repair. Don's a Cuttyhunk native. He left the island only to attend high school. He spent eleven years as the Cuttyhunk harbormaster in the 1970s, but the $75-per-year salary wasn't cutting it, so he started a boatyard. He ran the boatyard for seventeen years before investing in the Sea Tow franchise.

"What'd the locals think?" I asked him.

"They didn't warm up to the idea right away. They didn't see a need for it." Don did. He knew from his experiences as harbormaster and at the boatyard that there was a market for services to boaters in distress that neither one provided.

"Why Sea Tow?" I wondered out loud, eyeing the canary-yellow boats with apprehension.

"You can run a local hamburger stand," Don counseled me, "but you're never going to make as much money as a McDonald's."

As Don talked, his phone rang. "Right," he said into the receiver, "that's the cost of a year's membership. It covers all your boats—if you've got three boats, it covers all three." Long pause. "We get you back to your car, sir, no matter where we pick you up. Would you care to join up?"

Don takes pride in the fact that he helps people out, but he makes sure they understand that his help is a business transaction. When one of Don's boats comes alongside you, they get your credit card number even before tossing you a line. (Almost everyone expects a line *immediately* in trouble situations.)

Don's great-uncles were Cuttyhunkers and made their livings as wreckers (marine salvagers). "Back then," he told me, "the ships were full of ivory and what-not." I asked if he considered himself a modern-day wrecker, and he looked mildly annoyed.

"That's a term they use more down on Montauk," he said. "Those guys—in the old days—helped out with shipwrecks, and they got a just reward. That's how most of the homes out here were built, you know. Lumber from ships."

My *Webster's Dictionary*, printed in 1989, defines wrecker as "One who causes ship wrecks or plunders wrecks; one who recovers goods from wrecked vessels." It's highly doubtful whether that definition has been updated since 1989. It's also doubtful whether Don's ancestors had any need to cause shipwrecks, since Sow and Pigs Reef would have provided for them very nicely in that regard.

Don grew up listening to AM radio reports that covered fish landings in New Bedford. These broadcasts also reported when local vessels sank. Talking about the salvaging business, he got a mildly insane gleam in his eyes. "I do it," he told me, "because I love being out there, in the thick of it, the lightning, the storms. . . . I guess I like to help people."

"Do you really go out in bad weather?"

"The greater the risk, the greater the save, the greater the gain," Don chanted, like a mantra. These days, most of his business comes from rescuing recreational boaters who have a dead battery or are out of gas. Commercial salvaging jobs have dropped off. Even Sow and Pigs doesn't give him the business it did back in the days when he called it "Bread and Butter Reef." One reason he cited for this decline is modern navigational equipment. Don lauded the benefits of the new technology, but I couldn't help thinking that it has hurt his business as much as it has lobsterman Bruce Borge's. The development of steel hulls also had an impact on the salvaging business. When fishing boats were made of wood, they'd freeze up at the dock in New Bedford and go down.

"I'd get all the sinkers out of New Bedford," Don recalled, "mostly scallopers." He pointed to the government's practice of limiting the number of days fishermen can spend at sea for the drop-off in his salvaging business. Fishermen now have more time to maintain their boats, and they can avoid going out to sea on the worst weather days.

A typical salvage job for Don might involve a ship that has run up onto the shore of Naushon Island. Don's men will "lighter" the ship—offload its cargo—and patch any holes that unforgiving boulders have punched in its hull. Then he'll hire tugs to haul the ship off the beach. Don gets paid a percentage of the value of the cargo that he's saved. When the wreck involves hazardous materials, he gets paid a percentage of the total environmental cleanup costs that the owners would have incurred. For reasons that he doesn't care to discuss, Don does less oil spill cleanup work than he used to. His crew was first on the scene of the *Bermuda Star* oil spill on Cleveland Ledge in 1990. In contrast, his company's involvement with the 2003 *Bouchard 120* oil spill cleanup was limited to pushing rented barges carrying cleanup crews around the shoreline of the Bay.

Don Lynch is one of those lucky people who makes his living doing what he loves. But it's cost him. The last thing he told me was that he'd been through two marriages. In the end, both women told him, "Don, you've got to quit doing the pirate thing."

THE CUTTYHUNK FISHING CLUB was founded in the summer of 1864, when seven New York millionaires sailed into Cuttyhunk searching for a suitable spot for a fishing club. They bought nearly the entire island and built their club on the southeast shore. They built sixteen fishing stands, constructed of narrow plank walks and platforms and supported by iron pipes. Eventually, the club grew to seventy-five members, and each was allowed to host one guest per season. The season ran from June 15 to the fall. Each evening, the members would hold a drawing for the stands, some of which were more desirable than others. In the morning, before dawn, the fishermen would trek out to their allotted stands accompanied by chummers. Chummers were Cuttyhunkers hired to throw bait, usually lobster tails, into the water to attract striped bass. Charlie Tilton, the captain who gave me the slip, has ancestors who were chummers. The average bass the men caught weighed nine pounds. The largest bass caught in 1870 weighed forty-seven pounds, in 1874 fifty-five pounds, in 1882 sixty-four pounds. The men caught these fish using reels, originally made of wood, that had no drags other than the fisherman's thumb. They disliked the numerous bluefish because the fishes' teeth easily severed their linen fishing lines.

At the end of the day, the fishermen would return to the club for a meal of several courses, liquor, and rare wines. After dinner, the day's catch was weighed and displayed on the front lawn. Alec Gwinn, a black man and the club steward for many years, would play "See the Conquering Hero Comes" on his trombone. The member who had caught the largest bass was awarded a diamond-studded pin in the shape of a fishhook. The member who had caught the smallest bass received a tiny gold fish.

The members of the Cuttyhunk Fishing Club were some of the most powerful businessmen and politicians in the world. They included William McCormack, of International Harvester; J. D. Archbold, president of Standard Oil; and Hugh D. Auchincloss, Jacqueline Kennedy Onassis's stepfather. Presidents Grover Cleveland and William H. Taft attended as guests. Archbold's family lived on a large yacht whenever he visited the club, and he was so enamored with the island that his daughter married a titled Englishman in the island church. The club became known as "the Millionaires' Club" and Cuttyhunk as "the Isle of President Makers" because so many behind-the-scenes business and political decisions were made there.

The Cuttyhunk Fishing Club prospered for about thirty years, until the early 1900s. The decline of striped bass stocks, the death of several founding members, the resignation of others because of age, and the outbreak of World War I—all contributed to the club's demise. Also, the invention of the gasoline engine introduced a popular, competitive method of fishing. In 1912, the club put out only one stand. Charlie Church maintained the Cuffe Rock stand at his own expense, but he caught his world-record seventy-three-pound striped bass from a boat off Nashawena Island. By 1922, the club had only two members; one of them was William Madison Wood, president of the American Woolen Company, a conglomerate of textile mills.

Wood was the man destined to steer Cuttyhunk's course far into the future. Of Portuguese descent, he was born on Martha's Vineyard shortly after his parents arrived there on a whaling vessel from the Azores. Because he was

Portuguese, the Cuttyhunk Fishing Club originally turned down his membership application. Later, he made so much money they couldn't refuse him. The Wood mill was the largest single woolen mill in the world. In 1922, William Wood offered to buy the whole club and was accepted. The deal included all the club's holdings, making Wood the majority property owner on the island.

Fortunately for Cuttyhunk, Wood proved to be a man of vision when it came to preservation. He strove to maintain the island's character, including its wild places. He engineered a series of pathways to connect key spots, eliminating the need for automobiles and the traffic that inevitably follows. Hence the golf carts. Wood allowed the introduction of modern conveniences, as long as they didn't interfere with the rustic character of the island. For example, he had all phone and electrical wires run underground, out of sight. Wood also made it clear that the Cuttyhunk Fishing Club was not to be tampered with in any way. Today, the club stands as a fine example of old Cuttyhunk at its best.

By the time William Wood passed away in 1926, his preservation efforts had taken firm root on the island. No one would claim that Cuttyhunk has remained unchanged. Just look at the boats packed into the pond on a summer day or the new houses springing up. But despite ever-mounting pressure to develop the island, Cuttyhunkers have consistently tried to modernize in the most intelligent ways possible. Interestingly, Wood's vision has been kept alive not by laws but by a communal will to preserve this island paradise.

WHEN I FIRST FOLLOWED one of William Wood's pathways to the Cuttyhunk Fishing Club, meandering through the trees between modest residences, I got lost. I ended up at a shingle-style mansion fronted by an enormous stone wall of creamy beach stones covered with yellow lichen and ivy. This must be the place, I concluded. But it was Avalon, the house Wood built just behind the club, reportedly to spite its members after they turned down his membership request. The Club, closer to the shoreline, long and low, with white clapboards front and back and natural cedar shingles on the sides, is less impressive.

There is a fascinating renaissance in progress at the Cuttyhunk Fishing Club. The story began in the 1940s, when Cornelius Wood, son of William, sold the club to Robert Moore, cofounder of the Sheraton Hotel chain (and father of author Robin Moore, who actually wrote some of his books in the house's library). When the senior Moores died, their children reluctantly decided they had to sell. In 1997 the club had been for sale for four years, and the only committed buyer was a developer. On the morning of the day the deal was scheduled to go down, William Wood's granddaughter, Oriel Wood Ponzecchi, walked down to the club to say good-bye to her friend Robin, who was leaving the island. To her own astonishment, she blurted out, "Don't sell the club to anyone else, Robin. *Please!* I'll buy it!" And she did. The only problem was that Oriel had no idea what to do with it.

Happily, a woman named Bonnie Veeder approached Oriel with a proposition to take over the club and run it as a bed-and-breakfast. The Veeders, like the Tiltons, are one of the original Cuttyhunk families. Bonnie's ancestors, like Charlie's, figure prominently in period photos of the club chummers, as well as in just about every other photo of island locals. Oriel was thrilled with Bonnie's idea because it would bring the club's destiny full circle, and the rest is history.

Today Bonnie, who used to run her own restaurant on the island, both cooks for and manages the club. She rents rooms to groups of fishermen—mostly fly fishermen these days—and families. Oriel acquired all the club's original furnishings, so Bonnie is perpetually in the process of restoring the club to its original glory. You can eat dinner at the same long wooden table that President Cleveland dined at. The walls are decorated with photographs of stuffy, imposing men in dark suits with thick gold watch chains slung across their midsections, and plenty of interesting literature and memorabilia lies scattered about. Best of all, you can fish off the same beach enjoyed by the original members, and the striped bass are back.

THE LASTING SIGNIFICANCE of Cuttyhunk Island to Buzzards Bay may have less to do with Gosnold, Shakespeare, the supernatural, shipwrecks, striped bass fishing, or powerful men than it does with the efforts of a group of people trying to preserve the character of their land. It is a common sentiment that when you visit Cuttyhunk, you become part of the island community and likewise committed to preserving the place as a paradise. That's a pretty idea, and one that is doubtless beneficial to the island's future. It is also part of a culture of preservation from which the rest of us might gain inspiration. There are symbolic Cuttyhunks all over this "stately sound" that need protection from irresponsible development. If each of us brought a measure of the islanders' zeal to our own little pieces of paradise on Buzzards Bay, perhaps we too could inspire preservation.

> From Elizabeth's island unto the main is four leagues. On the north side, near adjoining unto the island Elizabeth, is an islet in compass half a mile, full of cedars, by me called Hill's Hap. . . .
>
> —ARCHER, ON PENIKESE ISLAND

PENACHASON POKED at the roasting striped bass in front of him, anticipating the moment when the white flesh would become flaky and loose. The fire was tiny, built of dry twigs so it would produce no telltale column of smoke. The Wampanoag sat with legs drawn up, arms clasped tightly, his chin on his knees. The Bay lay unfurled before him, restful, glistening in the starlight. Penachason was young, in the prime of his manhood, with long black hair that flowed down over the bronze muscles of his arms and back. At the moment, he was troubled. The red blood of the bass had triggered memories of other blood, flowing freely from the white settlers. The previous day, Penachason, his comrade Tatoson, and their men had killed fifteen in an attack on a garrison house at Plymouth. Metacom—King Philip to the settlers—would be proud of them. But now, Penachason was a fugitive, with a substantial bounty of four coats levied on his head by the King of England. For as long as he lived, he must run.

Penachason chewed the smoky bass thoughtfully, simultaneously kicking sand over the fire with the heel of one bare foot. Very soon, he and Tatosan would leave this remote island to return to the warpath. The young warrior held no illusions about what lay ahead; either they would succeed in helping Metacom rid their land of the settlers, or they would die in the attempt. His hand fell to his side, nudging his war axe. He did it habitually, unconsciously. Glancing wistfully around him, Penachason resolved to name this island after himself. He prayed to Kiehtan that if his enemies took his life, his spirit might be allowed to return to this island that had sheltered him, to forever guard its shores. Penikese Island would be, thereafter, a safe haven for castaways. Finishing his meal, the warrior rose with new resolve to meet his fate. The year was 1676.

IN THE 1600S, the Wampanoags called Penikese—a tiny island of seventy-five acres due north of Cuttyhunk—*Punnakesset, Pennakees, Peneeces*, or *Peene*. Available translations of these names are vague. According to one story, Penachason, the son or nephew of Tatosan, a key figure in King Philip's campaign against the settlers, fled to the island temporarily during King Philip's War and named it after himself. No evidence exists of permanent Native American settlements on Penikese, so historians believe that the Wampanoags used the island as a hunting and fishing camp. In 1956, while digging clams on Penikese, Eugene Margarida of New Bedford dug up a Wampanoag axe that is believed to be three hundred to four hundred years old.

Throughout its known history, Penikese has most often been a retreat for those who needed to be apart. The cedar forest Archer described is long gone. The island's stark landscape is now characterized by rolling grassland and scrub, scattered granite boulders, a few rustic buildings, and the ruins of old foundations. The island is ringed by a rocky beach and massive boulders.

A sachem named Tsonoarum owned the nearby island of Pasque until 1667, and he may have owned Penikese as well. At that time, the agents of Charles II of England seized the island (along with the other Elizabeth Islands) and sold it to Thomas Mayhew, the Christian minister who, along with his descendants, proved so influential in converting the Wampanoags to Christianity. It was later owned by Peleg Slocum of Dartmouth, the same man who owned Cuttyhunk. Early settlers on Penikese were farmers, fisher-men, pilots, and wreckers. Sheep were raised there, and lobsters were plentiful. In the 1800s, locals called the island Pune. In 1865, Beriah Manchester, a whaling captain, ran a menhaden oil factory on the island. He probably built the existing stone wharf.

In the late 1860s, John Anderson, a wealthy tobacco merchant from New York, bought Penikese as a private retreat. Anderson described it as a "charming climate, feast to his eyes of scenery made up of mainland and islands, and the ever changing aspect of the sea, that filled his soul with rapture and made his cup of happiness full to overflowing." Despite these accolades, in 1873 Anderson gave Penikese to the naturalist Louis Agassiz, together with a $50,000 endowment to establish a school for the study of marine natural history.

Louis Agassiz was a world-famous naturalist who is credited with, among numerous other scientific accomplishments, developing glacial theory. He was educated as a physician and studied briefly under Georges Cuvier, the most famous naturalist in Europe at the time. Agassiz accepted a professorship at Harvard University in 1848 and established the Museum of Comparative Zoology there in 1860.

The Anderson School was the first in the world dedicated to studying creatures in their natural environment. Agassiz envisioned the laboratory as a place where one could study the creatures of the Bay alive, in their natural surroundings—a progressive idea at a time when most scientists typically studied dead specimens. He set up a network of gas-powered, saltwater runs on Penikese that led to the lab tanks, which he stocked with local marine creatures. Tragically, Agassiz died after the school had operated for just one season, and it was shut down in 1875 after his son made a brief attempt to run it. At the time of his death Agassiz was acknowledged as America's leading scientist. Thankfully, his work on Penikese was not in vain. The Anderson School proved to be a major inspiration for the world-renowned Marine Biological Laboratory (MBL) in Woods Hole. Agassiz's vision lives on at the MBL, where scientists continue to study live sea creatures in their natural environment.

Just after the turn of the twentieth century, the state acquired Penikese and established a leper colony there. They did so only after being rejected by several potential sites on Cape Cod, and despite severe opposition from neighboring Buzzards Bay communities such as Cuttyhunk. Four cottages were built for the lepers on the Buzzards Bay side of the island. In 1921, the lepers were moved away, and Penikese was turned over to the Massachusetts Division of Fisheries and Wildlife as a bird colony. In 1973, with the approval of the Massachusetts Audubon Society, the division leased part of the island to the Penikese Island School, a rehabilitation facility for troubled teenage boys. Today, the school, the bird sanctuary, and the ruins from the island's past lives coexist in unique and fascinating ways.

ON MY WAY to tour the Penikese Island School, I was headed out onto the Bay aboard the *Harold M. Hill*, the school's vessel that is docked in Woods Hole. Built by Harris Cuttyhunk Boats, the trustworthy and well-liked vessel looks a bit like a lobster boat. This morning she carried a full load of fifteen passengers. It was a cool, cloudy spring day, with clearing skies predicted for the afternoon.

Three women on board were going out to lure roseate terns to Penikese from Ram Island, which had just been heavily oiled by the *Bouchard 120* spill. Later, I learned the results of their work from Ian Nisbet. They planned to lure the terns to Penikese using an electronic device that emits tern calls. They had already wired Ram with flashing lights to scare off birds arriving to scout for nest sites. Penikese had also suffered from the oil spill—parts of the shoreline looked as if they had been smacked with a black-dipped paintbrush—but it was not nearly as bad as Ram. One of the researchers—delicate, pale, and exquisite, like the roseates she studied—folded herself into an oversized green MassWildlife jacket and promptly fell asleep. I saw her again on the return trip, when she strode onto the *Harold Hill* carrying a dead male eider by one wing. The duck was so blackened by oil it might have been a cormorant. I learned that the state would "bag and tag" the bird and use it as evidence in the criminal case pending against Bouchard Transportation.

Out on deck a tall, thin man stood hunched in a mustard-colored hunting jacket. The father of one of the kids on the island, he was courteous and attentive, but his mind was far away. The pilothouse held the main attraction, a new student transfer. He had a shaved head and an unshaved face, and he wore a gray hooded sweatshirt with the hood up. He was staring back at the receding shoreline with round frightened eyes.

When we docked at Penikese, the first thing I saw were the remains of snare booms—think blue and white pom-poms tied to a rope—tangled around the pilings of the wharf. The booms had been deployed in triplicate around the island to protect it from the oil spill. We were also greeted by Canada geese, herring gulls, dipping barn swallows, and a pair of ospreys hovering near their nesting tower down the beach. For the first time in my life I saw dead gulls, strewn about the landing. I thought, *My god, this is the place where gulls come to die.* I felt like the proverbial man who discovered the mythical elephant graveyard. Meandering single file up the trail to the school, our group passed the only sizable tree on the island: a giant, domed, wind-sculpted European maple, introduced to the island because of its resistance to salt. The rising landscape beyond the maple was covered in scrub cherries about twelve feet high and small sumacs.

I approached the main house with Otto Reber, a supporter of the school, whom I'd met on my trip out. A member of the school's board, Otto had come to the island as part of a routine checkup. He sported a devilish grin under a battered orange baseball cap labeled "Cape Fear." Now a builder in Falmouth, Otto had first come to Penikese in 1973 as a self-described "hippie carpenter" to help construct the main house for the boys. Otto's grin widened as he told me how his wife had been the lone caretaker on nearby Nashawena Island. She was the only woman in the vicinity, and he got her.

Otto hinted at the grim realities of living on the island, which is renowned for its extreme weather conditions. "The weather these buildings get in one year is equal to three on the mainland. That's why we chose the saltbox design—saltboxes are good in rough weather." The house is modeled after the Jethro Coffin House, the oldest building left on Nantucket, built around 1696, and now a National Historic Landmark.

As Otto and I talked, a cool sea breeze chased scarves of fog around the cluster of buildings in the compound. All we could hear was the shrieking of gulls and the trilling of red-winged blackbirds. The only trees visible were a couple of lone cedars cresting nearby hills. I imagined they were descendants of the plentiful cedars described by Gosnold, but later I learned that they had been brought to the island by the staff to serve as Christmas trees. The compound includes a large, fenced vegetable garden with raised beds, pens holding pigs and chickens, and a somewhat incongruous basketball court overlooking the Bay. The surface of the court was made of boards, like a deck. A sign on an old barn read PENIKESE HEALTH AND FITNESS CENTER. Scattered about the compound were chopping blocks and piles and piles of firewood, split ridiculously thin. There's nothing like splitting wood to keep mischievous boys out of trouble.

On closer inspection, I saw that the pigpen sat on a concrete foundation that dated back to Agassiz's time. The sows inside were frighteningly large, with all the characteristics I recognized from folk art renderings—immense round bodies, ridiculously tiny legs, diminutive curled ears. As I eyed one brown, sedentary behemoth, it struck me that the animal was every bit as large and humped as the boulders lying offshore. Here was the inspiration behind the naming of Sow and Pigs Reef, that storied, ship-wrecking reef off the tip of Cuttyhunk.

As we filed into the main house, nervous teenaged kids scattered away from us . The interior was rustic, with heat and light provided by wood-stoves and kerosene lanterns. The staff only recently acquired a generator, which they put out in the barn to run power tools and teach the kids industrial arts. The whole place might remind you of camp you went to when you were a kid: rough-hewn walls, book shelves packed with worn paperbacks, long wooden tables, camp coffee made in a pot, and lots of good food in the kitchen.

I toured the house with David "Pops" Masch, a founding staff member. I asked Pops about a monolithic rib that hung on the wall. "That's from a forty-six-foot humpback that washed ashore. We rendered it into oil." From a rough-hewn ceiling beam hung the largest knot I have ever seen—as big as five human heads—called a monkey's fist. One of the students darted briefly out of anonymity to tell me that nine kids had worked together to tie the knot. I noticed, too, that the walls of the house were covered with realistic, hand-carved reliefs of fish. I recognized stripers, blues, swordfish, and flounder, and others I didn't know.

"I used to teach them to carve them out of driftwood," Pops admitted proudly. The kids, buzzing about or shooting pool, slowly warmed up to us and seemed happy and friendly. Truth was, according to Otto, they were grateful for the break in routine that our visit provided. The students on Penikese study and work six days a week, with only Sundays off.

I was keenly aware that I had entered a distant age of simplicity. Otto sug-gested, "This place is pretty much self-sufficient. It would be a good place to be if, you know, it was the end of the world or something." At another time I would have passed Otto's comment off as small talk, but this country's post–September 11 vulnerability underscores the value of an independent community, and it gave me cause for reflection.

The goal of the Penikese Island School is to re-create an 1850s version of extended family, farmhouse, and school. This setup is the personal vision of George Cadwalader, a war hero who founded the school in 1973. The students' adopted extended "family" at Penikese is an attempt to counterbalance the broken homes that many of the boys come from. The idea is to instill in the students a sense of personal value by providing them with the opportunity to contribute as members of a social group. The staff believe that by improving the boys' social skills, they can help them overcome tremendous personal hurdles and thereby lead better lives.

After the house tour, Toby Lineaweaver, the director of the school, donned the hat of island tour guide. He led us to two square concrete columns laced with cracks, plastered in lichen, and capped by two spheres the size of bowling balls. Here was an example of the fascinating interplay between past and present that characterizes Penikese. These were ruins from the leper colony. The columns adorn a long stone wall that arcs across the island. Probably built by the Anderson School as a retaining wall, the leper colony used it to divide the "clean" and "unclean" areas of the island. Today the stone wall is the southernmost nesting spot in the world for Leach's storm-petrel. These petrels are delicate, dark, ocean-going birds that flutter over the surface of the sea like moths. They burrow into the wall and lay one or two eggs. According to Toby, when the ornithologists show up to count the population, they find the birds by following their noses. "When they smell a fishy odor in the wall they know they have an active burrow." Curiously, the petrels have become nocturnal as a means of avoiding predators such as herring gulls. On moonlit nights, the Penikese petrels emit haunting burrow calls and scare the devil out of the city kids from New Bedford.

The destinies of the school and the bird sanctuary collided on Penikese in the 1970s. "What we proposed happened to be a perfect marriage with what the state wanted," Toby explained. "This relationship could never be duplicated in this day and age." The school and the bird sanctuary coexist in perfect harmony and mutual respect. The students and staff of the school are very protective of the birds' nesting grounds. (In fact, I was pointedly warned not to invade the low, sandy isthmus that the birds use.) If a student sneaks out of the house and across the island, gulls will unwittingly help the staff find him, popping up from their nests like jacks-in-the-box as he passes.

Moving through low, rolling fields crisscrossed by stone walls, our tour group eventually reached the border of the bird sanctuary. I was disappointed to learn that I was too early to observe nesting terns; I would have to settle for herring gulls. The gulls lined our path, large, white, unmoving. They occupied every boulder. There is something about a sentry of gulls, especially in the deep silence of Penikese, that seems prescient, suggestive of a preternatural power. If there were ever a great pharaoh of Buzzards Bay, he would surely line the subterranean tunnel leading to his burial chamber with statues of standing gulls. Some gulls sat on the Plow, an immense granite boulder streaked with guano that is said to be the second largest glacial boulder in New England. It's named the Plow because of its shape: thirty-nine feet long and only sixteen feet high, sloping upward at a gentle angle.

One herring gull, sitting on the ground, became extremely agitated as I approached, repeatedly crying out *row-row-row-row-row*. She rose up off what proved to be her nest, a small depression in the ground lined with dry grass. Inside were three beautiful eggs, much bigger than a chicken's, light brown splattered liberally with gray and black spots. (According to Otto Reber, the yolks of these eggs are bright, phosphorescent orange and taste terrible. He and Pops once went on a mad expedition to collect and sample every variety of egg on the island.)

The current gull population is far smaller than it used to be. In the 1970s, when all the landfills were still open, the birds swarmed the landscape. Thanks to efforts by MassWildlife to cap landfills and manage coastal pollution, the gulls are being forced out of their pirated ecological niche, and native species are moving back in, such as the black-crowned night herons that now enjoy the blackberry patch near Cistern Hill.

Remnants of the island's leper colony are visible all around. What is left of the colony's laundry, purposely built to face directly into the island's punishing west wind, is a favorite hangout for the boys. The students call a tree-lined hollow nearby the "Secret Garden" and go there sometimes to sneak cigarettes. And the tiny leper graveyard sits high on a bluff. As Otto and Toby and I approached it, a steady cool wind blew about us and diaphanous fog filtered the weak sunlight.

I contemplated the headstone of Iwa Umazakia (1884–1916), easily the most fascinating member of the colony. Iwa was a talented Japanese artist and intellectual who was working for Isabella Stewart Gardner at her art museum in Boston when he was diagnosed with leprosy. Unfortunately for Iwa, in his day the disease was called the Holy Horror. People looked upon it, as they have since biblical times, as a sign of God's displeasure and feared that it was highly contagious. The state of Massachusetts tried to ship Iwa back to Japan, but his homeland didn't want him. So he was sent to Penikese, where he established a reputation as a naturalist and was known as the "Birdman." By 1913, however, Iwa decided he had had enough of the colony and paddled away. The people around Buzzards Bay panicked. Newspaper headlines, blatantly racist, announced: "Table Sauce Lured Leper to Mainland" and "Simply in Search of Soy Sauce." Iwa made it as far as a streetcar in New Bedford, before he was caught and shipped backed to Penikese, where he lived out his last few years in peace with a pet bird named Prince.

Only about 5 percent of the population is susceptible to leprosy, a bacterial infection that is actually minimally transmittable. It affects the cooler parts of your body, such as your nose, hands, and feet. One of its effects is to cause your body to absorb bone and cartilage in those areas so that they shrink, which is why the popular conception of the disease is of body parts falling off. Also known as Hansen's disease, leprosy today affects about 12 million people, six thousand of them in the United States. The disease can be controlled, but not cured, with antibiotics.

For most of its existence, from 1905 to 1921, the leper colony on Penikese was run by Dr. Frank Parker and his wife, Marian. Parker gave up a successful medical practice on the mainland, along with his social standing, to move to Penikese and help the lepers. He and his wife built and fostered a sense of community among the inmates, treating them like family as much as possible. All was well until 1912. In that "can-do" era, doctors at Harvard University had decided they were going to rid the world of the scourge of leprosy once and for all—and they were going to do it on Penikese Island. A doctor named James Honeij came to the island, and members of the leper colony began to die mysteriously. We do know that Honeij began extracting their lymph nodes in experiments; there were rumors, never proved, that he was feeding the lepers suspicious potions of strychnine and arsenic.

Between 1912 and 1916, the official death count was ten; before Honeij's arrival, only one leper had died in the history of the colony.

Unfortunately, the story of the Penikese leper colony doesn't have a happy ending. In 1921, the state of Massachusetts decided that the colony was too great a financial burden. They packed the lepers up and shipped them south, to an amenable institution in Louisiana. As the lepers came through New Bedford, they put their hoods up so people couldn't gawk at them. Most of them were crying. Employees of Massachusetts Division of Fisheries and Wildlife burned the buildings, had the foundations dynamited, and poured lime over the whole mess.

MY TOUR OF THE PENIKESE SCHOOL was over. I lingered on the shore of a small, fog-ringed cove just below the school compound. I could see why Louis Agassiz had been attracted to this place. The cove smelled strongly of salt air. The springtime waters, green, clear, and placid, were patrolled by a lone Canada goose repeatedly honking out a warning. On the fog-shrouded horizon, a heavy-bodied, white-breasted loon drifted in and out of sight. Two mallards winged out of the mist, fast, squawking, twisting like bats. A group of crooning eiders splashed noisily about, six splendid black-and-white males, one chocolate-brown female. Under my feet I noted quahog, bay scallop, oyster, mussel, and slipper shells. The yellow rockweed that ringed the cove's perimeter floated on the surface like a woman's hair suspended in bathwater. The finer red seaweed that collected around and below the rockweed breathed in and out with each pulse of the gentle surf. The delicate gold lichen that covers all things stone on Penikese, on closer inspection, was actually a golden-orange.

The Penikese Island School leads a fragile existence. Things aren't as simple for the school administrators as they were in the early days, when a key strategy to help the boys was simply to "fatten them up." So far, the school has resisted merging with another school or bringing in more students to generate income. The staff feels strongly that such changes wouldn't benefit the boys and would compromise George Cadwalader's founding vision. Sadly, however, with growing competition and the absence of an endowment, the future of Cadwalader's vision—and of the school itself—is anything but certain.

I overheard Otto relating the story of one Penikese graduate, which clearly illustrated to me why this school is unique. He went home to New Bedford and knocked on his mother's door, only to find that she had moved and left no forwarding address. With nowhere else to go, the boy returned to school. Otto and the other staff members put him up in their homes—"He had nothing"—and employed him as a junior staff member for a while. They later helped him get a job in Falmouth, where the boy eventually succeeded in renting an apartment. The last the staff heard of him, he was making it on his own working in Florida. It's that kind of commitment, over and above the call of duty, that sets Penikese apart and sometimes makes all the difference in the life of a student.

When I left Penikese, sunlight had finally routed the fog. Shirts off, the students were shooting hoops, listening to rap music, hooting and hollering the way kids do everywhere. From the departing *Harold Hill*, I watched the glittering blue of Buzzards Bay unfurl. Here were the benevolent waters that had met the futile stare of Penachason, soothed the nerves of Anderson, blessed Agassiz with an unspoiled laboratory, comforted the tortured souls of the lepers, and now sheltered the wayward boys and seabirds. And from the depths of these healing waters rose Penikese, island of refuge.

Plants

The chiefest trees of this Island, are Beeches and Cedars; the

outward parts all overgrown with lowe bushie trees, three or

foure foot in height, which bear some kinde of fruits, as

appeared by their blossomes; Strawberries, red and white, as

sweet and much bigger than ours in England, Rasberies,

Gooseberies, Hurtleberies, and such; an incredible store of Vines,

as well in the woodie part of the Island, where they could run

upon every tree, as on the outward parts, that we could not goe

for treading upon them.

—BRERETON, ON THE PLANTS GOSNOLD'S MEN FOUND ON ONE OF THE
OFFSHORE ISLANDS, PROBABLY NOMANS LAND NEAR MARTHA'S VINEYARD

I'VE GOT A WALKING STICK in here." The older gentleman, stand-ing on the slope beside me, retrieved a stick that looked like a ski pole from his backpack. "Some people call these trekking poles, but what I call them is canes. Why not call them what they are?" Then, as I watched, he hiked rap-idly to the crest of the rise. I never quite caught up with him for the remainder of the day.

I was back on Penikese Island, this time with Dr. Richard H. Backus to learn about plants. It was a fine September day, seventy degrees with distant blue skies. The undulating landscape was aglow with the yellow blossoms of goldenrod, and crickets chirped all around us. I don't know how old Dick Backus is. But he told me that he retired from the Woods Hole Oceanographic Institution "a long time ago," when he was sixty-five. Dick is the epitome of the eminent scientist—degrees from Dartmouth and Cornell, a distinguished career at the institution. He served as chairman of the biology department there not just once but "a couple of times."

In a blue stocking cap with a rolled-up brim, Dick Backus looks like Jacques Cousteau. Actually, that's not quite accurate; when you factor in his bushy white eyebrows and long, thin nose, he looks more like a cross between Cousteau and Tolkien's wizard Gandalf. When he's in the field collecting specimens, Dick carries an Adirondack-style pack basket, which is essentially an open, woven wicker basket fitted out with nylon straps. The basket's open top is the key. "Guys that work in the woods find it real handy," he explains, making as if to pitch a hammer over his shoulder.

In 1999, already "retired," Dick headed up a botanical survey of Penikese Island. That means that he and the members of his scientific team found, identified, and catalogued every single species of flowering plant on the seventy-five-acre island. This incredible feat seems only slightly less incredible when you learn that a similar survey was completed on Penikese in 1873, in 1923, and every twenty-five years thereafter. In all probability, this ongoing study makes the island one of the most intensely studied places, botanically speaking, in the northeastern United States.

To the layperson's eye, Penikese is essentially barren. It looks like abandoned, rolling farmland covered in grasses and vines, with a few sporadic, unremarkable eruptions of small trees and shrubs. Originally, the island was forested, mostly with eastern red cedars. We know this because in 1602, in his *Relation*, Archer referred to Penikese as "the little islet of cedars" and wrote that Gosnold went there to harvest cedars to carry back to England. It is unclear why Penikese supported cedars while Cuttyhunk and the other Elizabeth Islands were covered mostly in dense oak-hickory forest. Because red cedar typically recolonizes land that has been cleared, one theory suggests that the Wampanoags might once have burned Penikese. The tribe might have burned the land accidentally, or intentionally to make room for crops. Around 1675, colonial farmers on Penikese began stripping the island of its cedars and either burning them or using them for construction. Once the cedars were gone, the sheep ate just about everything else. In 1873, David Starr Jordan, a student at the Anderson School of Natural History on the island, conducted the first botanical survey there. Jordan described the island as "about as barren looking a pile of rock and stone as one could well imagine." Both farming and grazing had ceased on the island by the early twentieth century. Since that time, the plants on Penikese have been staging a comeback, their only enemy now the brutal, incessant salt wind.

The three botanical surveys after Jordan's were conducted by the Woods Hole Marine Biological Laboratory (1923, 1947) and Smith College (1973). Together, the five surveys have documented 326 plant species on the island, with Backus's 1999 survey yielding 218. An interesting phenomenon that emerged from the data is that alien species on Penikese consistently account for nearly 50 percent of the plants. This is a very high percentage; if you compare the data from other New England areas, you'll typically find alien species at closer to 30 percent. Botanists attribute the high ratio of alien species to the island's history of varied use as farmland, leper colony, game preserve, and school. Another interesting conclusion of the botanical surveys is that Penikese is distinguished as much by the plants it doesn't possess as by those it does: some plants that commonly grow on the other Elizabeth Islands—most notably blueberries, beach plums, and grapes—are absent there.

The principal change to the vegetation on Penikese over the last 125 years has been what scientists call "an increase in woody vegetation." Vines, shrubs, and trees are recolonizing the pile of rock that David Starr Jordan described in 1873. Unfortunately, most of these "woody species" appear to be nasty, creeping vines, many of which are alien and invasive. You and I don't necessarily think of vines as "woody," but, as Dick explained, they "make the tissue we call wood."

Beach rose (*Rosa rugosa*) is one of the woody plant species that seems intent on overrunning the island. The blitzkrieg-style advance of *Rosa rugosa* on Penikese serves as fair warning to any municipalities or homeowners contemplating its introduction. The 1924 botanical survey of the island described this rose as "escaped" and "occurring occasionally." In 1948, the survey reported "large patches on the eastern shore." By 1976, the species was "well established," and in 1999 it was everywhere.

Another plant that has spread quickly over Penikese is poison ivy. In 1874, Jordan found poison ivy, along with five other plant species, only on nearby Gull Island, a smidgen of land that has eroded to such an extent that it is now submerged at high tide. In 1948, poison ivy was described as "uncommon" on Penikese. In 1976 it occurred there "in dense patches," and by 1999 it was "generally distributed over the main part of the island." Other woody plants vigorously attacking Penikese today include Asiatic bittersweet, a vine; Japanese honeysuckle, also a vine; and multiflora rose, a shrub.

Recently, scientists discovered that the landscape of Penikese Island is becoming drier. Ponds have dried up, and moisture-loving species such as ferns, which were formerly common on the island, are now rare. This change might be related to the spread of the woody vegetation. So what do scientists say should be done about the nasty invasive vines? Burn them, Dick Backus and his team recommend. Burn the whole island and make way for native grasses. Create more areas for terns to nest. Make the island a place where people can walk around. The state, which runs the island as a wildlife refuge and thus calls the shots, has yet to act on this recommendation.

Trees have been far less successful in recolonizing Penikese. In 1935, the Massachusetts Division of Fisheries and Wildlife reported that it was "almost impossible to get any trees to grow on the island." That observation holds true today. The relentless, salt-laden southwest wind that rolls over the island in the summer is too much for most trees. And in the winter, the freezing northwest wind destroys much of the new growth the trees managed to sprout in the warm months, a phenomenon aptly called winterkill. Many of the trees that grow on Penikese lie pathetically on the ground, a pose described by scientists as "recumbent." Other specimens prop themselves up as best they can, crippled, disfigured, mercilessly beaten by the salty breath of the open Bay. One encouraging sign noted by Dick Backus's team in 1999 was that two species appear to be gaining a foothold. One is our native black cherry. In 1948, scientists reported the status of cherries as "suckers only, four feet tall" and "dead twigs," also about four feet in height. In 1999, about a dozen small cherry trees were growing on Penikese, albeit horribly disfigured by the winds. The cherries resemble shrubs, growing wider than they do high. Interestingly, the other species making a comeback on Penikese is red cedar. In 2001, two of the largest of the ten cedars thriving on the island bore cones. Amazingly, the cedars appear to be completely immune to the salt winds, which shear, stunt, and burn the life out of nearly every other plant on the island that dares to raise its head from the ground.

DICK BACKUS AND I stood on the high point of Penikese, Cistern Hill, which Dick refers to as Reservoir Hill. The discrepancy is one of the eccentricities of the island—geographical names are variable, uncertain, ever-changing. We were accompanied by the sometime captain of the *Harold Hill*, Captain Jeff, who stuck a guinea fowl feather in the rear band of his baseball cap and struck off after us up Reservoir Hill barefoot. I surveyed the acres of bramble-infested grassland and looked at his feet skeptically. "I take my shoes off for good in May," he responded. Later, I got a look at the soles of Captain Jeff's feet; they were thick and orange-yellow, like mine used to be as a kid in the summertime.

The leper colony's cisterns, which were connected to a well and used to distribute fresh water to the buildings, still sit on Reservoir Hill. The Penikese Island School roped them off for safety and strung up colorful lobster buoys for increased visibility. The cisterns, deep, round, and brick-lined, look like something a Roman would have built to stage a fight between a Christian and a lion. They are about wide enough to provide adequate maneuvering room for the contestants and about deep enough to keep the combatants safely contained. The theatrical analogy works, too: surely the ancient Romans would have chosen such a hilltop, with its commanding view of the open waters of the Bay, for their amphitheater.

At the summit, Captain Jeff and I watched Dick scramble down a rather abrupt slope, intent on sampling one of his favorite berries, a European variety of blackberry. Penikese is one of only a few places in New England where it grows, and how it got there is anyone's guess. I tried one, and it was deliciously sweet with few seeds. A teenage boy from the island school crossed the barren landscape on a solitary walk. When he reached us, the preoccupied kid paused briefly. "This isn't a place to go barefoot," he commented before moving on. Captain Jeff merely shrugged. Clambering back up the hill, Dick pointed out a conspicuous dark patch in the landscape far below us: black swallowwort. He considers it "a nasty weed," partly because his garden at home is plagued by the invasive species. Dick's team discovered the plant here during the 1999 botanical survey. It is one of those plants, like the woody vines, that they fear will overrun the island if it isn't burned out soon.

The summit of Reservoir Hill is a tightly woven nest of native grasses and the vines of Japanese honeysuckle and native blackberry. This variety of blackberry, though abundant, produces little fruit. The vines of the honeysuckle were everywhere. "The only thing that can be said in its favor," said Dick, jabbing disapprovingly at the vines with his staff, "is that it has a flower that is deliciously fragrant." A little farther down the slope waved glorious stands of bright seaside goldenrod. The robust qualities of this hardy species finally registered with me when Dick stopped by the side of the path to examine a mixed stand of seaside goldenrod and two inland species. Compared to its slighter cousins, the fleshiness of the seaside's leaves and the larger size of its flowers became apparent. Below the goldenrod, the slopes of Cistern Hill succeeded to the European blackberry vines. Then pale green fields of American beach grass took over and rolled away to the upper beach of the island's shoreline. The largest species of plant life on Cistern Hill was a single, wind-sculpted viburnum crouched low against the hillside.

I glanced up from note-taking just in time to see Dick hiking rapidly away with Captain Jeff in tow. They were bound for the west side of the island, where several ponds awaited exploration. I caught up with them as they paused over a mix of shiny sumac and goldenrod beside the path. This sumac bears beautiful, dense clusters of rich purple fruit that is semi-edible. "The Wampanoags made a drink from those, I think," recalled the scientist. Captain Jeff had already swallowed a few berries. "Hmmm . . . a little sour," he concluded. Then, laughing, he said, "Just throw me overboard if I keel over on the trip home." The shiny sumac, which I have seen standing over ten feet tall on the mainland, had reached the height of only two or three feet on windswept Penikese.

Passing the ruins of the leper colony's laundry on the bluff, I struggled to follow Dick through a thick wall of bayberry and other shrubs. Bursting into the open on the other side, I looked about in amazement. I was standing in a tiny field of tall pink wildflowers. The depression, surrounded as it was by foliage, was invisible from the outside. "This," announced Dick, "is Leper Pond." The scientist bent down and plucked up one of the pink wildflowers by its roots. It was knotweed. He showed me how the stem of each flower had been wound round with the tendrils of dodder, a parasitic plant. The dry floor of Leper Pond was also populated by a shorter pink wildflower, saltmarsh fleabane, a member of the Aster family. The plant's richly colored blossoms were strangely pungent. So there were at least two species of wildflowers growing on the floor of a pond that had been filled with water less than two months earlier, in July. This is a typical occurrence among the ephemeral ponds on Penikese. All of the ponds, with the exception of two—South and Tubs—dry up periodically, at which time they host various species of wildflowers and other plants. "What comes and goes in these ponds," Dick lectured, referring to plant species, "has a lot to do with how long they have been dry or wet." There are seven ponds on Penikese. There used to be eight, but not surprisingly, Dry Pond dried up completely. In 1999 it was so dry that Dick's team couldn't even find it.

Quite close to Leper Pond lies diminutive, dry Tern Pond. Tern was studded with green spikes of wild iris, brown-tipped and gone to seed. Tern dries up around mid-May each year, and the irises bloom in June. When Dick Backus's team surveyed Tern in May 1999, it was full of grazing Canada geese. The pond was bordered by a neck-high, waving stand of panic grass, a robust, brown-tipped grass.

The next in the string of tiny ponds, Rankin, is set just twenty feet or so back from the beach. "At least I think it's named Rankin," muttered our guide. "Or maybe it's Zinn." Seeing my confusion, Dick explained. "Rankin named it after Zinn, and Zinn named it after Rankin." He was referring to two of the many scientists who have surveyed the pond over the last century. The names of the ponds on Penikese are as ephemeral as the ponds themselves. The 1999 botanical survey states as much: "Considerable confusion exists in the island's biological literature with respect to their [the ponds'] names." The floor of Rankin Pond was carpeted with a much shorter stand of panic grass than the one bordering Tern.

Leaving the ponds behind, Dick tore off through uncut brush up a long slope that led to the north end of the island, and we followed. Now I began to appreciate how difficult it is to move over a landscape woven thick with woody vines. Every step was laborious and frustrating. Eventually, with Dick and his bobbing woven basket leading the way, we broke through to open ground. "That's a cherry tree," said Dick, pointing to a long, low shrub. "You could've fooled me," I admitted. The shrub resembled a giant green caterpillar. I stuck my head into the dark shadows beneath its foliage to get a look at the tree's growth structure. The trunk and branches were literally lying on the ground. Some of the branches, actually embedded in the dirt, looked more like roots. This brave pioneer of the bluff had almost completely capitulated to the relentless force of the sea wind.

On the way back to the island school, we passed through fields of stunted gray sumac bushes cascading down gentle slopes to the Bay. Dick, perplexed, snapped a twig off one of the sumacs. "It's a mystery why there isn't more growth. These plants get winterkilled, but that still doesn't explain their lack of growth in the summer." Closer to the school, the scientist announced grimly, "Here comes the world's biggest patch of poison ivy." I eyed Captain Jeff's bare feet. "They keep it off the path," he replied, undaunted. In 1999, Dick's team actually measured the monstrous, glossy patch of ivy and found it to be ninety feet long by ninety feet wide.

After lunch we headed out to the isthmus, a place that held considerable interest for me. I had been banned from entering it on my previous visit because of nesting birds. The isthmus on Penikese is a crucial breeding area for endangered piping plovers and terns. We passed Typha Pond, which was full of cattails. "It could be called Cattail Pond," Dick commented, referring to the fact that Typha is the generic name of the species of cattails found there, *Typha latifolia*. When we reached the sandy isthmus, which borders a tranquil cove, Dick pointed with his walking stick at the conspicuous, glistening mounds of *Rosa rugosa*, or beach rose. The species is rapidly advancing in this part of the island. The roses, though invasive and alien, were undeniably beautiful. I paused at a dense cluster and admired the interplay of colors between red rose hips, magenta flower blossoms, and interspersed sprays of yellow goldenrod. It was a true Buzzards Bay bouquet, colorful, lush, fragrant. I lingered long in that remote, tranquil rose grove listening to the crickets' throbbing chirps, the sea wind's constant hum, and the rhythmic washing of the surf across the isthmus.

Then I returned to my pursuit of the intrepid Dick Backus. The grove of beach roses gave onto the rocky cobble of the isthmus's upper beach. There, I was halted by an overwhelming stench that threatened to turn my stomach. Twenty-five feet to windward, on the waterline, lay a massive, decaying leatherback sea turtle. It sprawled there like a knocked-out NFL linebacker, face down, its great brown arms extended. The leviathan's empty eye sockets, black and haunting, magnetically drew my gaze. The skull was as wide as my own. The turtle's decomposing shell was four feet long and sharply keeled, or ridged, several times lengthwise. It was a soft orange color and radiated a faint honeycomb pattern, as if lit from within. I poked the shell, and it felt like an empty leather cowboy boot. Leatherback.

The upper beach on the isthmus was covered with sea poppy. Like *Rosa rugosa*, sea poppy is a bewitchingly beautiful alien species. It is originally from Europe. On Penikese, sea poppy blooms in June, producing brilliant yellow, four-petaled flowers. All parts of this uncommon plant are conspicuous on the barren sand or stones: the coarse, sea-green foliage; the thin, curving seed capsules, or pods; the unforgettable yellow flowers. Locally, it grows on only a handful of remote beaches on Buzzards Bay and Nantucket Sound, including Stony Point Dike in Wareham and Little Island in Falmouth. We knelt to examine the plant's long, bizarre seed pods, or "horns," which have also given it the name "horned poppy." "Like everything else on this island," said Dick happily, "it looks better this year than I've ever seen it." He was referring to the year's plentiful rainfall.

The scientist jabbed at a thick cluster of shrubby, red-green growth erupting from a foot-high pile of brown eelgrass. "That's *Chenopodium macrocalycium*," he said, "commonly known as goosefoot." I had seen broad fields of this bushy plant on other remote Bay beaches. I pointed to a curious plant that grew out of the pure white sand near the goosefoot. It looked like an oak seedling but had long, closed lavender flowers, similar to a morning glory's, and a single, roundish, thorny green fruit at the heart of each leaf cluster. "Thorn-apple—also known as Jimsonweed," Dick offered. The flowers bloom only at night. "It's a hallucinogen."

"Did the Wampanoags use it to get high?" I asked. Dick rolled his eyes. "No need. They had Indian tobacco." He threw out a Latin name so long I didn't even attempt to catch it. "That was bad enough. After they smoked it, it gave them bad dreams and visions and often made them sick."

It was time to head back to the *Harold Hill*. Captain Jeff was already on board, ostensibly preparing for the return trip, but more likely, nursing his feet in private. Our return path meandered through sublime, three-foot-tall stalks of small yellow roses that Dick identified as evening primrose. Mixed in were clusters of white yarrow, a species that is popular with gardeners because it assumes several shades of color.

Back at the school, Dick spent a long time studying the weedy border of the pigpen. "One day," he said, "I was hunting around here and I found *Coronopus didymus*." I looked at him blankly. "People call it swine-cress," he explained with a broad smile. I started laughing.

It was warm in the autumn sunlight, the sky was blue, and the cascading fields of the island were golden. For the moment, life was perfect on Penikese, with no trace of the brutal salt winds whose effects were so obviously written in the plant life all around us. As we waited for the boat to disembark, Dick and I relaxed on the open porch of the school's rustic saltbox, waiting for the ferry. Surely, I thought, the spirit of Louis Agassiz lives in this man.

"What exactly do you call yourself, Dick?"

"Well . . . mostly I call myself an oceanographer. But sometimes a marine zoologist and sometimes an ichthyologist."

That means he studies the oceans, I thought to myself, and *animals in the oceans and fish, not to mention plants*. He is a generalist, nearly defying modern scientific categorization, a throwback to the old-time naturalists. I swallowed hard, knowing that Dick didn't like personal questions. "Do you consider yourself to be a successor to Louis Agassiz?"

"No," he replied, without hesitation. I dropped my gaze, disappointed. "Well, actually . . . I did have a teacher at Cornell who studied under an ichthyologist, who studied under a herpetologist, who studied under . . . " (and so forth), "who was a student of Burt Green Wilder, who was the man who first brought zoology to Cornell." That's it, I thought. That's the connection. Burt Green Wilder was a student of Louis Agassiz's at the Anderson School of Natural History on Penikese in 1873, the same year that David Starr Jordan performed the first botanical survey on the island.

Dick Backus was a direct academic descendent of Agassiz. I stared at my companion, who gave me a quizzical look. "Don't make a big deal of it," he warned me sternly.

"I have a bit of a fascination with the man and his life," I explained haltingly.

Dick smiled. "Louis Agassiz was a charming man. He talked a lot of people into a lot of things." I was surprised Dick used the word *charming*, as if he had known Agassiz, who passed away over one hundred years ago. I realized then that my tour of Penikese that day with Dick might be as close as anyone could come to glimpsing what life was like that fabled summer of 1873 studying natural history at the Anderson School.

"What do you think the landscape of this island will look like in a hundred years?" I asked him.

"A lot of cedars, I'd say," Dick replied immediately. "A lot of cedars."

MANY OF THE WILDFLOWERS around Buzzards Bay are unique in Massachusetts, because of the Bay's sandy, acidic soil and the warming effect of the Gulf Stream, that steaming oceanic river that arcs northward from southern waters. For the same reasons, many wildflowers commonly found inland are absent on the Bay's shores.

The Bay is the northern boundary of the natural range for many wildflower and animal species. The Gulf Stream bends in tightly against Florida and then travels up the eastern coastline until it reaches the elbow of Cape Cod, where it detours sharply to the east and out to sea. Because of the Gulf Stream's proximity, the climate of Buzzards Bay is more like the climate of Virginia's coastal plain than it is like areas to the north. As a result, many southern species of wildflowers, such as redroot, Maryland meadow beauty, thread-leaved sundew, and creeping Saint-John's-wort, are commonly found on the Bay.

WHEN YOU WANT TO LEARN about local plants around Cape Cod, all roads lead to Mario Digregorio. One of the most respected botanists in our area, Mario makes a living as a consultant. He's the guy you call when you want to stop a piece of land from being developed. Mario goes in and finds some rare plant, and suddenly the bulldozers fall silent, pitched at an awkward angle on a slope of fresh brown earth. When I first met him, the botanist was working for a wealthy client on Martha's Vineyard who was attempting to stop another wealthy man from building a mansion beside his own. Mario is a champion of the endangered flora of southeastern Massachusetts, but he poses a substantial threat to the livelihood of some of its citizens. If he ventures onto a property such as a cranberry bog and finds, for example, an extremely rare orchid, the property owner might find the operation shut down indefinitely by order of the Endangered Species Act. Mario can also be just simply bad for business. For example, commercial landscapers felt the effect when the botanist published an article in a local newspaper entitled "The Green Death," which documented how the use of hydroseeding in public works projects, such as installation of new gas lines, effectively displaced native flowers and grasses.

Remarkably, Mario is self-educated, an anomaly in a scientific community characterized by doctoral degrees. He doesn't always receive the professional respect he deserves, but he doesn't care, he's got Ph.D.'s calling him all the time for advice. "You'd be surprised at how much some Ph.D.'s don't know," he quipped. When Mario was a boy, he kept tanks of fish and aquatic insects in his garage and charged the kids in his neighborhood a dime apiece to see them. Eventually, he figured out how to make a living doing what he loves—studying the natural world. Recently, several admirers convinced Mario to put together a guidebook for identifying rare wildflowers on Cape Cod. It's called *A Vanishing Heritage—Wildflowers of Cape Cod*. He hopes that his book will encourage people to botanize for recreation, as they did in centuries past, and through wildflowers to gain a greater appreciation for the natural areas that remain.

OUR FIRST BOTANICAL FORAY was to Mud Cove, behind Phinneys Harbor in Bourne. Mud Cove is old Cape Cod, a throwback to the halcyon days before widespread development. A protected conservation area, the cove is bordered by a small, unspoiled salt marsh. The tiny kingdom at Mud Cove also boasts such typical Buzzards Bay habitats as a sandy beach, a rocky strand, upland, and even a tiny sand plain well above the high tide mark. A brief isthmus, submerged at high tide, wraps itself around a field of saltmarsh cordgrass and a small, shallow mudflat. The isthmus leads to a top-heavy, tree-filled island, whose edges are rapidly eroding in cascading runnels of sand. Colorful fiddler crabs dart about on the marsh trail, diamondback terrapins glide warily in the shallows, and a jungle of fascinating plants, most on a Lilliputian scale, thrive.

Within thirty feet of our parking spot, Mario identified at least that number of plant species. Most obvious were the prolific bunches of beach roses. *Rosa rugosa* is an excellent example of what ecologists call a "naturalized species"—it is non-native but widely believed to be native because it has adapted so well to its new environment. The familiar beach rose has rich green, serrated leaves; fragrant pink, magenta, and white flowers; and plump, searing red fruit known as rose hips. *Rosa rugosa* is an Asian species, purposefully introduced into our area in the 1870s. A long time ago, according to Mario, people called it Japanese rose. You can make jelly from rose hips that ounce-for-ounce contains more vitamin C than oranges. Cape Cod wildlife love to eat rose hips, an important factor in the rapid local spread of the species.

Equally conspicuous were the brilliant yellow clusters of seaside goldenrod. This goldenrod can be distinguished from other, inland species by its leaves, which are lance-shaped, thick, and fleshy. Also, the individual yellow blossoms are larger than those of its inland relatives. I learned from Mario that many plants that live near salt water have thick fleshy leaves as an effective defense against salt's tendency to suck moisture out of things.

At the shoreline, Mario knelt and rattled off the names of several tiny plant species, all contained within a few square feet of marshland. Miniature salt-marsh asters—narrow-leaved, the white flower petals tinged with pink—grew just below the mean, or average, high tide mark. These asters exude sodium chloride—salt—from their leaves, another typical defense employed by saltmarsh plant species. Essentially, the plants drink in salt water, then spit the salt back out. Mario also pointed out spike grass, or saltgrass, a diminutive, wheatlike plant, and arrow grass, whose arrow-shaped leaves also displayed the characteristic fleshy foliage. Closer to the waterline grew green, succulent single spikes of glasswort, also known as seapickle. Seapickle is edible and actually does taste like pickled cucumbers. The plant's fleshy, water-hording stalks change color in the fall, causing acres of marsh to turn blazing red and orange. Close by the seapickle grew a delicate cluster of sea lavender, another species renowned for its color. It is the dainty lavender blossoms of this wildflower that give marshes their purple hue. The blossoms are fragrant and keep their purple coloring when dried, qualities that make the flowers popular for dried bouquets. Sea lavender is protected by bylaws in many local towns.

Farther into the marsh, Mario stopped short, obviously delighted. High up on the beach, just above the storm tide line, rose a magnificent stand of New England blazing star, the main reason Mario had brought me to Mud Cove. *Liatris*, as Mario affectionately calls the wildflower, rises to three-foot stalks that are covered with bursts of deep purple flower heads, thirty to sixty flowers per stalk. The flowers are easily confused with purple blossoms of thistle. "But it's a completely different animal," Mario insisted. In his book, he describes *Liatris* as "a royal purple scepter." The species is unique among wildflowers that blossom from stalks because it flowers from the top down rather than the bottom up. On these blazing star plants, showy, star-like, light purple flowers at the top of the stalks deepened to richer, equally beautiful buds at the bottom. "This is one of my favorite wildflowers!" Mario exclaimed, beaming. "And it's a beautiful, beautiful display of *Liatris* this year. We got it just right."

New England blazing star is a very rare wildflower. The state of Massachusetts lists it as a species of "Special Concern." The state's classifications are as follows, in order of most to least rare:

ENDANGERED	a species judged to be in immediate danger of disappearing
THREATENED	a species in decline that will probably disappear if nothing is done to prevent it
SPECIAL CONCERN	a species that is so few in numbers or distribution that it could soon qualify for Threatened
WATCH LIST	a species that isn't rare yet but is threatened by development and declining in numbers

New England blazing star rates Special Concern status because, although it appears in large numbers where it does grow, its distribution is limited to a few isolated habitats such as Mud Cove in Bourne and the moors of Nantucket Island.

The blazing star family in general tends to thrive in the West, on the grass prairies of Kansas and Nebraska. New England blazing star, *Liatris borealis*, is the only species of *Liatris* that grows in the Northeast. It is one of the wildflowers found on Buzzards Bay that is at the northern extreme of its range, growing much more prolifically to the south. The plant is also nearly unique to Buzzards Bay. This is because the species prefers a habitat that is plentiful on the Bay, the rocky strip, or cobble, typically found on the upper beaches of its shores. Scraggy Neck in Cataumet and the Mashnee Dike in Bourne possess this type of shoreline. I was surprised to learn from Mario that this apparently sterile carpet of stones serves as an important habitat for other seaside plants as well.

Mario paused often as he lectured, his palms lingering on flower heads, his fingers twirling stems. It was a glorious, warm September day, the salt marsh was resplendent with the exquisite blossoms of native wildflowers, and he was savoring all of it. He was quite different from Dick Backus in the field. Mario strokes plants gently. Dick is just as likely to snap a plant off at its base to get a better look. Perhaps Dick's methods belong to the old school of naturalists such as Audubon and Linnaeus. In a world of apparently endless natural bounty, those men thought little of taking life to advance scientific knowledge. Gradually it dawned on me that it was no accident that the blazing star was in full bloom. Everything around us was. "Most of the plants in the salt marsh are in flower in the late summer and fall," Mario confirmed. It seemed fitting to me that, eschewing spring, New England salt marshes reserve their stunning shows of beauty for summer's end. As we sauntered along, identifications poured from Mario like the unstoppable flood of an incoming tide:

"Virginia wild rye—*Elymus virginicus*. Black grass—*Juncus gerardii*—not a grass but a rush. Sometimes it's called path grass because it doesn't mind being walked on. Marsh elder, or high tide bush—*Iva frutescens*. You can see that it grows right along the high tide mark. Sea rocket—*Cakile edentula*. You can tell it's a member of the mustard family because the flowers have four petals. The buds are fat and squat, not like modern rockets but more like Chinese rockets." The botanist grinned. "I guess the name's a bit of a stretch."

Standing near to the water's edge, I gestured at the rich stands of grasses around us. "What's all this?"

"There are about six species of grass in the salt marsh," Mario replied. At sea level, sprouting directly from the lapping waters of the cove, he pointed out saltmarsh cordgrass (*Spartina alterniflora*), the species that most people call marsh grass. Advancing up the shore, just above the marsh grass grew *Spartina patens*, similar to marsh grass but shorter and finer. It is commonly known as saltmarsh hay. "Take away these two species, and you wouldn't have much grass around here. He knelt to finger a specimen of what appeared to be saltmarsh hay. "Nope, it's not *patens*. This is actually a short form of the *alterniflora*, that typically grows just behind it." Like the other plants, all the *Spartina* grasses were in flower, with tiny white blossoms lining just one side of each tall blade. Higher up on the beach, I recognized thick bunches of reddish grass blades.

"Isn't that the grass that you can use for your lawn?" I asked.

"Yes—that's red fescue," Mario replied. "It grows naturally along the edges of salt marshes."

Surveying the marshland, Mario muttered, half to himself, "The zonation here is very distinct." *Zonation*. I realized it was about the fifth time he had used the term. Another word he kept using was *salinity*. Recalling his earlier emphasis on fleshy, water-retaining leaves, I finally put it all together. "This place—it's all about salt," I blurted out.

"That's right," the botanist said. "Salinity dictates the zonation, or plant distribution, within the salt marsh. The salinity of the open ocean is thirty-five parts salt per thousand parts water. At the edge of the marsh, in the *alterniflora* zone, the salinity is fifteen to twenty-five parts per thousand. The salinity continues to drop as the elevation of the land rises, which allows other species that are less salt-tolerant to gain a foothold. For plant life, salt dictates the viability of life here."

Once I grasped the concept of zonation, I began to see the salt marsh in a new way. As opposed to a random distribution of plants across the marsh, I now saw order, a strict segregation of species according to how well each had adapted to the presence of salt. If you took four lengths of clothesline and laid them parallel to the waterline several feet apart, you could not create more pronounced borders between species than the salty blood of the Bay does. You will never, for example, find sea rocket growing among the seapickle near the water's edge. At the risk of over-simplifying, the zonation at Mud Cove goes something like this: Virginia wild rye on the upper beach, saltmarsh hay around the wrack line, seapickle at the mean high water mark, and saltmarsh cordgrass in the water itself.

Across Mud Cove's sandy isthmus, on the tiny wooded islet, stands a grove of curious oak trees. They are the Gullivers of the salt marsh's Lilliputian plant world. Even so, they are low and sprawling as trees go, with pale branches that grow parallel to the ground. Mario told me they were maritime white oaks. "Taxonomically, they're no different from white oaks.

Their horizontal growth form is dictated by the salt-spray horizon. They are disappearing fast because they mostly inhabit uplands, which are the areas that are getting wiped out by development. It's a shame, because some of them are over a century old."

As we were leaving Mud Cove, I asked Mario, "I know some local biologists dislike alien animal species because they sometimes displace native species. Are there any similar feelings toward alien species in the botanical community?" "You've got to be careful with invasive species such as *Rosa rugosa*," he replied. "When I was on the Conservation Commission in Falmouth, I resisted planting plans that included only beach roses."

"What can harm the native wildflowers in a salt marsh like Mud Cove? Is it people tramping over them?"

"These plants are pretty resilient," Mario replied. "The big thing is restricting tidal flow—building roads, culverts, that sort of thing." (Culverts are the large pipes placed under roads to regulate the flow of seawater.) "If you constrict the tidal flow," the botanist continued, "you'll start to see more of a freshwater influence. The saltmarsh plant species will begin to retreat. You'll also get invading species such as phragmites, maybe even purple loosestrife. You've got to keep that flow going."

"THIS IS BLACK BEACH, and botanically it's quite famous," Mario told me. "Interdunal swales are one of my favorite botanical associations," he added enthusiastically.

"Associations?"

"Communities," he explained.

We were in Falmouth, at the Sippiwisset Marsh District of Critical Planning Concern (DCPC), home to the Black Beach Bog. Mario helped obtain the conservation designation for the area, which restricts the activities of people who visit it. The Black Beach Bog is a rare habitat, a tiny swamp hidden deep within one of the few areas of duneland on Buzzards Bay. The Sippiwisset Marsh more closely resembles a microcosm of the dunes of Provincetown than it does the shores of Buzzards Bay.

The plants that live there are rare as well. We had come specifically to see orchids and carnivorous, insect-eating plants called sundews. Hiking out to the bog, the botanist and I tramped through a low field of *Hudsonia*, a green-gray, heatherlike plant that blanketed most of the sand dunes. We eventually reached a brief hollow set among the *Hudsonia*. "Just this small dip in topography is enough to create a bog," marveled Mario. "This place is one of the real treasure troves." The floor of the depression was peppered with native wild cranberries; the round, tart fruits were nearly ripe, displaying red tops and yellow bottoms. Among the cranberries grew bog clubmoss, some of its two- to three-inch green spikes growing erect, others horizontal to the ground, and white boneset, a two-inch species of wild-flower with white blossoms. The ground beneath these plants was richly carpeted with several species of sphagnum moss, some red, some green, wet and soft to the touch. "They meet the groundwater," explained Mario. Although my flip-flopped feet were wet, the bog is technically considered to be dry in the autumn. In the late winter and spring, it is full of water.

The biggest plant in the sculpted bowl was a lone, dramatic specimen of sweetgale, a shrub related to bayberry. The shrub stands about four feet high and spans about twelve feet in diameter. Everything else in the bog is minia-ture in comparison. It wasn't always that way. The parched silver bones of cedars that stick glaringly from the sandy edges bear testament to a time when the bog supported more robust forms of plant life. During the No Name Storm of 1991 (also called the "Perfect Storm"), the angry ocean tore through the dunes here and flooded the bog with salt water, killing off the cedars and all the other large herbaceous plants except for the sweetgale. The seawater flooded in not from the open beach fronting the dunes, but from the sleepy harbor across the road.

In 1988, Mario Digregorio made one of his most important botanical finds in the Black Beach Bog. He discovered an entire population—about thirteen plants—of *Arethusa bulbosa*, an extremely rare species of orchid listed as Threatened by the state of Massachusetts. *Arethusa* is also known as swamp pink, or dragon mouth. The orchid has a single, green, leafless stem, from the top of which blooms an exquisite magenta flower that has a hanging, bearded lower lip lined with yellow or white. If you want to know what *Arethusa* looks like, picture an animated pink dragon that has just turned its horned head, fixed its eyes on you, opened its mouth, and belched a yellow fire. It grows only in bogs and only in sphagnum moss. Most local populations exist in coastal cranberry bogs. One unsuspected colony thrives just steps away from a busy highway in Wareham.

Mario's orchids put Black Beach on the map. Botanists from all over have been making pilgrimages there ever since. Sadly, the strangely beautiful orchids he found there no longer exist. "I haven't seen them since the Bay broke through in '91," Mario lamented. "Every year, in the spring, I come back here looking for them." The botanist can take consolation from the remarkable fact that Black Beach Bog is also home to two other species of bog orchid, grass pink and rose pogonia, also known as snakemouth. The name snakemouth is appropriate: if the ephemeral *Arethusa* resembles an intense magenta dragon, rose pogonia, also beautiful, calls to mind a hissing pink snake, its lower jaw stretched open, leering at you. The yellow lower lips of the bog orchids are designed to attract bumblebees, their main pollinators and means of reproducing. A crucial difference between rose pogonia and *Arethusa*, however, is that rose pogonia can also reproduce vegetatively, which is believed to account for its relative abundance.

Although the orchids in the Black Beach Bog were not in flower when we visited, Mario quickly located a rose pogonia and crushed its ovary (the round, buttonlike part of a flower in the center of the petals) between his index finger and thumb. The seeds that slid out were as small as the tiniest brown ant. "That's one of the reasons it's so difficult to grow orchids," lectured the botanist. "There's no food storage to speak of in the seeds."

As a child, I relished feeding houseflies to my Venus's-Flytrap plants, so I looked forward with delight to seeing the carnivorous sundews. "There are three species of sundews that grow here," Mario told me. "It's the only place I know of where they all grow in the same spot." I was beginning to understand why Mario could refer to this scrape in the sand as a treasure trove. The three kinds of sundews found in Black Beach Bog are the thread-leaved, round-leaved, and spatulate-leaved. All three sundews, although radically different in shape, are similarly covered with red-tipped hairs coated with a sticky liquid. The hairs ensnare insects, then the sundews secrete enzymes that enable them to digest their prey. According to Mario's book, sundews feed on insects to obtain nitrogen, a nutrient that is not available to them in the poor soil of the bog. The sundews use the nitrogen harvested from the insects to build flowers and seeds.

Mario knelt in the damp sphagnum moss to show me a thread-leaved sundew, which is on the state's Watch List. It was a fragile green spike about five inches high, covered with fuzzy red hairs. "Run your hand along that," he directed. My fingers came away slippery with slime. Next he pointed out the round-leaved species, tiny red or green dishes with the same sticky tendrils. "The liquid is the same viscosity as the thread-leaved's," Mario explained. "It's just like flypaper." This time I took his word for it.

As with my experience at the salt marsh, a newly educated eye revealed a different bog to me. I could now appreciate the uniqueness of this place, and also its vulnerability. Looking at the tiny ecosystem, I couldn't help stating the obvious. "A bulldozer could wipe out a place like this in a matter of minutes."

"It's not always the bulldozer that does it," replied Mario. "It's important to remember that the Wetlands Protection Act protects only a wetland area and one hundred feet around it. People need to realize that seemingly unrelated changes in local hydrology can negatively affect these types of environments, including the drilling of wells nearby, erosion from development, even heavy metals carried by sediment runoff from construction."

Later, as we trekked out through the dunes, I said, "You sure know a lot about plants for a guy who's self-educated."

Mario laughed delightedly. "Hey," he said, "Thoreau was a botanist, right? And what did he have, an English degree?"

EELGRASS IS TO THE BAY as olive oil is to my kitchen. Not much happens without it. Eelgrass grows in shallow water areas of the Bay, in both sand and mud, from just below the low tide mark to twenty or thirty feet below the surface, depending on water clarity. It grows no deeper than that because it depends on sunlight to live. The plant also prefers areas where current and wave action are moderate. Typical places you will find eelgrass are salt ponds, harbors, and the mouths of estuaries and tidal rivers. In ideal growth conditions, it can cover acres of shallow bottom.

Eelgrass has leaves, or blades, up to one-half inch wide and three feet long. The older blades of the plant die, turn brown, and wash ashore to create the familiar line of gray-brown seaweed along the high tide mark of Bay beaches. Eelgrass grows from a runner in the bottom sediment that periodically sends up shoots. It is classified as a marine seed plant, which means that in addition to reproducing vegetatively, from its runners, it also propagates itself using flowers and fruit. The plant is a perennial and flowers in the late spring or early summer. When you read anything about eelgrass, you unfailingly encounter references to the supreme ecological importance of the species. Typically, though, the information is too general to be very useful. The analogy that makes the most sense to me likens the ecological importance of eelgrass beds to the salt marsh. Some Bay creatures eat eelgrass. Others hide in it, or nurse their young among its blades. A few of the many local creatures that are biologically dependent on eelgrass are algae, ribbon worms, jellyfish, skeleton shrimp, slipper shells, quahogs, crabs, lobsters, bay scallops, cod, tautog, black sea bass, bluefish, striped bass, and the Atlantic brant goose. On Buzzards Bay, the species that is perhaps most closely associated with eelgrass is the bay scallop. Young bay scallops cling to eelgrass blades to avoid suffocating in the muck and to hide from predators. Eelgrass also plays an important role in the formation of salt marshes, in stabilizing bottom sediments, and in cycling oxygen and nutrients in the water. Even the dead brown blades that wash up in deep piles on the shore provide a fertile habitat for seaside plant species.

Massachusetts is in danger of losing its eelgrass forever. The decline of eelgrass in our waters can be attributed to several causes. On Buzzards Bay, the single most important threat is nutrient loading, which occurs when inshore waters are polluted with high levels of nitrogen. Nitrogen enters the Bay from groundwater and road runoff when it rains. It gets into the water from septic systems, wastewater treatment plants, and synthetic fertilizers applied to lawns, golf courses, and farmland. Nitrogen is deadly to eelgrass because it promotes the growth of algae in the water, making the water murky and decreasing the amount of sunlight that reaches the beds, thus impairing photosynthesis. If a bed of eelgrass does not harvest at least 20 percent of the sunlight shining on the surface of the Bay, it will begin to die. As the health of an eelgrass bed declines, the defined, clean green blades become progressively fuzzier, browner, coated with algae. Eelgrass is so sensitive to water pollution that it is considered an indicator species for environmental quality—yet another local species that serves as a "canary in the coal mine."

The other major causes of the disappearance of eelgrass on the Bay are boats and jet skis. When motor boats are operated in shallow, inshore areas, their propellers churn up the bottom. The churned up mud or sand clouds the water, limiting the amount of sunlight that reaches the eelgrass. Props also damage the plants by shearing off leaves, flowers, and growing tips, called meristems. Damage to meristems limits the vegetative growth—spreading by runners—of eelgrass, which is very detrimental to local beds. Damage to eelgrass flowers by props results in fewer seeds, which impairs sexual reproduction. Boat wakes damage eelgrass beds by eroding their edges. The best thing shallow-water boaters can do to protect eelgrass is to locate and stay away from the beds. Many towns have maps and charts that describe the locations of local eelgrass beds. Additional factors that have contributed to the decline of eelgrass on Buzzards Bay include towed fishing gear, such as shellfish dredges, boat anchors and mooring chains, and lobster pots set repeatedly in the same spot.

Eelgrass also faces natural threats in the form of disease. It appears that it is periodically attacked by a devastating wasting disease, or blight. Scientists don't know much about this wasting disease. The last time it struck, in the 1930s, most of the eelgrass in the Atlantic Ocean died. According to Joe Costa of the Buzzards Bay Project, who wrote his Ph.D. dissertation on the history of eelgrass in the Bay and has tracked its progress ever since, much of it grew back. The greatest expansion occurred from the late 1940s to the 1970s, when the beds had recovered to perhaps one-third to one-half of the size they were in precolonial times. But in some areas, eelgrass didn't return after the blight, and more significantly, in others it recovered but disappeared again in the 1970s and 1980s. Today, eelgrass beds in the Bay cover only 20 to 40 percent of the area they naturally would under pristine growing conditions. Scientists now believe that the lack of eelgrass recovery and the more recent decline are the direct result of human disturbances, namely, boat traffic and nitrogen pollution. Current consensus is that unless the disturbances to impacted areas are reduced, the eelgrass beds have no chance of coming back.

In general, eelgrass in Buzzards Bay is distributed along the fringes of the entire coastline and the shores of the Elizabeth Islands. None grows in the deep, central waters of the Bay or in harbors with poor water quality. Inshore areas of the Bay that historically maintained eelgrass beds but no longer do include New Bedford Harbor, Apponagansett (Padanaram) Bay, the Wareham River Estuary, and portions of West Falmouth Harbor, Sippican Harbor, Buttermilk Bay, Onset Bay, and the Westport River. Clarks Cove has been the one bright spot for eelgrass recovery on the Bay. Beds have continued to expand there since the early 1990s, when New Bedford improved the cove's water quality by upgrading its sewage treatment plant and combined sewer outflow (CSO) system.

"EEEUUUUOOO!" I spun rapidly onto my back in the water to face my wife on the shore. "There's too much *seaweed*!" she shouted, before retreating hastily back to the beach. The tide was out in Bourne, and I had tried, obviously without success, to find a place without eelgrass where my wife could swim. We had ended up at the North Channel between Patuisset and Bassetts Island. It was a hot summer day, and two elderly women, real Buzzards Bay types, were sitting near us at the waterline with their feet soaking in the water. They sat in low beach chairs, the corroded aluminum kind with yellow or green fraying nylon straps. They probably had old sneakers on. As they watched my wife with amusement, I managed an apologetic smile. It wasn't my wife's fault; she was brought up on open, sandy beaches and doesn't take well to eelgrass.

As I floated in the warm, shallow water, blades of eelgrass occasionally licking my arms and legs, the scene before me changed. The year was 1933. A young man sat at the waterline, arms propped behind him, legs extended, his back to the Bay. The man's head, shoulders, arms, and chest were massive and well defined, like a marble sculpture. In contrast, his legs were small, thin, and out of proportion with his robust upper body. On the packed wet sand in front of him lay a set of black steel leg braces and a pair of wooden crutches. He was alone, and he was smiling.

The man began to move into the water backward, by planting his hands, lifting the weight of his body, and swinging his hips. With each propulsion, his bare heels left drag marks in the wet sand. As he met the tepid water of the Bay, he felt the knotted roots of eelgrass beneath his palms, the swishing blades that hid and caressed his lower body like a thousand healing hands. The swift tidal current began to lift his body and tip it sideways. He gave one great push off the bottom and twisted onto his stomach, riding the flow. He was free. The young man laughed out loud and swam across the racing flood toward the island with broad, powerful strokes. His legs, no longer a burden, fluttered behind.

MY GRANDFATHER, Weston Straffin, had polio. He contracted a severe case at a very young age and lost the use of his legs. His brother, Philip, had a much milder case of the disease. Their doctor prescribed swimming as a form of physical therapy. "Teach the boys to swim," the physician advised their father, Franklin. "Take them down to Buzzards Bay." So he did. Franklin had a summer cottage built in Bourne in the early 1900s, and our family traveled by horse and wagon from Brockton to the Bay, a dusty, all-day trip. As a young man, my grandfather swam the North Channel to Bassetts Island often, simply because he relished the challenge. After retiring to the Bay with my grandmother, he spent every day he could on the water in his tin skiff, mostly quahogging, but also fishing for flounder and scalloping. My grandfather was intimately familiar with eelgrass.

Most times, Wes would drift down the east side of Bassetts while quahogging, hanging over the lee side of the boat, his great weight tilting the gunwale of the light craft sharply toward the waterline, one burly arm permanently sunk in the muck seeking his quarry. He typically wore a short-sleeved, checkered, collared shirt, long, dark trousers held up by suspenders, and shiny, black leather shoes. Attached to either side of each shoe was a heavy steel leg brace that disappeared mysteriously up his pant leg. He would move about on his bench seat in the boat by lifting one leg after the other, grasping under a knee with both hands, lurching his upper body hard to the side, and jerking the leg over. Each foot would clank down with a metallic bang! against the bottom of the aluminum boat, metal meeting metal.

In the mid-1970s, the shallows on the east side of Bassetts Island were one rolling prairie of eelgrass. You could see the bright rays of sunlight streaming between the waving, pale-green blades in the clear water and the shadows on the bottom created by their movements. You could glimpse skittish fish and bay scallops darting away through the thick beds. Today, the same area of bottom is a sand flat, nearly devoid of eelgrass. Over the area where the eelgrass used to grow, you will typically find a large fleet of powerboats, anchored up close to the shoreline for a day of family fun in the sun. My own boat is one of them.

As young boys, my brothers and I would often accompany my grandfather on quahogging trips. "Hey, Daaaaan," he would say with a gleeful grin. "Take a look at this!" and he would lift some squirming, dripping creature out of an eelgrass bed. Sometimes it was a channeled whelk, its surreal, orange mantle extended around an unlucky clam, other times an enormous, scary green spider crab, covered in algae, its long, spindly, jointed legs fluctuating in slow motion. Most times, though, he'd just pull up a quahog. Then, smiling, he'd pop the clam open with his big black-and-silver pocket knife, scrape the orange-yellow flesh from the purple-splashed shell, dangle it over his mouth dramatically, and swallow it with exaggerated gusto while we feigned disgust. That quahog was just as likely to be a big chowder clam as a cherry-stone, the smaller-sized quahogs favored by raw-bar connoisseurs today. Wes was out on the water most of the day, and I don't remember his ever packing a lunch.

Sometimes, staring at the braces protruding from beneath his dark pant legs, we would ask him innocently, "Gramps, what would you do if you fell overboard?" It was at these times that Wes, a man who seldom spoke but often laughed, would laugh the hardest. "Haar, haar, haar!" he would roar in his deep voice. "Haar, haar, haar!" We never really understood his reaction, just looked at each other smiling, raising our eyebrows and shaking our heads in wonder.

My grandfather would never return to shore without his full limit of quahogs. It was a point of pride. He was also renowned locally for refusing help in wrestling his boat into or out of the water. Strangers, watching with concern as he simultaneously balanced on both crutches with one arm and jerked his boat up onto the stony shoreline with the other, would sometimes offer him a hand. "No, thank you," he would reply curtly, his temper rising. Locals knew better than to ask. After clipping his skiff to the rope-and-pulley system and running it safely out beyond the low-water mark, he would labor up the steep hill to the house on his sticks, the heavy, dripping basket of quahogs, destined for the chowder pot, leaving a trail of salt water in his wake. For Wes Straffin, every day spent in his boat, drifting on the south-west wind over the lush green prairies of eelgrass, was a good day.

With an exploding human population and an ever-increasing number of motorboaters enjoying the Bay, it may be unrealistic to hope for a return to the days of the lush eelgrass prairies. The fate of this vital plant species may ultimately be tied to our ability to solve the looming, complex problem of nitrogen pollution from septic systems, which threatens the overall ecological health of our inshore waters. But it may not prove as difficult for us to protect our eelgrass beds from boat traffic. In light of the benefits eelgrass provides to the public, including improved fisheries, perhaps the coastal towns might consider establishing some restricted marine areas to protect eelgrass, similar to "dune restoration" areas on the shoreline, which bar foot traffic and are intended to promote the growth of stabilizing beach grass. Never, in all my travels around the Bay, have I seen such an area. Perhaps now, with the future of our eelgrass beds hanging in the balance, it might be a good time to ask ourselves why.

Boating

We perceived a broad harbour or river's mouth, which ranne up into the maine: but because the day was farre spent, we were forced to return to the Island from whence we came, leaving the discoverie of this harbour, for a time of better leasure. Of the goodnesse of which harbour, as also of many others thereabouts, there is small doubt, considering that all the Islands, as also the maine (where we were) is all rockie grounds and broken lands.

—ARCHER, ON THE MANY FINE HARBORS GOSNOLD'S MEN OBSERVED
ON THE WEST SIDE OF BUZZARDS BAY

"WE BETTER RUN BACK to the cove," said my father, nodding gravely toward the southwest, where black clouds had suddenly appeared on the horizon. I knew exactly what he meant. My father had taught me always to keep an eye on the southwest when I was out on the Bay, because that's the direction bad weather comes from. That lesson was at the top of the list, along with "the best boat for Buzzards Bay is one with a V-shaped bow." My father and I were fishing, anchored up in the Chris-Craft on the far side of Bassetts Island, where the open blue Bay rolls away in shining splendor to the western horizon. The wind was starting to pick up, and the V-shaped bow of our boat began to gently rock, straining against the anchor line. In the few moments it took us to reel in our fishing lines and stow our rods, the stiff breeze out of the southwest had grown into a strong wind, the hurtling black clouds were nearly overhead, and the towering, white-crested rollers were surfing in with an awesome dignity between Scraggy and Wings Necks. My father started the engine, faced the bow of the boat squarely into the oncoming waves, and told me to pull the anchor. I looked over the windshield at the small, slippery fiberglass bow of the boat, now pitching up and down like a rodeo steer, and felt as scared as hell. I knew I had to go because there were just the two of us. My father had to man the wheel and keep the bow faced into the swells, or when the anchor wrenched free of the bottom, the boat would surely be pushed broadside into the waves and roll over like a floating log. I had no choice but to rely on my father to keep the boat steady and keep me from pitching into the churning gray water. I clambered out onto the heaving bow through whipping salt spray and pulled that anchor. It was the hardest thing I had ever done in all my twelve years of life.

BUZZARDS BAY is renowned among boaters for its fierce southwest wind. Local sailors will tell you that you'll travel a long way indeed to find better sailing. The Bay is also known for the numerous picturesque coves that provide sheltered anchorages for afternoon or overnight stays. But in addition, the Bay is known for dangerously strong currents that arise where it meets other bodies of water. These places include the passage through Woods Hole, the holes, or channels, between the Elizabeth Islands, and the west end of the Cape Cod Canal.

For those engaged in marine commerce or commercial fishing, boating is work. For recreational sailors and fishermen, it is a pleasure. And for both groups, boating is a means of building character, of learning and honing important life values and skills. The reality is that the sea is unforgiving and teaches hard lessons. In his book *South,* an incredible tale of survival and seamanship on the sub-Antarctic Ocean, Sir Ernest Shackleton aptly describes the sea as "open to all and merciful to none."

Boating can be an especially effective tool for teaching important life values to children. Getting kids out on the water is also a good way to teach them about the environment, through hands-on experiences with marine creatures and a first-hand view of important conservation issues such as water pollution. Also, bonding with the Bay can lead to a lifelong commitment to its environmental welfare.

That day on the water with my father, I learned to use courage to overcome fear. I learned the value of obeying an order in a dangerous situation. I learned the meaning of responsibility. I learned how to trust another human being. Today, many boating programs around Buzzards Bay instill and nurture these values and skills, recognizing that they're what boating is all about.

Telemachus called unto his company and bade them lay hands on the tack-
ling, and they harkened to his call. So they raised the mast of pine tree and
set it in the hole of the cross plank, and made it fast with forestays, and
hauled up the white sails with twisted ropes of oxhide. And the wind filled
the belly of the sail, and the dark wave seethed loudly round the stem of the
running ship, and she fleeted over the wave, accomplishing her path. Then
they made all fast in the swift black ship, and set mixing bowls brimmed
with wine, and poured drink offering to the deathless gods that are from
everlasting, and in chief to the grey-eyed daughter of Zeus. So all night
long and through the dawn the ship cleft her way.

—HOMER, THE ODYSSEY

LIKE THE VESSEL that carried Telemachus in search of his father Odysseus
in Homer's *Odyssey*, the *Ernestina* is a swift black ship. And her remarkable
history is so far-flung and heroic as to rival the epic tales of *The Odyssey*
itself. The schooner, measuring 100 feet at the waterline, 156 feet overall,
is berthed at the New Bedford State Pier. Hers are the great masts you see
rising conspicuously behind the snarl of overpasses when you take the
Downtown exit off Route 195. Built in 1894, the ship is one of five surviving schooners of the nearly four thousand built in Essex, Massachusetts, and
one of only two still sailing. A gift from the people of Cape Verde, an island
nation off the coast of Africa, the *Ernestina* is now the official ship of the
Commonwealth of Massachusetts.

I sailed on the *Ernestina* as a guest on an unsettled fall day, when Hurricane
Lucille was rocking the Atlantic to our south with 140-mile-per-hour
winds. It was the kind of day when you see birds getting blown around.
Driving south on the highway to New Bedford, I was shadowed by a strange
portent in the eastern sky, a white cloud in the shape of wings, like a head-
less hawk cruising at right angles to the horizon. The great white wings
traveled with me for some time, while all other clouds in the sky streamed
wildly and loosely to the north, running from Lucille's fury.

When I arrived at the ship, I watched the other guests assemble in the parking lot. A young woman and a small dog got out of a car in front of me. The
woman had thick red dreadlocks, making her look like Medusa, and wore
silver-spiked, black leather bracelets and black combat boots. Around her
left bicep was a blue tattoo depicting a ring of barbed wire intertwined with

sharks. She carried a heavy black cane. She made her way around the lot and tenderly hugged each member of the group. Another guest was an ex-Navy man with the blue baseball cap to prove it. He later informed me that he had once owned 16,000 books on maritime history, which he had donated to the New Bedford Public Library. There was a middle-aged woman straight out of a bird club, with the standard-issue binoculars and lunch sack, an elderly man who doggedly hauled every line he could get his hands on onboard ship, and a nervous couple with two young children who wanted to know where the life jackets were stored.

What strikes you when you first see the *Ernestina* are her masts. They are thick, tall, and blackened, as if smeared with tar. Her soaring masts dwarf the superstructures of the nearby fishing vessels. A jungle of rigging descends from each mast, fastened with mysterious logic by old-style wooden blocks, or pulleys. The schooner has the nose of a swordfish; her long bowsprit juts out from her bow nearly half as far as her masts are tall. On her massive, black, wooden bow, behind the raised nameplate that reads ERNESTINA, you can still make out portions of the painted-over words EFFIE M. MORRISSEY, the schooner's christened name.

A schooner is a sailing vessel with two or more masts. The *Ernestina* is a two-masted, gaff-rigged schooner. *Gaff-rigged* basically means that she flies a single, enormous, trapezoidal sail from each mast. A trapezoidal, or four-sided shape—as opposed to a triangle—increases a sail's surface area, enabling it to derive more power from the wind. The *Ernestina* is a typical fishing schooner, built for speed. She is long and narrow, in contrast to similarly sized whaling schooners whose hulls were wider, built for volume. She is, however, modeled on the *Fredonia* schooner, so she is not quite as narrow as predecessors that were designed strictly to beat their competition from the fishing grounds to the market. Those schooners, though fast, proved so unstable and sent so many sailors to their deaths that they were scrapped. The *Ernestina* is the type of schooner that would have been used locally in the late nineteenth century for fishing the Grand Banks or as a packet ship, hauling timber, coal, or people between major New England ports.

When you board the *Ernestina*, the first thing you notice is the deck. The decking looks similar to the dark wooden floors of a very old house, except that there are round wooden plugs set in each plank, and the seams between the planks are filled with white caulking. The deck planks are actually fastened down with steel nails, and the plugs, called bungs, are used merely to cover them. Each bung is meticulously placed so that its grain matches the grain of the plank. When you look up from the deck, you experience the *Ernestina*'s grand scale. Looking down the length of the mainsail boom, up to the peak of the main mast, and forward to the tip of the bowsprit, just trying to take it all in, you feel suddenly transported to a land of giants. To get an idea of the incredible scale of the schooner, consider that the mainsail boom—the wooden piece that runs along the bottom of the sail at a right angle to the mast—is all of sixty-three feet long. If you sawed down a tall tree, cut off its branches, and suspended the trunk with ropes horizontally six feet off the ground, there you would have the boom.

If her deck is a place of grand vistas, below deck the *Ernestina* is just the opposite—dark, cloistered, a breeding place for seasickness. Her belly is called the fish hold, and it is where the scaly catch, and later cargo, was stored. I descended into the fish hold, backward, clutching both railings and feeling for each step. I thought the staircase was very narrow and steep until I saw the original—six inches wide and completely vertical, carved into the face of a support beam.

The *Ernestina*, like Telemachus's swift black ship, originally carried twenty crew members. She now carries twelve. The bunks are stacked down in the fish hold. Two deep, the bunks aren't much bigger than my son's crib. Each has a bunched, blue cloth curtain strung across a wire for privacy. As I sat in the fish hold absorbing a history lecture given by a crew member, a deluge of silver seawater crashed down the staircase onto the floor beside me. No one seemed to take much notice. There are two shadowy bookshelves in the fish hold, and the same wire that holds the curtains up keeps the books from tumbling out. The cloistered dark world of the fish hold—the only place on any ship where I have ever felt queasy—rolls endlessly as the *Ernestina* fleets over the waves.

The *Ernestina* is so big that when she backs out into the harbor it seems like part of the wharf is detaching. She eases out in a wide arc, swinging her bow around until she is pointed like a javelin at the entrance to the Hurricane Barrier. Throbbing diesel engines shepherd her toward the barrier like a pony at a racetrack guiding the thoroughbred to the gate. By the time the ship reaches the narrow entrance, the engines have been cut and the sails hauled up, and the majestic ship bursts free of the harbor under wind power alone. As she shoots the gate into the open waters of the Bay, the crew and guests raise their voices together in a traditional shout of jubilation.

When you sail as a guest on the *Ernestina*, you do just that. Each guest is expected to haul the lines that raise and lower the acres of heavy sails. Guided by the crew, we formed two long rows on either side of the ship, twenty people to a line, and raised the mainsail. The mainsail, honest to God, weighs 3,300 pounds. Standing behind me, hauling gamely hand over hand, was the elderly gentleman I had noticed earlier. While hauling away rhythmically, we sang songs that celebrated the sea and the prowess of the *Ernestina*'s crew, which was graciously stretched to include ourselves. Raising the Ernestina's mainsail was hard work, and it was difficult for me to imagine doing it in foul weather after a long day fishing the Grand Banks. After we raised the mainsail, I stood for awhile staring up at the canvas, trying simply to come to terms with its vast size.

Under sail, the *Ernestina* moves smoothly and confidently through the water, accompanied by a slight, side-to-side rolling motion. She comes about slowly, taking her time, in a wide arc. Tacking, all sixty-three feet of the wooden mainsail boom, drifting silently just inches overhead, gave true gravity to the shouted command, "Ready about—Hard alee!" Behind the shorter, forward mast is an area the crew calls the "triangle of death." "You don't want to be there when that boom comes over," one of them advised. The *Ernestina* handled the stiff breeze that day with ease. If she had been a racehorse, her pace would have been a fast walk, or maybe a trot. I felt absolutely safe on her decks. There was none of that vulnerability that you experience on smaller craft. I felt her strength as she forged through the water and believed unquestioningly in her mastery over the sea.

And in her day, *Ernestina* was a master of the sea. She sailed through a staggering number of owners, maritime geographies, and cultures. The ship's first owner, Captain William Morrissey of Gloucester, Massachusetts, put her to work fishing the Grand Banks. Her crew caught haddock, mackerel, cod, and almost anything else they could get. In those days, all the fish were taken by handlines out of dories launched from her decks. (There are reproductions of her original fishing dories on board the ship today.)

William Morrissey eventually turned the schooner over to his son, Clayton, also a fisherman. Clayton, who was just nineteen when he became her captain, was one of three models to pose for the *Man at the Wheel* fishermen's memorial—the statue of a mariner, in sou'wester hat, grasping a ship's wheel, in Gloucester.

In 1912, under Captain Harry Ross, the *Effie Morrissey* sailed from Portland, Maine, to Yarmouth, Nova Scotia, a distance of two hundred miles, in just twenty hours. The swift black ship had set a new record, and she had done it through storm and darkness.

Bob Bartlett, of Newfoundland, bought the *Effie Morrissey* in 1924, and her career as a hard-working fishing schooner ended. Bartlett had a reputation as a crazy old man with a taste for the Arctic. Known as the "Ice Navigator," he was the skipper of Admiral Peary's ship, the *Roosevelt*, on its early-twentieth-century expeditions to the North Pole. Bartlett sheathed the *Morrissey*'s hull with an inch and a half of greenheart, a Central American hardwood, to protect her from icebergs, and sailed her to the Arctic for three months every summer to capture exotic wild animals, including polar bears, walruses, and narwhales. Bartlett stowed many of these creatures alive on the *Morrissey*, transported them home, and sold them to the Bronx Zoo. The eccentric old man devised a brilliant scheme for obtaining crew members for these expeditions. He charged wealthy families a steep fee to take their teenaged sons for the summer and put them to work on the schooner. "I'll make a man out of your son," Bartlett assured delighted parents. In addition to crewing on the *Morrissey*, the boys did what most teenaged boys really want to do: they shot rifles and captured polar bears.

The *Ernestina* crew had a black-and-white photograph from the Bartlett days, of live walruses lurching about on the deck. Another photograph, labeled "Bound for the Bronx Zoo," shows an adult, snow-white polar bear lashed to the main mast with a black leather harness. The bear is straining against the harness and lunging savagely at a passenger who is clearly taunting it. Sixteen years after first purchasing the schooner, in 1940, Bob Bartlett sailed the *Morrissey* to 80 degrees 22 minutes north, which is closer to the North Pole—about 578 miles—than any other wooden sailing vessel in the world had ever gone, or would ever go.

In 1946 the schooner was purchased by two brothers, Melvin and Sidney Jackson, who painted her white and planned to reward her hard work in the north with a gentle life in the South Pacific as a mail and passenger carrier. Before they could put their plan into action, however, the *Morrissey* caught fire. With New York Fire Department hoses gushing over her, the ship sank. As the legend goes, the high-spirited *Effie Morrissey* went to the bottom because she couldn't face the drudgery and embarrassment of the mundane life that awaited her.

The *Morrissey* was raised from the bottom and bought by a man named Henrique Mendes, who renamed her the *Ernestina* after his daughter. He repaired her, stripped her of her engines, and sailed her south to Cape Verde in 1948. There she was employed as a packet ship, transporting cargo and bringing Cape Verdean immigrants to the ports of Providence and New Bedford. Over the next sixteen years, the *Ernestina* made about a dozen voyages between Cape Verde and America, frequently buffeted by hurricanes and often on a shoestring budget. Until 1954, the schooner made the seven thousand–mile round trip without the benefit of engines or even a radio. The crew showed us a color photograph radiant with the vibrant hues of the tropics, the ship surrounded by an inviting pool of azure water, *Ernestina*'s towering masts painted sparkling gold. A black man in a white three-piece suit stands on her stern next to a brilliant flag of yellow, green, and red. Everyone on deck is smiling.

Today, descendants of Cape Verdean immigrants sometimes approach the schooner, at rest in New Bedford Harbor, in tears. For Cape Verdean Americans, the schooner represents all the ships that brought their people to this country. In 1982, the Republic of Cape Verde presented the schooner as a gift to the people of the United States, to be forever a symbol of the ties between Cape Verde and New England, including the seafaring tradition we share. The gift was also meant to exemplify cooperation and understanding between peoples of the world. Because of her historic importance to New Bedford, that city was selected from a pool of several worthy candidates, most notably Providence, to be the *Ernestina*'s home port.

Since that time, regrettably, adequate recognition and funding have always been central challenges to the *Ernestina*'s existence. A current supporter told me that the schooner's plight is symptomatic of a state that spends more money on prisons than on education. Recently, when the governor visited the offices of the *New Bedford Standard Times* across the street and was asked if he would visit the ship, he reportedly replied, "Ernestina who?" In addition to relying on public funding, the Schooner *Ernestina,* a nonprofit organization, offers memberships to private citizens as a means of generating income. For a moderate annual fee, you can participate in member sails, like the one I attended, and experience firsthand the majestic Age of Sail on Buzzards Bay.

That is, you can experience it if the ship survives its latest financial challenge. Ed Morrissey, a descendant of the original owners of the ship and a resident of Nova Scotia, happened to be on board the *Ernestina* the same day I was. Ed's presence was a cause for celebration among the crew, and he was introduced to our group with great fanfare. Ed was a close-lipped gentleman, but he did answer a few questions. Yes, his father had been a fisherman, and no, he himself was not. "My father went down in a schooner off the Banks. They were rammed in the fog by another ship. I chose another direction in life."

I asked how he felt about the state owning the vessel.

"It's a good thing," he replied confidently. "They'll put the money in to maintain it." Ed Morrissey should have knocked on the wooden mast. A few months after we spoke, the state cut funding for the *Ernestina*'s annual hauling and repair work, posing a real threat to her future. Unless new funds were found, the ship would remain at the wharf.

Today the *Ernestina* plays an important educational role for the kids of greater New Bedford, many of whom are underprivileged. I first encountered New Bedford's issue of lack of water access when talking with one of the captains of the schooner, Amanda Madeira. Amanda voiced a concern that I would hear again and again in my travels around New Bedford: "The children in this city have no access to the water."

Addressing this lack of access to the Bay, the focus of the science programs conducted on board the *Ernestina* is to provide local children with the novelty of what Amanda calls "a water perspective." These programs include taking the kids ashore in the ship's dories with a seine net to see what they can catch, and hauling up an otter trawl on board for live lessons in oceanography and marine biology. There are also saltwater "touch tanks" on board. Environmental issues come up as a matter of course. For example, when the *Bouchard 120* oil spill occurred, the crew added oil pollution to the curriculum.

WHEN THE ERNESTINA returned to port on the day of my sail, locals gathered along the wharves to celebrate her return. She ghosted past a modern Coast Guard cutter and foreign oil tankers like an apparition from the past, a reminder to all that this city once counted itself among the most prosperous in the world. The swift black ship is indeed worthy of our admiration. For she is a living link to our own version of Homer's *Odyssey*— to inspiring tales of nautical adventure, the romance of exotic ports, and grand human dreams both won and lost. In an age plagued by the cancer of monoculture, she also stands as a vital symbol of Buzzards Bay's maritime heritage. The venerable *Ernestina* has important lessons to impart to us about peaceful cooperation between cultures and about the continued ecological survival of this tiny portion of the vast, wine-dark sea.

"THAT'S A MARSHALL 22," said Steve Vaitses, nodding at the wooden catboat with familiar buff-colored deck and hatchet bow resting behind a chain-link fence. "It's sloop-rigged, which makes it a little bit nicer than the average catboat." Next to the catboat squatted a Shearwater, an English-built sailboat that has three keels. The design allows the boat to rest squarely on the bottom when the tide goes out. The boatyard also held half a dozen Vanguard 420s—twelve-foot racing sailboats—a few old Boston Whalers, and shellbacks, homemade wood and fiberglass rowboats used as dinghies.

I had come to the New Bedford Community Boating Center, or CBC, to meet with Steve Vaitses, the executive director. Founded in 1996, the CBC is a nonprofit organization that teaches children about sailing and the marine environment, not only to enrich their lives but to teach them life skills such as cooperation, respect for others, goal setting, competence, teamwork, and preparedness. The center is one of the few places where New Bedford's inner-city kids can get out on the Bay on a regular basis. For the vast majority of the CBC's students, many of whom are poor, the program provides the only way for them to get out on the Bay, period. The center has been headquartered at Clarks Cove since the spring of 2003. It also runs sailing programs out of Fort Rodman, on the outer edge of New Bedford Harbor, and on Popes Island. The program serves more than 350 kids of all ages.

Clarks Cove lies between Apponagansett (Padanaram) Bay and New Bedford Harbor. It is a pretty, clean cove, the last frontier before you reach the commercialized waters of New Bedford Harbor. CBC headquarters sits on the border between the town of Dartmouth and the city of New Bedford. On the New Bedford side, punks in hotrods speed down thickly settled side streets. On the Dartmouth side, white-haired men in yellow pants dote on their Grady White fishing boats and debate the finer points of this year's clam bake.

The CBC boathouse is a white vinyl-sided, split-level house that looks straight out over the Bay. It was purchased and remodeled—mostly by the students—to suit the program's needs. The first floor has been converted into a classroom and storage space for wetsuits and dry gear. The attached garage holds sails, gas tanks, and a long line of donated Johnson and Evinrude outboard engines mounted on sawhorses. Many of the boats in the boatyard outside have also been donated by friends of the program and will be sold to raise funds. The yard used to be the site of a commercial boatyard, and the CBC staff dream of one day renovating the broken-down stone wharf.

By sheer coincidence, I arrived at CBC headquarters on the day that Hurricane Isabel, by then downgraded to a tropical storm, rolled into Buzzards Bay. As I drove past the western edge of New Bedford's mighty stone Hurricane Barrier, I could see the swells surfing into Clarks Cove, tall, gray, and angry. If you have never driven past the Hurricane Barrier, it's a rather strange experience. Busy city streets run smack up against a colossal wall of jumbled rocks, so big that you can't see over it, so big that you would never even consider scrambling over it to get a glimpse of the water on a nice summer day. It's quite medieval.

Steve had encouraged me to come even though no one would be sailing because of the bad weather. "There will be kids here," he told me. "They'll come down anyway—they love this place." Indeed, when I arrived, about eight high school kids were sprawled around the classroom listening attentively to a lesson on racing tactics. They were about evenly split between boys and girls, wore hip, street-fashion clothes, and reflected the multicultural diversity of New Bedford. Their instructor, Bo, was a tall, clean-cut, sandy-haired kid. He held the students' rapt attention, lecturing informally with the aid of a whiteboard. At the end of the lecture, he jammed his hands into his pockets, cast his eyes to the ground, shrugged, and concluded, "I'm not bragging or anything, but I race with older guys who win big races—pros, you name it. And I'm telling you, if you want to win races, this is the way it's done." The advice met with respectful silence.

After class the students set to work on hurricane cleanup, which entailed reversing the extensive preparations that had been made in anticipation of the storm. Many of the sailboats in the boatyard had been moved to New Bedford, as had the sails normally stored in the garage. All of the dry gear—yellow and red rain jackets and pants—had been stashed upstairs, and the kids were running armfuls back down to the basement, joking and horsing around as they worked. The disheveled mountain of dry gear upstairs looked as if the hurricane itself might have deposited it there. Through the open upstairs windows, the strong southeast wind whistled like a musical instrument.

"Why would you store this stuff upstairs with a hurricane coming?"

"It's not the wind we're worried about," Steve answered. "It's the storm surge flooding the lower level of the house." I recalled that the hurricane barrier ended just blocks before the CBC boathouse.

"Why did you choose Clarks Cove for your headquarters?" I asked.

"There's pretty much no access to the water inside New Bedford Harbor," Steve explained. "You've got the Hurricane Barrier and the fishing fleet as obstacles. And it's polluted! You've got to get out to the points, the coves, to get access to the Bay."

I was incredulous. "You mean the kids from New Bedford have no access to their own harbor?"

"Not really," Steve replied. "And most kids don't have the means to get down to the Harbor anyway, even if they did have access."

"You mean, they don't have bikes . . . or public transportation?"

Steve gave me a dubious look. "Let me put it this way," he said slowly. "It's dangerous. With traffic and all, I wouldn't want my kids trying to make it down to the waterfront, not from the North End." I began to get the idea.

Later, the CBC staff introduced me to the teens and asked me to talk a bit about why I was there. They sat on the front steps, arms wrapped around knees, and I stood awkwardly in front of them. I tried to remember what I would have been willing to listen to when I was sixteen. I told them why I thought their community boating program was important to the future of the Bay. When I said that the Bay was one of the last relatively pristine bodies of water on the East Coast of America, they laughed.

"Pristine? Are you kidding? Have you seen the harbor?"

"New Bedford Harbor won't always be polluted," I assured them. "By the time you're my age, the Environmental Protection Agency and the city will have cleaned it up." They seemed incredulous.

As the students dispersed, I asked a big, surly kid named Marcos why he liked it down at the CBC.

"It's fun," he replied impassively.

"What do you like about the boating program?"

"It's fun," said the boy again. He crossed his big, meaty arms on his chest.

"What do your parents think about your involvement in the boating program?"

"They're happy I found something I like. I don't get injured a lot."

The conversation seemed to be going nowhere, but then Marcos offered, "I like this place because they give you goals." I perked up. *Goals* was a word that I'd heard Steve Vaitses use a lot.

"Do you have goals in other aspects of your life, Marcos? For example, at home?"

"No," he replied flatly. Then, suddenly, he blurted out, "My goal here is to go to the Olympics."

Steve later confirmed that Marcos's noble goal was indeed to reach the Olympic sailing competition, and that he was apparently headed in the right direction, having already earned the rank of junior captain. But Steve wasn't impressed that Marcos's goal was to get to the Olympics; rather, what was important to him was that Marcos had learned what it was to *have* a goal.

The next student I interviewed couldn't wait to share her views on the CBC. Christina bounded out of the crowd of kids with a smile when I asked to speak with her. She was sixteen, a high school junior. Her body was toned and strong, flush with youth and the vigor imparted by a summer spent on the Bay. Christina has been in the community boating program for seven years. She had spent the previous summer as a junior instructor, teaching ten-year-olds how to sail.

"The CBC is unlike anything I have ever done," she explained enthusiastically. "My stepmother encouraged me to try it, and I loved it! I want to grow up and be something. I'm not going to let drugs and alcohol destroy my future, my goals." There was that word again—*goals*.

"What has the CBC taught you about Buzzards Bay?" I asked Christina.

"Before I joined," she confessed, "the only time I got to the water was swimming at West Beach." She made a wry face. "I didn't like swimming there . . . too polluted. I've seen the difference in water quality between Clarks Cove and the harbor. There's a lot of trash, pollution over there. The problem is that most kids in New Bedford don't have anything to compare it to. It's not like they go to Florida in the winter, or anything like that."

"How has the CBC made a difference in your life?"

"I always used to say, there's nothing to do in New Bedford. This program changed all that."

Christina is one of the main cheerleaders in the community for the boating center. She has taken the initiative to educate school guidance counselors about the group, and she often tells high school students, "Get *something* on your résumé for college!" Christina counts getting other kids involved in the CBC as her greatest personal success.

Later, admiring the view of the cove from a boathouse window, I watched a sailboat clear the point. The distant sail was illuminated by a shaft of sunlight, and it glowed in that singular fashion that only a sail gliding on the surface of the sea can. Certainly, you would never see this breathtaking scene from the projects in New Bedford. Steve pointed to a poster for the CBC program: "Where Kids and the Water Meet."

"There's another, informal slogan that the kids are throwing around privately," he told me proudly: "CBC—Where the Kids Want to Be." I wanted Steve to tell me more about using boating as a teaching tool.

"The CBC is not just a sailing experience, it's a life experience," he explained. "If you think about it, everything you do on the water has to do with values, such as teamwork and courtesy. These kids don't get that at home."

"Are they that bad off?"

"The worst stories you can imagine; one of these kids will tell you all about it," Steve replied. "Homelessness, alcoholic parents, abuse. In the Advanced Youth Program, we use sailing to teach the children life values including competency, self-esteem, and preparedness."

I wondered what the CBC teaches these kids about Buzzards Bay.

"We practice what we call destination sailing. That means the kids sail to a place, get out of their boats, and take a look around. We'll study crabs, minnows, whatever's there. And in the advanced programs, such as the high school ones, in addition to teaching such things as racing tactics, vectors, and ballast, we teach students about weather and how science and the local environment relate."

As I was leaving, I turned to Steve. "Do you really think the students here will remember the Bay when they grow up?" He understood and made a sincere effort to put my doubts to rest. His reply illuminated the truth as brightly as the sunlight had illuminated that lone sail.

"Every day these kids go out on the Bay," he said, "they bond with it. They learn an affinity for the water that they will never forget. What we do is get them out there. Not just in sailboats, but in kayaks, too—in anything."

Many of us who love Buzzards Bay were brought up with unlimited access to it; we had summer places to stay at, or grandparents to visit, and clean beaches to swim from. And many of us had boats, or at least friends with boats. How can thousands of less privileged local kids ever come to know the Bay, and thus learn to appreciate and protect it, without access to the water? The CBC is onto something that is much bigger than just teaching kids boating skills. The vinyl-sided split-level on Clarks Cove houses not just dry gear, sails, and old outboards, but also an idea upon which the future of Buzzards Bay depends. *Get them out there.*

FOR YOUNG ADULTS who decide to turn their love of the sea into a career, the Massachusetts Maritime Academy awaits. The academy is perched on Taylors Point, at the west end of the Cape Cod Canal. From a distance, it looks less like a college campus than a huddled group of build-ings clinging forlornly to the side of a massive ship. That ship, docked in front of the academy, is the training vessel *Enterprise*. The *Enterprise*, 540 feet long and 76 feet wide, is powered by a 15,500-horsepower engine and is capable of moving through the water at twenty knots.

Massachusetts Maritime is the oldest maritime academy in continuous operation in the United States and the largest state maritime academy. The school's mission is to "graduate educated men and women to serve the maritime industry as licensed officers or to serve the transportation, engi-neering, environmental, and industrial interests of the Commonwealth and the Nation." One of the school's complementary missions is to assist the Commonwealth and the region in furthering maritime interests.

Students at the academy can choose from several courses of study relating to the sea, including engineering, business, or the environment. They also have the option of earning a merchant marine officer's license or a naval officer's commission. All first-year cadets participate in an exciting "semester at sea," during which they sail nine thousand miles around the globe and visit three foreign countries. The academy prepares students for careers both at sea and on land.

The Massachusetts Maritime Academy was founded in 1891 by the state leg-islature as the Massachusetts Nautical Training School and was originally located in Boston. In 1942 the school moved from Boston to Hyannis.

During World War II, academy graduates served their country with valor, as they had in World War I. At the end of the war, the academy moved to the State Pier on Buzzards Bay.

I MET CADET JOHN MULDOON for breakfast at a diner in Pocasset. He walked in wearing the tan, white, and blue colors of the Mass Maritime Buccaneers and the number 43 inscribed on his jacket. John, who played both football and baseball for the academy, looks like an athlete. When he sat down across from me and jammed his hands deep into the pockets of his jacket, his neck looked thick and his shoulders sloped down at a long, sharp angle.

John is from Wareham. He grew up in a large Irish Catholic family that wasn't poor but not exactly wealthy either. He has earned most of the money for his college tuition himself. When we spoke, John was working four jobs—running his own landscaping company, waiting tables at Lindsey's in Wareham, helping teach special education at Wareham public schools, and coaching football for the Old Colony Regional Vocational Technical School. "I'm already reaping the benefits of a Mass Maritime education and I haven't even graduated yet," the cadet told me. There were other, more qualified applicants for the teacher's aide job, but John believes he got it because he's a cadet. "Mass Maritime got me the restaurant job, too," he assured me.

An outgoing, personable young man, John describes himself as "a fireball" when he was younger, "always fighting and yelling." That fire found alcohol, and the results were predictably disastrous. After one fateful night, involving yelling and throwing and blacking out, John joined Alcoholics Anonymous and has been dry ever since.

Like many recovering alcoholics, John struggled emotionally. A professor who's also a member of AA helped get John back on track. Several other ex-alcoholics at the school supported him emotionally as well, including one member of the athletic staff. "Mass Maritime instills morals in you," explained Johnny sheepishly. "If you're doing something wrong there, you know it."

Support at the school has come from many places: the quarterback on the football team; the athletic director, who taught John "not just about sports, but about life" and the president of the college, Admiral Bresnahan, himself.

During John's first year, when his grades were so poor that he was in danger of flunking out, Bresnahan walked up to him and said, "Johnny, we need you to get your grades up. All right, buddy?" That the president of the college would take such an interest in a new cadet made a big impression on John.

John chose his major, marine safety and environmental protection, because he plans to work professionally on shore. He has studied coastal ecology and environmental law. He also did a summer internship at the SeaMass Resource Recovery Facility in Rochester. That's a fancy name for a place that burns trash and turns it into electricity. SeaMass is where the trash train that chugs up the spine of the Cape stops. John's three bosses there were all Mass Maritime graduates.

In the spring of 2003, many cadets at the academy received a windfall of hands-on opportunity from the *Bouchard 120* oil spill. First on the scene, the cadets were employed in everything from cleanup to standing guard against the press at Hurley Library, the command center for the legions of officials involved in the cleanup effort.

I asked John what the cadets thought about the oil spill, and how Bouchard handled it.

Bouchard's initial reports on the amount of oil on board the barge and the amount that spilled proved inaccurate. According to John, although aware of these discrepancies, most cadets were too busy during the cleanup to contemplate much more than the tasks at hand. It's safe to assume, however, that many of them, including John, were both angry and sad as they watched the deadly sheen of oil fouling the waters they knew and loved.

I wondered, overall, what going to school on the ocean has meant to John—and, by extension, the other cadets.

"I can't even begin to tell you," John said with feeling. "The view I've had from my room over the last four years is a million-dollar view that I pay ten thousand dollars a year for. I never saw anything so beautiful." There is also the excitement of watching massive commercial ships enter the canal, carrying their cargos of oil, cars, and cement. The cadets get to feel that they're part of the hustle and bustle of commerce and the promise of prosperity that the ships hold out. There are times, too, just walking to class, when the

Bay seems to reflect moods, sometimes blue and calm, sometimes gray and turbulent. "Out on the tip," John observed, using the cadets' name for the academy's location, "I'll see the Bay go from calm to sixty-mile-per-hour winds in a matter of minutes. It's kind of like life."

People familiar with the Massachusetts Maritime Academy often describe it as a gem in the state's educational system. Graduates like John are everywhere around the Bay. They are employed in all the professions that have an impact on the environment; they work in local police departments, town halls, juvenile detention programs, in environmental companies, on commercial vessels, and as members of the Navy and Coast Guard Reserves. In these roles, the John Muldoons of the Bay are in fact foot soldiers in our battle to preserve it. What teacher could better prepare them for this important task than the sea itself?

Fisheries

In five or six hours absence, we had pestered our ship so with

Cod fish, that we threw numbers of them over-boord againe:

and surely, I am persuaded that in the months of March, April,

and May, there is upon this coast, better fishing, and in as great

plenty, as in Newfoundland: for the sculles of mackerel, herrings,

Cod and other fish that we dayly saw as we went and came

from the shore, were woonderfull.

—BRERETON, ON THE DENSE SCHOOLS OF FISH THE EXPLORERS
ENCOUNTERED OFF CAPE COD

WHAT'S THE LAST THING that goes through a tautog's mind before
it dies? A Chinese cleaver. The tautog, a native bottom fish of six to eight
pounds, traditionally favored by locals for fish chowder, is now a staple of
Asian restaurants and Asian food markets in Boston and New York. One
reason the fish is considered ideal for this market is because, strangely, it
can be kept alive out of water for long periods simply by wrapping it in
wet burlap. Upon reaching the restaurant, it is released alive into a tank and
given the opportunity to strut its stuff to customers, who personally select
the specimen they desire. This is all very sad, particularly for the tautog,
who has a reputation locally as a homebody. The *Massachusetts Saltwater
Fishing Guide* describes the fish this way: "Tautog are very slow-growing
compared to most fish, and do not migrate far from where they originate
but move inshore in the spring and offshore in winter."

THERE ARE FOUR KINDS of fishing on Buzzards Bay: fin fishing (the
catching of species we typically call fish), lobstering, shellfishing, and aquaculture. Fin fishing on the Bay is unique for several reasons. Most striking is
the fact that, in the traditional sense, no commercial fishing is allowed on
the Bay because net fishing was banned in 1896. This legislation was driven

by public concern over the impact of the popular pound net and weir fisheries on fish populations. At the time, there were over thirty weirs in use locally. As a result of the legislation, and in contrast with most heavily populated coastal areas around the world, the fish of Buzzards Bay have been protected from trawling and gill netting for over a century. Today, the New Bedford–Fairhaven fishing fleet, the biggest in the country, heads out of New Bedford Harbor and keeps on going clear of the Bay. An interesting result of this situation is that shellfish have emerged as the Bay's major commercial fisheries resource.

Buzzards Bay is unique in supporting a highly varied fishery based on many different species of fish. Historical records indicate that 203 species of fish have at one time or another spent some part of their life cycle in the Bay. Whereas Cape Cod Bay is known primarily for cod, flounder, striped bass, and blues, you can also find tautog, scup, sea bass, and fluke in Buzzards Bay. The Bay's rocky bottom makes an ideal habitat for these additional bottom-dwelling fish, whereas Cape Cod Bay and Nantucket Sound have sandy bottom. Because of the abundance of these species, Buzzards Bay has historically been characterized as "a bottom-fishing place."

Another unique characteristic of the Bay fishery, compared to other local areas, is accessibility. Buzzards Bay offers the public a great many boat ramps and shore areas. Large waterfront homes, though they certainly exist, have not yet limited access to shoreline areas to the extent they have on Vineyard and Nantucket Sounds. Unfortunately, there are no guarantees that these advantages will survive. As the population on the Bay grows, so do the number of fishermen. Already, the fishermen could use more boat ramps and expanded parking areas. New faces bring new attitudes. In recent years, the tide of public opinion has sometimes turned against fishermen. One example is the recent, failed attempt to close the popular Padanaram Bridge in South Dartmouth to the fishing public. Even some state parks have begun to limit access. For the most part, however, Buzzards Bay is still a place where the average man, woman, or child can find a place to fish.

As a resource, the colonists on the Bay ranked fishing second only to farming. They salted and dried mackerel and cod and caught many species to eat fresh, including mackerel, bluefish, sea bass, butterfish, scup, and menhaden. The importance of cod—the fish that played such a vital role for other early

Massachusetts settlers—to Bay colonists is unclear. Although cod are rarely found in the Bay today, we know that historically the fish made up some portion of the colonist's catch from late winter to early spring. Mackerel were abundant in colonial times, but their transient, migratory nature made them an undependable food source, so they were seldom targeted and were taken mostly by chance in weirs.

Historical records indicate that in the late 1800s Buzzards Bay was a major commercial source of menhaden, alewives, tautog, squeteague (weakfish), and eels. Before 1920, its waters were dominated by mackerel, butterfish, silver hake, alewives, herring, and scup. After 1960 (the next available reference), the most abundant species were scup, winter flounder, and butterfish. Today, bluefish, striped bass, and mackerel are also prevalent in the summer and fall. And in terms of sheer mass, each year new-born butterfish, scup, and sea bass outweigh all other animal life in the Bay.

Species counts have varied widely since the time of the colonists, the result of natural fluctuations and—by the late 1800s—overfishing. In the past, many people blamed bluefish for the decline of fish species on the Bay because they fed so voraciously and unselectively. By 1870, many fish species were disappearing from Buzzards Bay, and experts pointed to overfishing as the likely cause.

Despite recent excitement among fishermen about the resurgence of the striped bass, arguably the most important fish on the Bay, both historically and today, is the scup. A feisty, silver bottom fish, typically weighing one to two pounds, the *Massachusetts Saltwater Fishing Guide* describes the scup like this: "A party boat staple, the scup are easy and fun to catch. Scup are very good eating though be careful of the many bones." Scup are both a good choice for teaching kids to fish and a staple for fishermen out to put food on the table.

The documented history of the scup provides a useful example of how fish populations on the Bay have fluctuated over time. Colonial records indicate that scup were extremely plentiful from 1621 to 1642. In the late 1600s they disappeared. In 1794 they appeared again in large numbers, only to decline rapidly again around 1864. Judging by the number of petitions introduced at that time to protect the scup, people living on the Bay considered the fish a valuable resource. Then, sometime around 1960, scup experienced another population explosion. Pie charts published by the Buzzards Bay Project, called "Changes in Reported Fish Catches for Buzzards Bay," comparing species yields between pre-1920 and post-1960, dramatically illustrate this event. More than half of the pre-1920 pie chart is composed of a large slice labeled "Mackerel" and a small sliver labeled "Other." In the post-1960 pie chart, both slices have been replaced by a giant black wedge labeled SCUP. Mackerel are no longer represented at all. It would appear that sometime around 1960, a great battle was staged on the ledges of the Bay between the mackerel and the scup nations, and the scup emerged victorious. The practical repercussions of this victory rang throughout the Bay. For example, by the late 1970s, my father had sold his boat and nearly stopped fishing. His justification for doing so surprised no one. "All that's out there now," he lamented, "is scup."

MY BROTHERS AND I didn't even know what we were looking at. We were anchored up in my father's Chris-Craft near the North Channel of Bassetts Island. The year was 1976. My father was ecstatic—after years of catching mostly scup, he had just landed a hefty pair of tautog. To our impressionable eyes, the fish were big: three times as big as the scup we typically reeled in, and they had fought hard, putting a deep arch in my father's fiberglass rod. And unlike the silver scup, flashing purple in the sunlight, these fish were dark gray. We stared at my father with awe. The way he appeared at that moment is the way I prefer to remember him now: forty years old, vital, filled with happiness. His body was powerful, and he still talked of his days on the USS *Maken*, when he worked out with weights and the other sailors respectfully called him Hoss. I use this memory to counter another, more recent one. This one is of my father receding into a hospital bed, collarbone jutting out, eyes far away and distilled to the clear blue of an infant, reduced by cancer to a fluttering candle flame of a man. The memory of my father with his pair of tautog is what fishing is all about. The activity offers the ordinary person the chance to be a hero. And it creates joyful memories between friends and family, memories that can invest with meaning lives too often circumscribed by routine, disappointment, and pain.

ALTHOUGH A COMMERCIAL NET FISHERY does not exist on the Bay, commercial fishing does exist in the form of charter and party boats, rod and reel, and pots. The commercial rod-and-reel fishery on the Bay targets several species. In the spring and fall, the "live tautog" fishery, driven by Asian markets, is popular. In the summer, scup fishing dominates, with fluke taken as a bycatch. Some boats target sea bass. Striped bass are also harvested, mostly along the north shores of the Bay and around the islands, with an incidental catch of bluefish. This striped bass fishery, however, tends to revolve more around Vineyard Sound than Buzzards Bay.

Several large party boats fish the Bay out of Wareham and New Bedford. These multideck vessels take crowds of tourists bottom-fishing for scup, with a bycatch of sea bass and tautog. Most of their clientele are from out of state. Buses and car pools arrive daily from New York, New Jersey, and Connecticut in the summer months. The goal of these fishermen is to stock their freezers with as many fish as possible.

The charter boat fishery primarily targets striped bass and blues, with the exception of a few boats that fish for scup, sea bass, and tautog. Most of the charter boats are out of New Bedford, Fairhaven, Dartmouth, and Cuttyhunk. The season typically runs from mid-May through the fall. Many charter boat captains are part-timers, fishing to supplement income from off-season positions, such as schoolteacher. They fish mostly at night and target the Elizabeth Islands, favoring spots such as Quicks Hole and Sow and Pigs Reef off the tip of Cuttyhunk.

In the mid-1980s, a successful pot fishery migrated to the Bay from Nantucket Sound. This fishery, which employs pots similar to lobster traps, is carried out by a small group of fishermen who lay approximately two hundred pots. They target sea bass and scup from the beginning of May until around mid-August. Scup pots are baited with clam bellies. No bait is used to catch sea bass, as the fish willingly enter the traps in their search for a place to spawn. Ecologically speaking, the advantage of pot fishing over trawlers is that undersized fish and bycatch are returned to the water unharmed.

The popular recreational fishery on the Bay targets the same species as the commercial fishery, with the addition in the summer months of false albacore and bonito that ride the Gulf Stream north from southern waters. Recreational fishermen typically fish the Bay from small boats, generally up to twenty-five feet long, and from bridges, rivers, beaches, and other spots on the shore.

THIN RIVULETS OF BLOOD pooled on the gray bottom of my tin boat as I chopped mackerel on a cedar shingle. Every few seconds, I dropped a small piece—a head, a tail, a kidney—over the side into the current that ran like a conveyor belt to the field of boulders at the end of the distant neck of land. The chum line led from my boat directly to the nose of a large bluefish, one of the legendary monsters that cruise authoritatively through Buzzards Bay on the tail of the fall run. Next, I dropped the prize, a hook baited with a larger piece of mackerel, overboard, stuck the rod under the bench seat, and sat back confidently to wait. Relaxing in the subdued fall sunlight, I finished off a box of crackers and chuckled to myself as I contemplated the bait bag full of mackerel. I had truly run afoul of my Yankee heritage. My father and grandfather would have been shocked that I was using up four fish to catch one. They never even bought bait, depending instead on night crawlers, which we pursued with flashlights after a warm summer rain. And to committed bottom fishermen, even the fact that I was fishing for blues, fish of dubious culinary distinction, would have appeared extravagant.

Just then my rod swung violently to the side and smashed against the gunnel. It was difficult to pull the butt out from under the seat and wedge it under my armpit without completely losing control of the fish. Oh, the high price of laziness. A large blue, when hooked in shallow water, has nowhere to run but away, something it is capable of doing at high speed. Unlike the long, powerful runs of a striper, a blue fights in shorter, violent bursts that frequently change direction. One of its most disconcerting and successful escape tactics is to clear the water while running hard in the direction of the angler, all the while shaking its head and gnashing its teeth in an attempt to gain slack in the line and thus throw the hook. Amazingly, a large blue of fifteen to twenty pounds will test the strength of a grown man and leave some a trembling, shaken mess.

Ten minutes later, after an intense tug-of-war, I pulled an unwilling, ghostly ice-blue torpedo with glowing yellow eyes to the boat. It was a sixteen-pound blue. I gingerly leaned over the side and tailed the fish by grasping the thick round muscle just below its forked tail, taking care to keep the toothed head away from my body as I swung it heavily aboard. Bluefish are one of the few fish who can see as well out of the water as in, and they will sometimes lie still, watching your movements, calculating the best moment to deliver a nasty snap at an unwary hand. They have an attitude. When you look into the eye of a bluefish, which seeks out your own, you can't help but sense that in addition to being outraged, the fish is deeply and personally offended that you, a human, had the nerve to catch it.

It was my first big blue. I sat for a while, spent, letting the adrenaline course through my body and the boat rock gently on the incoming tide. I release most of the blues I catch relatively unharmed. This one, however, was pre-destined for the smoker: its pungent flesh would ennoble holiday tables in the form of bluefish pate. Later, I sponged down the inside of the boat, weighed anchor, and cruised home at high speed, encouraging the Mercury to split the silence of the Bay, whooping into the teeth of the wind like a savage. Except perhaps for when I lost my virginity, never before had I felt more like a man, never more acutely alive. It is impossible to describe this feeling to someone who has never tested their strength and wits against a wild animal and conquered it. The feeling is addictive and is responsible, in large measure, for that breed of person known as a "fishaholic." I know a man who was once the star receiver of our high school football team. Of all people I have known, he has perhaps experienced the most personal elation. He knew the cheers of crowds chanting his name, the rush of adrenaline as he flashed across the goal line again and again. Now he spends every free moment fishing. He fishes because it gives him the same rush he used to know. One of the best things about the elation of sport fishing is that you don't have to be a star athlete to experience it.

> Also, [there are] divers sorts of shell-fish, as Scallops, Muscles, Cockles, Lobsters, Crabs, Oisters, and Whilks, exceeding good and very great.
> —BRERETON, ON THE LOBSTERS AND SHELLFISH GOSNOLD'S PARTY FOUND ON BUZZARDS BAY

A WIDE GRIN split my grandfather's large, chiseled features. A big man with a thick shock of white hair, Weston Straffin was a dead ringer for the prototypical Cape Cod sea captain. "Are you really going to *eat* that?" he exclaimed mischievously, alluding to the boiled lobster on my plate. We were seated opposite each other at a red wooden picnic table so old it was decomposing into the landscape, beneath the great, apple-green catalpa tree, its string beans swaying in the warm sea breeze. It was Labor Day, Wes was 93 years old, and we both knew, I think, that this was the last annual cookout he would attend. A *Mayflower* descendant, he was one of the last to fully embody Pilgrim values. My grandfather looked at you with the same clear gaze with which he would no doubt regard his maker on Judgment Day; when lesser men met his eyes, they invariably looked away. He had a pulverizing handshake, kept his word, didn't lie, rarely cursed, never knew the taste of alcohol. And he certainly didn't eat lobster. To him, lobster was trash fish.

CAPE COD AND BOSTON were the first areas of the country to support lobster fisheries, both beginning around 1800. The industry spread to Maine in 1840 and to Provincetown in 1845. Lobstering in Buzzards Bay began around 1807 along the Elizabeth Islands, based at Cuttyhunk.

Early records from the Plymouth Colony describe lobsters as a nuisance, pitched up on the beaches layers deep by storms. In 1635, William Wood, a colonial-era writer, said of lobsters that "their plenty makes them little esteemed and seldom eaten." They were also much bigger then. Wood noted that some lobsters captured by the colonists in shallow water weighed twenty pounds. Martin and Lipfert, in their 1985 book *Lobstering and the Maine Coast*, noted that four-foot, forty-five-pound specimens were common in colonial times. In 1841, in a book titled *Report on the Invertebrata of Massachusetts*, Augustus Gould commented that ten- to twelve-pound lobsters were commonly seen in the markets. By the late 1880s, because of overfishing, most lobster fisheries had begun to experience a decline in the numbers and size of lobsters caught. Today, the Cape Ann fishery, based at the ports of Gloucester and Rockport, leads Massachusetts in annual lobster landings for territorial (inshore) waters, contributing around 20 percent of the state total, which is currently just over seven million pounds. The second-largest contributor is Boston. Prior to 1991, Boston's fleet of 120 boats was the undisputed leader, contributing 30 to 40 percent of the state total. During the 1990s, however, the Boston fishery collapsed. By 1998, half of the lobstermen in Boston had sold their boats and left the industry.

Historically, Buzzards Bay has sustained a very productive lobster fishery, in recent decades contributing 3 to 4 percent of the state's total haul. The fishery's stocks are plummeting, however, and the industry is collapsing. It is now harder to catch legal lobsters in Buzzards Bay than anywhere else in Massachusetts. The annual catch is one-quarter of what it was in recent decades. This crash, which began in the mid-1990s, is reflected in the entire lobster stock unit. A stock unit, as defined by the Massachusetts Division of Marine Fisheries—the organization charged with managing the state's living marine resources and overseeing water-quality classification—is a group of fish with similar biological characteristics, such as gene pool, growth rates, and size at maturity. Bay lobsters are part of a stock unit that extends from southern Massachusetts through Long Island Sound.

So what happened to the once-plentiful lobster population of Buzzards Bay? The story varies according to whom you talk to. The fishermen attribute the crash to shell disease, pollution, the environmentalist-engineered return of cod and striped bass (both natural predators of lobsters), and perhaps a bit of overfishing. The scientists will tell you that the stock has been drastically overfished. An objective analysis suggests that overfishing was the primary cause of the crash and that pollution and disease compounded the problem.

Lobstering on Buzzards Bay is a year-round but heavily seasonal fishery, with the bulk of the catch taken from April through September, when warm water spurs the growth rate of lobsters. Far fewer lobsters are taken from October through March. Roughly two hundred commercial lobstermen work the Bay and nearby waters, the great majority out of New Bedford–Fairhaven. The Bay also supports a small recreational fishery. In general, lobstering is not as attractive as fin fishing to the average recreational fisherman, because traps require significant maintenance, and they must be checked frequently to prevent cannibalism.

A significant difference between commercial lobstering and shellfishing on the Bay is that lobstering is regulated by the state—the Massachusetts Division of Marine Fisheries—as opposed to the towns. Before 1997, the federal government regulated the lobster fishery in Massachusetts. Regionally, the lobster industry, which extends from Labrador to North Carolina, is overseen by the Atlantic States Marine Fisheries Commission. This commission includes representatives from every state that hosts a lobster fishery; the main players come from the states ranging from Maine to New Jersey. In 1997, the commission put together a plan to manage the lobster population that is based on a dizzying array of overlapping regions, zones, and stocks. The lobsters in Buzzards Bay fall into Management Zone II, which also includes Nantucket Sound, Martha's Vineyard, the Elizabeth Islands, Narragansett Bay, and Block Island.

Buzzards Bay is good lobster habitat. Above all things, lobsters prize shelter, which they find in abundance on the rocky bottom of the Bay. In general, small, sublegal lobsters like to sit in depressions scraped on the bottom, while large, legal-sized lobsters prefer heavy cover such as kelp beds and rocks. Sometimes, desperate lobsters even burrow under traps to find shelter. The relatively warm, shallow waters of the Bay accelerate growth rates; as a result, females reach sexual maturity faster. This characteristic accounts for the Bay's consistently high productivity as a spawning ground.

These same qualities that make for good lobster habitat, however, can pose unique challenges to lobstermen. Warm water results in a buildup of algae on traps, lines (known as warps), and buoys, making them heavy and maintenance-intensive. In particular, this effect creates difficulties for recreational lobstermen, who typically pull traps by hand. The relatively shallow waters of the Bay also leave traps more vulnerable to storms, since traps set in less than sixty feet of water can easily be tumbled by strong, wind-driven currents. These storm currents can also entangle trap lines or even wrap entire trawls. Trawls are strings of ten to twenty traps roped together, with a buoy marking each end. Divers have discovered snarls of trawls as big as buildings sitting on the bottom after storms. Sometimes, before a hurricane, lobstermen will temporarily remove the warps and buoys that give the current something to grab onto.

Commercial lobstering is a physically demanding business. Many lobstermen suffer from arm, shoulder, hip, and (especially) back problems. These injuries result from continually lifting and moving traps on shore and boat and also from the inherent "one-sidedness" of the work. A large part of a lobsterman's daily routine consists of reaching one-handed over the side of the boat to retrieve traps from the pot-hauler as they come out of the water. A pot-hauler is an electronic device that mechanically lifts traps from the bottom to the surface.

Today there is a decided trend toward wire traps. The main advantages of wire traps over wooden ones are lightness and longevity. The weight of wooden traps does offer one advantage, however: it helps the trap hold the bottom during storms. Half-moon-style wooden traps, or "half-rounds," were specifically designed to create less drag in the bottom currents. Modern wire traps depend on holding the bottom by allowing seawater to flow through them.

Today lobster traps, whether wire or wood, are more efficient and ecologically correct than their predecessors. Advancements in trap design are the result of studies completed by the National Marine Fisheries Service in the mid-1970s that showed that lost traps continued to catch lobsters at about 10 percent of the baited trap catch rate. These animals presumably entered the unbaited traps looking for shelter. The studies showed that lobsters that entered these "ghost traps" died within thirty days. Regulations designed to address this problem, established in 1977, state that traps must include a 3.5-inch-diameter hole covered by a panel secured with biodegradable material, such as twine, so that lobsters can eventually escape. In addition, traps must be equipped with "escape vents," small slots that allow sublegal lobsters, known as "shorts," to exit at will. These escape vents minimize the handling of sublegal lobsters and prevent them from being eaten by larger lobsters or aggressive fish in the traps. The vents actually increase the catch rate of the traps, because mature lobsters are more inclined to enter a less-crowded trap. Because of this advantage, the escape vent regulation enjoys widespread support from lobstermen.

Bruce Estrella, the Massachusetts technical advisor to the Atlantic States Marine Fisheries Commission's Lobster Board for the last twenty-plus years and a widely recognized authority on all things lobster, is convinced that the stock crash in Zone II was mostly the result of overfishing. As evidence, he notes that the number of traps fished in Zone II, our area of the stock unit, have tripled or even quadrupled, just as they did in the past fifteen to twenty years in the western end of the stock unit (Long Island Sound). This increased fishing pressure, Bruce reasons, has taken a severe toll on egg production by legal-sized lobsters.

The lobster industry on Buzzards Bay has degenerated into what scientists call a "recruitment-dependent" fishery—one that depends on harvesting young animals that have just been "recruited to," or reached, the legal size limit. In other words, almost all the lobsters being caught on the Bay today have barely reached legal size. The current definition of legal size is three and three-eighths inches, as measured from the rear of the eye socket to the rear edge of the carapace (the headlike area of the shell). On average, the lobsters weigh one and one-fifth pounds. This is quite low compared to 1880, when the average lobster taken in the Bay weighed two and one-half pounds, or 1840 when the average weight was three pounds. Scientists don't consider a recruitment-dependent fishery healthy because the population is highly unstable, and thus vulnerable to natural stressors such as disease. In human terms, the situation is analogous to a town inhabited only by children and teenagers, with the teenagers being solely responsible for reproduction. If a deadly strain of, say, acne, broke out in this town, wiping out most of the teens, there would not be enough of them left to sustain the population. Any population, to remain healthy, must consist of large numbers of mature, breeding adults. According to Bruce Estrella, it is chiefly the commercial lobster fishery that is depleting the lobster population and thus making it vulnerable to unfavorable environmental conditions that can affect larval production and survival.

The theory that pollution and disease have impacted the lobster population of the Bay (and the rest of the stock unit) is more prevalent among fishermen than scientists. Regardless of the historical role these factors have had in the fishery's decline, however, they now pose a clear threat because of the population's recruitment-dependent status. With the lobster population barely hanging on, additional stress from pollution or disease could be the final blow that sends it into an irreversible tailspin, or at the least prevents it from ever fully recovering.

Lobsters are very hardy animals and are considered by many to be practically immune to pollution. In fact, some of the most productive lobstering in the state's recent history occurred in Boston Harbor before it was cleaned up, and specifically at the openings of the sewage outfall pipes. Lobstermen had so many trawls concentrated in those spots that they snarled on a regular basis. Nevertheless, coastal pollution is considered a primary cause of declining lobster stocks over the past few hundred years. Nitrogen loading—the excessive contribution of nitrogen to bodies of water from septic systems, lawn fertilizers, and other sources—is one area of concern. Excessive nitrogen, combined with warm summer water temperatures, can cause low-oxygen water conditions that are hostile to many marine organisms. Most lobsters, however, choose to inhabit deepwater areas of the Bay rather than the inshore areas that are most vulnerable to the effects of nitrogen loading. Pesticides are another pollutant that can pose a threat to lobster populations. For example, the spraying for West Nile Virus that occurred on Long Island Sound in 1999 prior to Hurricane Floyd is strongly suspected of decimating the lobster population there. Runoff from the hurricane, which delivered more than a foot of rain, is suspected of washing large quantities of pesticides into the Sound. Ten million lobsters, or 90 percent of the population, died, and one hundred and fifty lobstermen lost their livelihood. In general, however, lobsters are still probably one of the Bay's marine species least affected by pollution from the surrounding watershed.

Disease is another story. Shell disease is rampant in the Buzzards Bay lobster population. It's hard to pull up three traps without seeing some evidence of it, though scientists do not currently know the precise extent to which shell disease has hurt the lobster population. The main symptoms of shell disease are pitting and erosion of the lobster's shell. Although, technically, the disease does not kill the animal, the blisters can completely rot through the shell, exposing the lobster to secondary infection and deadly predators such as fish or sand fleas. The disease poses a particular threat to female lobsters because they don't molt (shed) their shells when they are carrying eggs. Shell disease is specific to lobsters and other crustaceans such as crabs and shrimp and is not considered harmful to humans. In theory, it does not affect the edibility of lobsters, but because it makes their appearance so unappetizing and therefore renders them unmarketable, fishermen often return diseased animals to the Bay.

Scientists have accumulated a significant body of research on the American lobster over the past twenty years. This research appears to indicate that we have been taking more lobsters than the species can sustain and that a new approach is needed. Typically, the pressure on managers to regulate the fishery relaxes in years when lobsters are abundant and increases when they are scarce, which might be, in hindsight, a shortsighted method of managing stocks. Current management strategy strives for an egg quantity equal to at least 10 percent of that produced by a virgin (unfished) population. A long-term, successful plan might realistically call for 15 to 20 percent. In the end, the only way to raise the percentage and size of breeding females in the Bay is to somehow reduce the fishing pressure on them, either by reducing the number of fishing licenses (traps), raising the legal size limit, establishing "no take" zones, or some combination of these three methods. As of December 2003, the Lobster Board voted to increase the minimum legal size of lobsters taken in Zone II to three and a half inches, to be phased in by incremental increases starting in 2005, but they chose to impose only ineffectual limitations on fishing pressure.

THEY FINALLY HAD HIM. After months of pulling suspiciously empty traps, they had caught the robber in the act. The two boats pincered the third like a lobster's crusher claw: Henry's boat to the offender's port bow, his friend's to starboard. Recognizing the man, they were not surprised—he was originally from out of state, a part-timer, another cop's kid gone bad. Hard words flew sharply between the men. Looking away momentarily to navigate an oncoming swell, the pirate looked back to find a pistol leveled at him, not five inches from his face. Only it wasn't a pistol, it was a frighteningly short sawed-off shotgun, and the man holding it meant business. The barrel of the gun, rocking with the boat, drew a shifting bead from the man's hairline to his cleft upper lip again and again. The angry voices ceased, leaving only the throbbing sound of diesels. Then Henry, without taking his eyes off the situation, spoke to the twelve-year-old at his side.

"Son?" he said.

"Yes, Dad?"

"Today, you may see a man's head part from his shoulders. If that happens, what you see never leaves this boat. Is that understood?" The boy nodded, and although he was scared, he stood unflinchingly, fists clenched, staring straight at the trap robber. After all, like his father, he was a fisherman. And out here they had always made their own rules.

"IT'S ALWAYS SOMETHING," muttered Henry Cebula, staring at the blank radar screen in the dark pilothouse of the boat. We were floating motionless, engines idling, in the predawn blackness of New Bedford's outer harbor aboard Henry's lobster vessel, the *Sea Blitz*. It was a few days before Christmas—air temperature 35 degrees Fahrenheit, water temperature 42. As it turned out, the radar was just cold, like us, and it soon snapped to life in a flurry of concentric electric-green rings. Earlier, I had been given the "new hand" tour of the vessel, which included a significant point at the heavy, bagged life jackets and the ten-gallon plastic pail that functioned as a head. Mentally, I resolved to eat only one of the two peanut-butter-and-jelly sandwiches I had packed. A few minutes after the radar lit up, we shot through the narrow gap in the hurricane barrier that encloses New Bedford Harbor like a castle wall and headed out onto the wintry darkness of the Bay.

Paul "Bunk" Silveira, Henry's mate, claims to be hard of hearing, but Henry thinks he's full of it. I believed Paul, especially after listening to the roaring diesel engines for ten minutes, after which I was reduced to answering any and all attempts at communication with "*What?!*" The *Sea Blitz* is what fishermen call a "highline" vessel, top of the line. It is thirty-six feet long, with a short, sharp bow, a heated, enclosed pilothouse, and a long, open deck. The boat is equipped with six saltwater holding tanks under the deck, for storing lobsters, instead of the typical three. Unlike the tanks on many boats, which depend on the forward motion of the vessel to regulate water levels, the *Sea Blitz's* tanks feature a hydraulic pump system. In total, the vessel is capable of hauling twelve hundred pounds of lobster.

Inside the pilothouse, an array of electronic navigational instruments, including radar, a compass, Loran-C, and a depth finder, were mounted over the wheel. Under the windshield, on the dash, lay a curious assortment of items, including a couple of beat-up baseball caps, a half-full bag of Redman chewing tobacco, a near-empty plastic bottle of yellow dish soap, and two rusted cans of WD-40. Behind the wheel was a rectangular fiberglass table, where the lobsters' claws were banded. The starboard, or wheel-side, wall of the pilothouse could be swung out and up and secured when hauling commenced, effectively turning the pilothouse into a semi-open workspace. This arrangement allows the captain to simultaneously steer the boat with one hand and work the pot hauler with the other. The pot hauler, mounted on the rail of the boat directly to the captain's right, consists of a metal arm and a set of pulleys into which the pot line is fed. Powered by hydraulics, this device quickly pulls traps up from the bottom, sparing the lobsterman an incalculable amount of labor. Belowdecks, the spartan hold of the boat consisted of storage space. One wall was lined with switches, resembling a giant fuse box. It was this wall, I was led to understand, that rookies were prone to stumble against, triggering potentially dangerous calamities. The long deck of the boat, stretching from just behind the pilothouse to the transom, was stacked high with green and yellow wire traps, on top of which were coiled warps and buoys. The deck also held two large, bright-blue plastic barrels of bait, holding five hundred pounds of yellowtail flounder. Henry purchased the *Sea Blitz* in 1997, just before Bay lobster stocks started to crash.

Henry Cebula is a proud father, an avid New England Patriots fan, and a successful lobsterman respected by fishermen and scientists. If you had to guess his age, you would peg him at around forty-five, though actually he is sixty. At the wheel of the *Sea Blitz*, with his gray baseball cap and silver stubble, he bears more than a casual resemblance to George Clooney's character in *The Perfect Storm*. He's one of those seamen who speaks haltingly shoreside but commands with a voice clear and strong once underway.

After twenty years of lobstering on Buzzards Bay, Henry's seen it all. He makes no bones about the fact that lobstering out of New Bedford is highly competitive. He speaks tersely about the "yuppies buzzing about in their phallic-symbol powerboats" and the sailors "parked on their ass with a sandwich" who won't give him the right-of-way when he's working a pot line, ten hours into a twelve-hour day. He angrily recalls the time that druggies broke into his boat and made off with several thousand dollars' worth of equipment. The worst was afterward, being out at sea and reaching for something, and it wasn't there. Then there was the incident with the trap robber, who, incidentally, was brought to justice in the courts and later fled the Bay in disgrace. Worst of all were the environmentalists. It had gotten to the point where, if one of the local whale-watching vessels saw three whales in the vicinity of any traps, the lobstermen were required to move them. A former schoolteacher, and self-admittedly a cut above most fishermen when it comes to environmental awareness, Henry isn't against doing the right thing. He just resents ignorant "do-gooders" who blindly sign petitions, such as those to save the whales, without understanding the impact they have on real-life working people like himself. If you ask him whether fishermen are responsible for polluting the Bay, he will wordlessly hold up a trap buoy entangled with the colorful nylon string and shriveled remains of a helium-filled birthday balloon, a sight he sees too regularly in the summer.

Perhaps the most maddening challenge he has faced as a lobsterman came when John F. Kennedy Jr. downed his plane off Gay Head, in one hundred feet of water, not fifty yards from one of Henry's pot lines. Officials closed off an area of ten square miles and patrolled it with a Navy destroyer and a Coast Guard cutter, refusing to allow the lobstermen in to tend their traps. This incident occurred in the summer, prime season, each day of which is crucial to the lobstermen. It galled the fishermen because, as Henry put it, despite the Kennedy family's celebrity status, JFK Jr. was "only a civilian," and the government's reaction infringed on the rights of fishermen—also civilians. In addition, many of the fishermen looked up to Senator Ted Kennedy, JFK Jr.'s uncle and the man who influenced the search operation, as the "workingman's champion," and they felt he had betrayed them. Henry tested the resolve of the gunboats, running the *Sea Blitz* in and out of the blockade, until at last the Coast Guard cutter bore down on him. He confronted the gunboat captain—who carried the unpardonable stigma of "being from out of state,"—angrily asking if the captain would be willing to foot Henry's grocery bill that week. In the end, there was nothing to be done for it.

Buzzards Bay also poses natural challenges to the lobstermen. The Bay is a windy place, and that wind is always of primary concern to the local fishermen. Anything over fifteen to twenty miles per hour keeps many of them on the dock. November and March, described by Henry as hosts to the "war of the winds," are hard months on the Bay. In November, the prevailing wind shifts from the southwesterly flow of summer to the northwesterly flow of winter, and in March the process reverses itself. This makes for highly unpredictable wind patterns. The lobstermen also have storms, cold, and ice to contend with. During Hurricane Bob in 1991, Henry lost two hundred traps off Sow and Pigs Reef. Ice takes traps by cutting trap lines and making navigating difficult. One frustrating winter day it took Henry and the *Sea Blitz* an hour to break through the ice just to reach Fort Rodman, at the outer end of New Bedford Harbor. Then there was the heart-stopping incident one February when a mate, entangled in a pot line, hurtled over the side near Gull Island, a small, rock-strewn spit of land near Penikese. Henry fished him out of the frigid gray waters, lent him his extra layers, and hung out in his underwear while the mate dried out below decks. The kid finished out the day. "Most fishermen," noted Henry, "are tough."

The chief sensations you experience on a lobster boat are the rumbling of the engines, the sideways pitching when the boat is idling, the smell of fish and diesel fumes, and the sunlight playing off the dazzling colors of the gear. On the way out to the first trap line, the mate typically keeps busy baiting the traps stacked on the deck with mesh bags of flounder. The captain navigates to the first string of traps using the Loran-C markings, then pauses to visually locate the nearest buoy before pulling alongside to gaff the line. This can be a daunting task, particularly if there are strong tidal currents. If you have ever experienced the challenge of snagging a mooring buoy from the bow of a pleasure boat, imagine doing it several hundred times a day in rough weather—that's lobstering. After the captain gaffs the buoy, he feeds the warp into the pulleys of the pot hauler, which hauls the pot and neatly coils the line at his feet. Just before the pot erupts from the surface, the hauler begins to screech, adding an element of chaos to the steady roar of the diesels. Reaching one hand over the side, the captain, with a swift twist, flips the dripping wire trap squarely onto the rail. If there are lobsters in the trap, he pulls them out and, more often than not, measures them. Legal-sized specimens are placed on the sorting table behind him to be claw-banded. The shorts are unceremoniously tossed overboard.

For each string of traps the captain pulls, he records pertinent details in a notebook: the Loran-C location (longitude and latitude) of the traps, the number of traps in the string, and the number of lobsters harvested. Working in parallel, the mate first discards the old bait, which has been reduced by sand fleas to a pile of shiny translucent bones. Sand fleas, tiny, white, squirming smidgens of life, are one of the great levelers of the sea, consuming any and all dead biological matter they find within a matter of hours. The mate then rebaits the trap using the same mesh bag. It is this routine of continuous rebaiting that draws the familiar entourage of wheeling, diving gulls so often appended to a working lobster vessel.

The day I accompanied Henry and Paul, we were retrieving 180 traps, set mostly around the Elizabeth Islands. Henry hauled efficiently, even in the blinding glare of the rising sun. The lobsters themselves, bathed in the clear winter light pouring through the open side of the pilothouse, were vibrantly beautiful. They came up newly varnished from the deep, especially those that had recently molted. Most of them appeared stunned by the cold waters and were barely moving. Their bodies, far from the boiled red familiar to restaurant goers, were rainbows of color: mixed mottled reds and olives above, a clear, pale, pumpkin-orange below. The joints of their legs and claws glistened with accents of sea green and robin's egg blue. I was shown, of all things, how to tell the sex of a lobster, an exercise that turned out to be comically anthropomorphic: males have narrower hips than females, harder "claspers" (small leglike appendages) under the belly, and bigger crusher (the larger of the two) claws.

Other creatures came up in the traps as well. These included sculpin, a fine looking gray tautog, and one leering, half-fish half-eel abomination, called ocean pout, which is used to make fish sticks. All bycatch was returned alive to the Bay. Only once did I see any fish mishandled; it happened shortly after Paul, while scrubbing algae off a buoy, splashed a bleach solution into his eyes and stood slowly blinking in wide-eyed wonder at his pain. Later, in defiance of his injury and the insulting, unholy ugliness of some nameless bottom dweller brought up in a trap, he punched the creature's jaw, at half-speed, as he propelled it over the side.

Despite lobstering's many challenges, Henry loves his job. That morning, the finest of the winter so far, it was indeed a joy to be on the Bay. The rosy fingers of Homer's dawn found us off Nashawena Island. Sunlight streamed down pastoral green slopes, catching on the flanks of Highland cattle feeding near the shoreline. No other boats were in sight. Surrounded by the shining Bay waters and the wild, grassy, boulder-strewn Elizabeths, I experienced the serenity of a century long past. Although they worked steadily, the lobstermen were well aware of their surroundings: Henry pointed out a subtle, sooty-yellow line of ozone smog on the horizon; Paul marveled that on any given morning, herds of deer could be seen, picking their way over the hilltops of the islands. These lobstermen take pride in the fact that, as proprietors of small, local boats, they tend to respect their environment more than some other fishermen. Their motivation for doing so, less altruistic than practical, is to ensure a sustainable catch. They spoke angrily of the big, migratory fishing vessels that sweep into the Bay from out of state, raping the waters and moving on, and of the local hydraulic-dredge shellfishermen, who "strip mine" the bottom by dragging bladed trawls across it. But, pride of place notwithstanding, these days Henry works in quiet desperation, frustrated by a seemingly endless succession of empty traps. He fondly recalls "the good old days," when he would steam home with a full boat, pumped up, elated. Now he usually goes home depressed. He carries on because this is what he knows. His son, also a lobsterman, has forsaken the Bay. He drops his first trap ninety miles offshore.

WE ALL TEND TO HAVE a romantic view of lobstering. We view lobstermen as characters in an idyllic scene. They are well aware of this tendency
and regard the phenomenon with mixed emotions. Some lobstermen probably
relish their role as the hardy, stalwart fisherman, toiling in the wild and
capricious sea. Most of them, though, are merely annoyed by it. Tourists
approach working lobstermen with presumptuous questions, how many did
they get that day, can they see the catch. Worse, they ask if they can *have* a
lobster or two. Apparently, many of us landlubbers are under the impression
that lobstermen pick money off trees or, more accurately, off the bottom. In
fact, these men work hard to make a living and view their catch simply in
terms of dollars and cents. Henry Cebula works three days on, one day off,
year-round. As opposed to plucking profits daily, two out of three days he
works to pay expenses, which include his mate's wages, traps, insurance,
and fuel. On the third day, if he's lucky, he makes money. Asking a lobsterman for part of his catch is akin to someone asking you for a few dollars
from your paycheck. As I learned from my stints on various fishing boats,
it's something you just don't do. To ask for a sample of the catch is to break
an unspoken rule, to cross an invisible line of confidence.

We fished until the cold of the morning drew near once again. A pale full
moon rose in the east over the cliffs of Aquinnah, and the exhausted winter
sun collapsed in a tent of orange fire on the western horizon. After ten
hours of work, Henry and Paul had landed just over a hundred legal-sized
lobsters. These days on the Bay, that's considered a good haul. As we
steamed up to the dock under the cover of darkness, we could see the tail-
lights of a flashy sport sedan backed up to the slip. "Aww . . . they expect to
pick up my lobsters in *that?*" Henry exclaimed. "It's always something."

A MIDDEN IS A SHELL HEAP, left by native peoples of coastal areas. If
you find a midden, it will be located several inches underground and will
probably encompass an area five or six feet in diameter. Some are much bigger. My family has a midden of our own, up behind the old Straffin place on
the Shore Road. It was started by my grandfather in the 1950s, or maybe by
his father at the turn of the century. Our midden, beneath the black locust
trees, is composed almost entirely of quahog shells. Besides tossing quahog
shells in a heap, the Wampanoags used them to make wampum and tied
them to sticks to hoe their corn. Because wampum was not accepted as a

means of payment for penny candy in the 1970s, and because any form of gardening was living death to young boys in the summer, we devised our own use for the shells. We threw them at unsuspecting motorists. It is a little-known fact about quahog shells that if you grasp one with your index finger wrapped securely around the rim, open side down, and throw it sidearm, it will command the air like a Frisbee. These missiles were deadly; they could be thrown farther than stones and acted as a kind of penetrating, exploding round of ammunition. Instead of denting and dropping as would a stone, the spinning edge of the shell would rip into the side of a vehicle and explode, with a sonic boom, into hundreds of shards of white shrapnel, leaving few clues for the distressed and terminally confused driver. Ironically, our midden, about five or six feet wide, is now buried several inches beneath the topsoil as a result of Title V septic system construction. Someday, someone out digging on the property will discover it and doubtless believe they have discovered a native midden. They will not be far from the truth.

TODAY, SHELLFISHING is the major fishery on Buzzards Bay. Both commercially and recreationally, the fishery revolves around three species: the quahog, the oyster, and the bay scallop. Soft-shelled clams, though prized in areas where they are found, are significantly less available than the other species. Soft-shells typically thrive on tidal flats, of which the Bay has few. In addition, the flats that are available for them to colonize are usually those areas most vulnerable to pollution.

Overfishing has had a heavy impact on the shellfishery on Buzzards Bay; it is causing a fundamental shift from wild shellfish stocks to cultivated. This means that some, but not all, of the shellfish taken on the Bay today are the product of seeding programs. The fishery is also intimately linked to pollution levels; any discussion about shellfish invariably ends up a discussion about clean water. Because shellfish are filter feeders, they are among the Bay creatures that are most vulnerable to the effects of pollution. For shellfish, the greatest threats include nitrogen, oil, pesticides, and bacteria and viruses, which typically come from road runoff and private and public sewer systems.

The towns manage shellfish resources on Buzzards Bay. This arrangement is unique to Massachusetts and Maine (formerly part of Massachusetts); elsewhere in the country, the state regulates shellfisheries. In terms of state compliance, the towns need only conform to size limits set by Chapter 130, the state law that regulates all fishing activities for approved areas, and submit annual reports to the Massachusetts Division of Marine Fisheries documenting quantities of shellfish harvested, officials elected, and other vital statistics. The towns set the harvest limits for most species. With the exception of the Elizabeth Islands, all of the towns from Westport to Falmouth have a management and propagation plan in place. As a result of this town-based system, the shellfisheries around the Bay vary widely in terms of quality and consistency.

Notable exceptions to this system are the areas that pose a threat to public health and are thus closed to shellfishing. The Massachusetts Division of Marine Fisheries manages these closed areas. Using fecal coliform levels as an indicator of the presence of harmful viruses, the division opens or closes shellfish areas accordingly. The shellfishing areas are classified according to the level of coliform bacteria present: approved (open); conditionally approved (sometimes open, dependent on levels of rainfall, seasonal water temperature, or marina activity); restricted (mostly closed, dependent on the status of contaminated stock relays); or prohibited (permanently closed). As of this writing, 7,669 acres of shellfish beds on the Bay (roughly half of the total closures) are classified as either restricted or prohibited, meaning they have little or no chance of ever opening naturally under current environmental conditions. For perspective, the entire Bay includes approximately 176,197 acres of marine environment.

The division is not responsible for fixing closed areas, but they will identify the source of problems for towns and try to help, depending on financial resources and the shellfishing potential of the area in question. The division reevaluates closed areas every one to three years, with the exception of prohibited areas, which are generally not considered worth the effort. They perform a shoreline survey of potential pollution sources, take water samples, and evaluate meteorological data. Every twelve years, state biologists conduct a more comprehensive analysis, called a sanitary survey. The Division of Marine Fisheries also carries out contaminated relay programs, which involve moving whole populations of shellfish from contaminated to clean areas. The shellfish cleanse themselves and produce spat, or young; then they are returned to the polluted area, where they can be safely harvested. It is important to note that the division's management efforts have resulted in shellfishing areas being opened as well as closed. Since it took control of water-quality classification from the Massachusetts Department of Environmental Protection (DEP) in 1988, the division has helped open thousands of acres of shellfish beds, including parts of New Bedford Harbor and Clarks Cove, by identifying and helping local communities eliminate pollution sources. Despite this progress, however, the division's fight against pollution is ongoing, with extensive efforts directed at the several thousand acres of shellfish habitat that remain closed.

Pollution has long been a threat to the shellfishery on the Bay. The primary concern, as it relates to human health, has always been the pathogens shellfish can pick up from human or animal waste in the water. Raw sewage is the main culprit. It enters the Bay from failed private septic systems, illegal boat discharges, the combined sewer outflows (CSOs) on New Bedford Harbor overflowing during heavy rainfall, and occasional malfunctions in municipal treatment plants. Even in areas where human waste disposal is well controlled, dog and waterfowl feces can degrade water quality.

The history of shellfish bed closures on Buzzards Bay begins in New Bedford. Between 1900 and 1903, consumption of shellfish tainted by raw sewage in that city resulted in 565 cases of typhoid fever and 93 deaths. This epidemic led to the first shellfishing restrictions on the Bay and was also the catalyst for the creation of New Bedford's first public sewer system. By 1909, 73 more people had died in New Bedford from typhoid fever; most were relations of fishermen who had been granted "contaminated bait only" shellfish permits. By 1925, national typhoid fever outbreaks linked to contaminated shellfish caused the United States Public Health Service to develop a routine monitoring program. This program led to additional Bay closures, including areas of Apponagansett (Padanaram) Bay and Mattapoisett Harbor, and brought total closures up to 2,000 acres. That figure remained relatively constant up to the 1970s, when many more acres of the Bay were closed to shellfishing. These closures were primarily the result of increased sampling efforts by the state Department of Environmental Quality Engineering as opposed to additional pollution; areas long overdue for closure were finally addressed, including those in New Bedford near the outfall pipe, and those around the Dartmouth Wastewater Treatment Plant outfall pipe off Salters Point. Other new areas closed in the 1970s included Cuttyhunk Pond, the

East Branch of the Westport River, and Red Brook Harbor. In the 1980s, the total area of closures almost doubled again, bringing Bay closures to nearly 15,000 acres. Shellfish areas closed in the 1980s included all of Buttermilk Bay and nearly 900 acres in Bourne, including all of Pocasset Harbor, the Back River, and the Cape Cod Canal. Since 1988, alarmed by the rapidly escalating rate of closures, many towns, in conjunction with the Division of Marine Fisheries, have managed to halt, though not reverse, this trend. One interesting fact is that the rate of shellfish bed closures on the Bay has directly shadowed population growth on its shores. Development is accompanied by the elimination of plants and trees and the addition of paved surfaces in the surrounding watershed. Less flora and more pavement create more water runoff from storms, which carries more animal waste and other pollutants into bays and harbors.

ON A SULTRY, STILL SUMMER NIGHT on the Bay, the stars press close in all their millions. And under each star, mirrored in the blackness of the Bay, lies a quahog. There are sprawling constellations of quahogs, vast belts that span the Bay like the Milky Way. In New Bedford Harbor alone, there are more than 100 million quahogs. In some places they grow fifty to a square foot. In Buzzards Bay, the quahog is king.

QUAHOGS ARE THE MOST IMPORTANT commercial shellfish species on the Bay, and thus, arguably, the most important fishery. The commercial catch dwarfs that of all other shellfish species combined. Quahogging has traditionally been carried out using small skiffs and handheld rakes. An exception occurred in the 1980s, when a hydraulic-dredge fishery was initiated, based largely around New Bedford. These fishermen harvested quahogs using suction tubes attached to a bladed metal cage that scoured the bottom. They employed thirty-five- to fifty-foot boats and fished in about fifteen feet of water, capitalizing on the fact that the quahog is the only shellfish species on the Bay (with the exception of the bay scallop) regularly found in water deeper than nine feet. At first, the rapid expansion of this type of quahogging caused overall landings of the species to drastically increase, but deepwater stocks were quickly depleted, and now few dredge boats remain. Critics of this fishery—some of whom are fishermen—consider this method of shell-fishing to be highly invasive and damaging to the ecology of the Bay.

Heavy fishing pressure on quahog stocks in the Bay has made seeding necessary in many areas. Whether quahogs are wild or seeded depends entirely
on their location. For example, the quahogs dug in Bourne, which has a
long history of seeding, are probably seeded. Most of the quahogs in towns
on the west side of the Bay, many of which started seeding programs as
recently as the late 1990s, are wild.

Towns that seed usually handle half a million to 10 million quahogs a year.
They are purchased from commercial hatcheries. These hatcheries spawn
the adult shellfish and then place the young in "downwellers," silos into
which they pump seawater carrying food and oxygen. When the shellfish
reach one millimeter in length, they are transferred to "upwellers," which
reverse the flow of water, allowing for a better flow of oxygen and nutrients
to the growing clams. Towns buy the baby quahogs when they reach three to
eight millimeters in length. Towns that own their own upwellers, including
Dartmouth and Fairhaven (operated by the Lloyd Center for Environmental
Studies) and Falmouth (operated on West Falmouth Harbor), are able take a
more active role in the process, and buy the shellfish earlier at the one-
millimeter stage. After they graduate from the upwellers, the tiny quahogs
are placed in nursery flats over the summer, where they will reach about an
inch in size. Around November they are planted in the Bay. The timing of
this release is critical, as the water must be warm enough to allow the
young to burrow into the sediment, yet cold enough to slow predators such
as crabs. Sometimes, if the timing is off, or the town has recorded a modest
harvest of mature quahogs that year, they will delay the seeding until the
following spring.

Before the quahog, the bay scallop was King of the Bay. Although never as
plentiful in number, the commercial catch of bay scallops brings a higher
price than quahogs, and traditionally gave the hard-shells a run for their
money. A sharp population decline began around 1982 to 1983, however,
and by 1986 bay scallops had practically disappeared from the Bay. This
crash might be linked to such pollutants as nitrogen loading and oil and the
accompanying loss of inshore eelgrass beds. Bay scallops prefer to use eelgrass habitat as nurseries for their young. Commercially, bay scallops are
taken in small skiffs that drag small metal dredges along the bottom, which
may indiscriminately remove eelgrass and scallops alike. They are also harvested recreationally by skin divers and from the shallows with handheld

nets and "scallop boxes." These are home-built, hooded contraptions with glass bottoms that allow the operator to clearly see where the scallops rest on the bottom. The bay scallop fishery got its start on the Bay in the 1870s, around New Bedford and the Acushnet River. On the eastern side of the Bay, West Falmouth Harbor has traditionally been the most productive spot. Today, restoration efforts for the nearly extinct fishery are underway in West Falmouth Harbor, Barlows Landing in Bourne, and Fairhaven. Strategies include transplanting scallops from healthy beds and seeding stock from hatcheries using technology known as "spawning sanctuaries." Success has been limited.

BEFORE THE QUAHOG and the bay scallop was the oyster. Middens of oyster shells left by Native Americans and records from early colonists indicate that large oysters were historically abundant across the shores of the Bay. In the late 1800s, the oyster was considered the most important commercial species on the Bay. In 1887, G. Brown Goode reported that in the Westport River, "an ancient bed of native oysters" had practically disappeared from "too great raking." Wareham was said to have produced the finest oysters on the Bay.

Strong evidence suggests that overfishing has been the cause of the decline in oyster stocks since the time of the colonists. In more recent times, disease has plagued the oysters of the Bay. These diseases include MSX, juvenile oyster disease (JOD), and dermo. It is not known whether there is a relationship between these diseases and water pollution such as nutrient loading. Lately, oyster populations around the Bay have increased modestly. For example, Slocums River in Dartmouth, historically a major oyster producer, recently experienced a 20 percent gain. This trend has been fueled by various restoration programs, which transplant seed oysters from healthy beds in other areas. Efforts have been made to start new oyster spat colonies by creating beds around artificial structures in areas including the Hurricane Barrier in New Bedford Harbor.

I EYED THE CROWD with suspicion. Singly and in pairs, they emerged from luxury sport sedans and began to suit up for what appeared to be some sort of arctic gladiatorial battle. It was a fine fall day on the Bay, with soaring blue skies and crisp temperatures, and the opening day of oyster season. A row of cars lined the sandy point where, as a boy, I could spend hours shellfishing without seeing another human being. Strong men with their game faces on sized me up as they snapped on heavy rubber gloves, pulled on brown waders, and donned colorful ski hats. They gravely pulled long, sharp-tined rakes and shiny new shellfish baskets from their trunks. Alarmed, I seized my rusty basket and bolted down to the water, dressed in cut-off shorts, a hooded, polyester sweatshirt with no shirt underneath, wool socks, and sport sandals. Watching the silent gladiators beside me, grimly intent on taking their limit, I thought, "My God, shellfishing—of all things—has become a competitive sport. Even worse, it has become a fashion show."

SINCE 1980, recreational shellfishing pressure has increased dramatically on Buzzards Bay and has proven itself capable of decimating local shellfish populations. One problem is that, unlike the commercials, recreational shellfishermen face little accountability. Another is that towns place no cap on the number of recreational licenses they issue, preferring instead to view license fees as an unlimited pool of funds. This arrangement results in an ever-escalating number of shellfishermen and ever-dwindling shellfish stocks. Already, similar to lobstering, some stocks have been reduced to a recruitment-dependent fishery, in which nearly every shellfish taken out of the water has just reached legal size.

FOR A NUMBER OF REASONS, shellfish aquaculture—the private raising of shellfish for sale to consumers—has failed to take hold in Buzzards Bay. In contrast, municipal seeding programs could be termed *public* aquaculture. Only a handful of people privately farm shellfish on the Bay—mostly oysters, some clams and scallops—representing only a fraction of the fishery's potential.

The most obvious barrier to the development of shellfish aquaculture on the Bay is a practical one. Relatively speaking, Buzzards Bay has a low tidal range (the difference between high tide and low tide is small). In places like Brewster and Wellfleet that have high tidal ranges, low tide leaves large sand flats exposed. These flats are ideal for growing shellfish because they provide the aquaculturist with easy access to beds and nets for harvesting and equipment maintenance. Shellfish farms require constant maintenance, including cleaning algae off nets, lines, and buoys, repairing and replacing nets, and relocating numerous predators such as crabs. These tasks are more difficult to complete when the shellfish are under water, as they typically are in areas with low tidal ranges like Buzzards Bay, and the technology needed to advance this brand of aquaculture has been slow to evolve.

An even more challenging issue facing potential aquaculturists on the Bay involves cultural values and land ethics. Few people here want aquaculturists working their local shoreline. They don't want to look at the pickup trucks, traps, and other equipment, and they tend to prefer open water views to the sight of shellfishermen working their beds. All fishermen today face the challenge of conflicting land values. Ironically, many home buyers are enticed to coastal towns by the nautical mystique of fishing boats and working fishermen. When they move in, however, they often experience a radical change of heart. It has been suggested that one way coastal towns could help aquaculturists establish themselves on the Bay and also allow other fishermen to remain a functioning part of the community would be to establish "fishery-zoned" areas. These areas would be prepped for and friendly to all fishermen.

Talk to any aquaculturist on the Bay today and they will tell you that we make it very difficult for them to start an operation in any harbor. To begin with, they must attend a series of public hearings and gain the support of the Division of Marine Fisheries and the Army Corps of Engineers. Even if they succeed, they might spend more than a year on the process. They would argue that the process is unfair, particularly since other businesses, such as gas stations or convenience stores, can often obtain approval in a matter of weeks. Perhaps more important, they would argue that we are discriminating against a business with deep local significance. They might also point out that our land values contrast sharply with other countries, including Japan, China, and Korea, who value coastal waters as a resource for the public good and encourage aquaculture operations.

Despite these challenges, shellfish aquaculture on Buzzards Bay might be inevitable. Massachusetts is running out of intertidal areas on which to grow shellfish, a fact that has increased interest in subtidal areas. And these areas do have one major advantage over intertidal flats—shellfishermen typically work them by boat, a method that has proven far more acceptable to local citizenry than the pickup trucks that invariably accompany flats operations. There is also an intriguing, newly emerging scientific theory being developed at the University of Rhode Island that suggests that shellfish farming might be good for the marine environment. Unlike fish farms, which create waste pollution, shellfish, as filter feeders, might actually remove nontoxic pollutants from the water by feeding on phytoplankton. When shellfish are harvested, the nitrogen stored in the phytoplankton they ate is effectively eliminated from the water. And shellfish are capable of filtering water on a grand scale: it is estimated that in the 1800s the vast oyster beds of Chesapeake Bay processed the entire volume of the Bay each day. (Today, owing to a reduced population, it takes them more than a year.) Perhaps this ability of shellfish to remove nitrogen from the marine environment might one day influence public acceptance of aquaculture, particularly in areas of the Bay where water quality has been compromised by nitrogen loading.

SETH GARFIELD GROWS OYSTERS on Cuttyhunk Island, in the shadow of the Gosnold Monument. The monument commemorates Bartholomew Gosnold's settlement there in 1602 and is a source of great pride to the Cuttyhunk community. Built of oval beach stones tumbled smooth by the surf, it looks precisely like a flashlight stood upright on a table. The pale buoys that float Seth's net lines radiate fanlike from the monument's base and cover approximately one-third of West End Pond.

Seth is woven as tightly into the culture of the Bay as his oysters are into their nets. Although he calls himself an oysterman, in reality he typifies the consummate citizen of the Bay: working locally, forging a living from seasonal careers that include fisherman, teacher, and occasionally, environmentalist. He is a disciple of the Great Truth of the Bay—namely, that clean water is the glue that holds it together. Clean water is the key to tourism, to lifestyles based on a sense of place, to community and tradition that span multiple generations. When kids grow up sailing, fishing, and swimming in clean water, they want to come back to live on the Bay as adults. Seth is one of those people who might as well wear a sign that says HAPPY TO BE HERE.

I SAT IN THE FOGGED-UP CAB of Seth's pickup truck—the bed was full of teenage kids from the mainland—jolting along the narrow, rutted pathway known as the Old Quahog Road. We were on our way to Cuttyhunk Shellfish Farms on the pond to do some oystering. It was December and raining. As the road nears the pond, it crests a hill dominated by squat native cherry trees. Acres of rolling green briar punctuated with bright red berries armor the down slope. The pond itself is cradled in undulating hills of blond grass. Here and there, dramatically sculptured granite boulders sit on the land as though they dropped out of the sky. The pond's inland end fades into a marsh; its outer end flushes through a narrow cut into the Atlantic. Its water is clean, devoid of the runoff pollution that typically plagues mainland aquaculturists. The flow from both the marsh and the ocean ensures a steady source of oxygen and food, in the form of phytoplankton, for the oysters. According to Seth, in addition to the trademarked Cuttyhunk Oyster, the pond also provides a habitat for coyotes, rabbits, mice, and even an otter that likes to make slides in the snow. Disgruntled, a great blue heron heaved off the shoreline as we approached.

Clothed in black hip boots and foul-weather gear, the youthful crew and I pushed off into an incessant southeast breeze under unsettled gray skies. Our craft was a square, plywood-covered raft powered by a small outboard. Underway, the front corners of the raft dipped under water, adding considerably to the amphibious theme of the day. The raft held a sorting table, over which spools of monofilament fishing line were mounted, stacks of plastic crates for handling and washing oysters, empty nets, spare lobster buoys, and plastic-handled knives for scraping barnacles.

An oyster net resembles a giant green slinky. It consists of three to six green metal hoops, covered by half-inch mesh netting. Mesh also stretches across each hoop, dividing the net into two to five compartments, depending on the number of hoops. Each compartment holds approximately fifty to sixty oysters. The nets are split lengthwise by an opening of about three inches in width, which is sewn shut with monofilament when the nets are in the water and opened for harvesting. The oysters grow suspended in these nets, which are hung from buoys attached to a line, one net per buoy. The nets hang a foot or so beneath the surface of the pond, which averages six feet in depth. The floating lines lie roughly parallel to the flow of the tide, which runs into and out of the mouth of the pond every twelve hours.

Harvesting the oysters consisted largely of kneeling on the side of the raft, feeling about beneath each buoy for a net, and hauling it—wet, heavy, and algae-covered—aboard. At the same time, other crew members retied loose buoys, replaced them, or scraped weed and barnacles off them as necessary. Once aboard, the nets were "unsown" and the oysters dumped out onto the sorting table. Oysters three inches in length or larger landed in the plastic crates. These were washed, freed of barnacles, and then emptied into plastic mesh bags in groups of a hundred. Juvenile shellfish were returned to the nets, which were then resown and rehung from the net lines, to be harvested at a later date.

We were out for two and a half hours, and we harvested eight bags, or eight hundred oysters. Cuttyhunk Shellfish Farms typically harvests fifteen hundred oysters a week in the winter months, and the same number or greater each day in the summer. The magic water temperature for oyster farming is 48 degrees Fahrenheit. Above that mark, oysters grow, below it, they go dormant until water temperatures rise again in the spring. This phenomenon explains why northern-grown oysters are significantly more expensive than those grown in the South. Down there, they grow like barnacles, year-round. It takes Seth's fast-growing variety of seed oysters six months to reach the legal size; slow growers take two and a half years. Seth restocks the pond every May with groups of 100,000 to 400,000 shellfish. He uses down time in the winter to repair nets and other equipment.

Cuttyhunk's West End Pond is an ideal location for oystering, and Seth confronts few natural challenges. Hurricanes can disrupt the operation temporarily, and excessively hot temperatures sometimes cause algae blooms, which suck the dissolved oxygen from the water and result in some oyster deaths. So far, the pond has been free of shellfish diseases, which Seth attributes to a lack of crowding and his reliance on disease-free seed stock. There are some predators that attack the oysters, including crabs—native blue, green, and an alien species of green crab that was carried to the island in the ballast water of a ship. This crab is about an inch wide, a paler shade of green than the native crab, and wields short, powerful claws. It is much more aggressive than the native species of green crab and will readily attack and consume young oysters.

The farm's major challenges are man-made. Seth depends largely on the good will of the island people to renew his lease, grant him dredging permits when the mouth of the pond silts up, and allow him access to the pond over privately held land. In true island style, in return for the support of the community, Seth gives back. Among other things, he acts as chief of the volunteer fire department. It also helps that for quite some time Cuttyhunk has produced Garfields as reliably as it now produces oysters.

The biggest challenge for the farm these days is labor. On Cuttyhunk, wages are high, work days are short, and most of the islanders would rather be fishing or hunting than hauling oyster nets anyway. As a result, a significant part of the labor force must be toted from the mainland in the company boat, the *Rawbar*. And that's not always easy. One time, Seth and his son Sam—who has hauled more oyster nets than anyone in the world and doesn't even eat them—fractured both panes of their windshield laboring through heavy swells.

Cuttyhunk Shellfish Farms takes pride in supplying fresh local products to local people, a philosophy that has apparently paid off. The eight hundred oysters we hauled on that rainy day in December were easily dispatched. In the summer, about one-third of the harvest is dished out on the half-shell to Cuttyhunk Pond boaters off the farm's "floating farmstand," another third is distributed through the catering arm of the business, and the remainder is shipped to area or metropolitan restaurants. The farm employs eighteen kids on Cuttyhunk and another dozen or so on the mainland, most of whom are students.

CRADLED DEEP IN THE BOSOM of Cuttyhunk Island, there is an aquaculture venture making good on Buzzards Bay. There are critics, no doubt, who would say that the success of Cuttyhunk Shellfish Farms, dependent on clean water and an ideal location, can't be duplicated. Others would hesitate to describe an operation that produces high-priced shellfish as utopian. Nonetheless, at least glimpses of utopia can be found here. Locals run the business, they produce a local product, and it is consumed by locals. Most important, the farm, through the simple culinary delight of the oyster, serves as a metaphor for the Great Truth of the Bay: We are, all of us, oyster and human being alike, dependent on clean water for our way of life here.

Conservation

Where coming ashore, we stood a while like men ravished at the beautie and delicacie of this sweet soile; for besides divers cleere Lakes of fresh water (whereof we saw no end) Medowes very large and full of greene grasse; even the most woody places (I speake onely of such as I saw) doe grow so distinct and apart, one tree from another, upon greene grassie ground, somewhat higher than the Plaines, as if Nature would shew herselfe above her power, artificial.

—BRERETON, ON THE PRISTINE NATURAL ENVIRONMENT GOSNOLD'S MEN
DISCOVERED ON THE MAINLAND SHORE OF BUZZARDS BAY

THE WATER IN BUZZARDS BAY has remained relatively clean and unpolluted since Gosnold's voyage. But there are exceptions in coves, harbors, and rivers—in short, in the very places we value most for recreational and commercial activities, such as swimming and shellfishing. Some inshore areas are threatened by too much nitrogen, resulting from residential development, and also by high bacteria counts. And although industrial pollution on the Bay is limited almost entirely to New Bedford Harbor, it's a major concern because the harbor is a working port and because nearly half of the Bay's population lives in New Bedford.

Tanker spills pose a constant threat of oil pollution to the entire ecosystem of the Bay, a problem to which oil-dripping automobiles and other motor vehicles in the surrounding watershed contribute significantly. And finally, coastal erosion and sea-level rise, natural processes that already chip away at the Bay's shoreline, have been compounded by global warming, and thus may pose an even greater threat to coastal communities in the future.

SQUETEAGUE HARBOR, a sheltered backwater on the eastern shores of Buzzards Bay, is being slowly throttled, robbed of its oxygen content. Its only outlet to the free-flowing water of Megansett Harbor is a ribbon-thin channel that will ground a skiff at low tide. As children, we prized the harbor for its dead calms; to water-ski on its surface of glass was to live our common dream of flight.

A squeteague is a fish. Like the rainbow trout, the live creature glistens with dazzling hues of pink and green that evaporate along with its last breath. Long absent from the Bay, and once prized as a game fish, the squeteague is making a comeback, moving northward along the East Coast. Soon, a wave of frontrunners, following an ancient, unknowable trail up the Bay, will regain their namesake harbor, gasp for air, and flash away like a reflection of the northern lights. The squeteague cannot go home.

THE GREATEST ENVIRONMENTAL THREAT to Buzzards Bay is that the sewage generated by its swelling population will strip the oxygen from its waters. The official name for this process is *nutrient loading*, and the principal enemy is nitrogen. Nitrogen enters the Bay primarily from septic systems, but also from wastewater treatment plants, from lawn, golf course, and agricultural fertilizers, and from storm-water runoff, dairy farms, and acid rain. Nitrogen promotes the growth of algae. When algae dies, it is decomposed by bacteria, a process that lowers oxygen levels in the water. In short, too much nitrogen leads to too much algae, which leads to too much dead algae, which leads to too little oxygen. The result is a harbor with cloudy, smelly water, a scummy bottom devoid of eelgrass, and fewer fish. Another possible consequence of high levels of nitrogen is the infamous "red tide," toxin-producing algae that closes shellfish beds.

There are two important points to understand about nutrient loading. The first is that conventional septic systems do little to prevent nitrogen from reaching the Bay. Title V is that part of the Massachusetts Environmental Code intended to safeguard public and environmental health by regulating on-site sewage-disposal systems. Title V systems do a better job of filtering nitrogen than older septic systems or the cesspools that many older Bay homes still use, but they were not designed to eliminate it. Fecal coliform bacteria, yes; nitrogen, no. The second point is that nitrogen destroys water quality in the places we value most on the Bay, its harbors and coves. Specifically, the nitrogen gets trapped in areas that the tides don't flush thoroughly.

Thanks to the Coalition for Buzzards Bay, a nonprofit advocacy group that conducts an ongoing water-quality study, we know that the quality in some of the thirty coves around the Bay has been steadily declining for the last decade. Water is of the poorest quality and at greatest risk in the rivers and shallow harbors around the Bay's inland edges. To the west, the Acushnet, Slocum, and Westport Rivers, as well as Apponagansett Bay, are hardest hit. To the east, the Wareham, Agawam, and Broadmarsh Rivers, as well as Squeteague Harbor, Wild Harbor, and Marks Cove, are among the areas at risk.

One significant source of nitrogen that we can control is fertilizer. Lawns are directly responsible for declining water quality in many harbors around the Bay. Bright green lawns—a suburban feature that fits poorly in a coastal environment—depend on large quantities of synthetic chemical fertilizer to maintain their color. This fertilizer releases huge amounts of nitrogen quickly, the excess nitrogen is washed off the lawn, and ultimately it ends up in the harbor. Better choices include natural fertilizer that releases nitrogen slowly, so more of it is absorbed into the lawn, and organic lawns, which depend mainly on grass clippings for their nitrogen needs. Golf courses also contribute to the nitrogen load, especially private ones that tend to use excessive amounts of synthetic fertilizers. Golf courses too, of course, have the option of going organic.

The major source of nitrogen in the Bay, however, is human waste, and it is a problem whose solution requires substantial time, effort, and changes in behavior. As citizens, we can help now by properly maintaining our septic systems, installing upgrades, supporting funding for nitrogen removal treatment facilities at town meetings, and supporting environmental groups that are addressing the issue. Currently, environmental initiatives are under way that will require public wastewater treatment facilities to conform to higher standards of nitrogen removal. Septic systems, which service 40 percent of the homes in Massachusetts, pose a greater challenge, one that our state and federal governments are currently addressing.

In 1998, the Buzzards Bay Project, in conjunction with other groups, including the U.S. Environmental Protection Agency, built a facility to address the threat posed by private septic systems. The mission of the Massachusetts Alternative Septic System Test Center, located on Otis Air Force Base on

Cape Cod, is to evaluate septic systems designed to eliminate nitrogen and facilitate state licensing so the systems can be sold commercially.

I WENT TO FALMOUTH on a wet morning in early spring to tour the test center. A heavy pewter-colored sky hung over the field. At first sight, the center bore a striking resemblance to an old New England graveyard. Wooden doghouse-like structures, concrete sewer tank covers, and PVC pipes rose from the earth at regular intervals. Several of these markers were even graced with thick clumps of wildflowers, most noticeably tall yellow-and-white daisies. It took several seconds for me to hit upon the real reason for the flowers—the earth here was inundated with nitrogen. Figures shrouded in slickers moved attentively between the markers, carrying clipboards.

Suddenly, George Heufelder, the manager of the center, erupted from a nearby trailer and didn't stop moving for the remainder of my visit. He spoke rapidly, drawing from an apparently bottomless well of information about septic systems. He explained that the land we were standing on was a kind of septic gateway between Coast Guard housing on the base and the neighboring waste treatment facility. A small percentage of the housing waste was diverted here from the main flow and pumped through half a dozen septic systems being evaluated for their ability to remove nitrogen.

Eliminating nitrogen from human waste is a dauntingly technical process. First, oxygen is blown into the waste to convert ammonium into nitrate. Then the nitrate is moved into a tank devoid of air and full of bacteria, which are searching hungrily for oxygen. These bacteria attack the nitrate and convert it into nitrogen gas, which is released, effectively stripping the nitrogen from the waste.

Most of the systems being tested at the center work quite well. But they are expensive to maintain. Almost all of them depend on a complex network of alarms, filters, and other gadgets that require constant monitoring by computers. At this level of the waste-treatment game, it's not enough to see clear water flowing from a septic system. If you looked at a glass of water that was chock-full of nitrogen, you would never know it.

So, one possible conclusion the center can draw is that most citizens will never be able to afford a nitrogen-removing septic system. At present, the only customers are wealthy people building large homes near the water who need to meet special environmental requirements to get their plans approved. To make nitrogen removal feasible on a wide scale, towns may have to own and maintain their septic systems.

As I neared the end of my tour, I began to notice an underlying tension that marred the apparent peacefulness of the place. It had to do with the center's mandate to produce test data that would make or break the commercial viability of a system. I sensed corporate pressure all around me. I heard it in the subdued tones of a staff member describing the unpleasant reaction of a company whose system had generated less-than-hoped-for test data. I saw it when I was whisked past a system that was shielded by plywood screens and referred to only as "Stealth." Many of the corporations whose systems are being tested at the center have already had fabulous success in the South, and stand poised to crack a major emerging market in the Northeast. They are in the business of turning waste into gold—alchemy of the darkest sort. The only ingredient they lack to complete the clandestine process is a piece of paper with high scores from the test facility. This modest plot of Cape Cod land is the epicenter of a high-stakes corporate game, and the winners will claim the lucrative task of protecting the water quality of the future.

THE SOFT-SHELLED CLAM BEDS my family harvested recreationally for almost a century are now closed. Once, home from college and yearning for a connection with my youth, I walked down to the beach to dig some clams. I filled my rusty wire basket with exceptionally large clams very quickly and congratulated myself on results that could be attributed only to youthful strength and skill. I will never forget how quickly those clams came. Or went. The shellfish warden appeared the minute I had dug my limit and announced sternly, "This area was closed to shellfishing years ago." That day, I learned two things. It is very difficult to watch hard-earned clams return to the sand. And clams could not care less about fecal coliform bacteria contamination.

A RESPONSIBLE MAN on the street scrapes dog feces into a storm drain with a shovel. A kind woman on the beach tosses french fries to the gulls. These seemingly innocent activities contribute to countless beach and shellfish bed closures on Buzzards Bay.

THE PARKING LOT at the beach on Electric Avenue is a place where water gathers. The surrounding neighborhood pulls itself up from the beach in rolling curves and bowls, webbed by dipping asphalt roads. Electric Avenue runs along Buttermilk Bay, which jabs a finger into the far northern reaches of Buzzards Bay. It is the site of the first facility built on Buzzards Bay to treat fecal coliform bacteria contamination. This bacteria, found in raw sewage, is not in itself a threat to our health. The viruses that sometimes accompany it are, however, and the bacteria are considered a prime indicator of their presence. Health officials regularly test the water around Buzzards Bay for fecal coliform bacteria because it is easy to find, while the viruses are not. Beaches and shellfish beds are closed when high levels of the bacteria are found, in order to limit human exposure to viruses or other pathogens that may be present. Effectively protected from human predation, and oblivious to the pathogens, the shellfish grow thick and strong.

I faced Buttermilk Bay on a brisk spring morning, working hard to digest the technical information being fired at me by Bernie Taber, my contact from the Department of Agriculture's Natural Resources Conservation Service. As Bernie spoke, she studied my face astutely, gauging my understanding and adjusting the level of complexity accordingly.

Buttermilk Bay was closed to shellfishing in 1984 because of high bacteria levels. A subsequent study found that the main source of the bacteria was storm water washing pollutants off the streets and into the Bay. Armed with this knowledge, the town of Bourne joined forces with the Buzzards Bay Project, Coastal Zone Management, and other organizations to build an infiltration system to treat the storm water gushing out from an outfall pipe on the beach. They built the system under the small beach parking lot and attached it to the existing storm drain network. The system directs runoff water into a pretreatment chamber that traps the heavier pollutants, including sediments and oil. The water is then diverted into the infiltration system, a series of concrete chambers that allow it to slowly seep out through a layer of crushed stone. Finally, the storm water is filtered through the surrounding sandy soil, which removes 95 percent of the bacteria.

The science of storm-water treatment has come a long way since the infiltration system at Electric Avenue was completed. For example, we now know that one of the keys is to treat only the runoff from average rainstorms, because the surges that result from big storms barrel through the system and push all the yet-to-be filtered pollutants out to the Bay. Nonetheless, some revolutionary work was completed at Electric Avenue. And the prototype system still works, and works well. Like *Pioneer 6,* a satellite launched in 1965 by NASA that is still hurtling through space and sending back data, the system has far outperformed the expectations of its creators.

So, to get our shellfish beds and beaches reopened, all we have to do is build one of these wondrous contraptions on every harbor on Buzzards Bay, correct? Unfortunately, it is not that simple. For starters, underground infiltration systems like the one at Electric Avenue are not practical for many parts of the Bay, because some towns have compact soils, such as loam, that are not good at filtering storm water. They will not work in areas with a high water table. And because many of these systems are located under town roads, they are expensive and difficult to build. Construction typically involves digging up the existing road, working around gas, sewer, and water utilities, and repaving the road. In addition, the completed systems must be constantly monitored and maintained once they are built. And although proposals for infiltration systems like the one at Electric Avenue are usually supported by local residents because they are underground and out of sight, this initial advantage can later lead to forgetfulness and lack of proper system maintenance.

Fortunately, there are alternative systems for towns that want to treat their storm-water runoff but find underground infiltration systems impractical. The towns can construct "end-of-pipe" storm-water treatment systems. These systems include artificial marshes known as storm-water wetlands. The plants in these wetland systems, like those in natural marshes, filter bacteria and other storm-water pollutants. One common challenge to implementing these systems is convincing nearby residents that their ocean views will not be aesthetically compromised by their above-ground nature.

One main contributor of fecal coliform bacteria pollution, not surprisingly, is animal waste: from pets such as dogs, wild animals such as raccoons and skunks, and waterfowl such as geese, ducks, and seagulls. When it rains, feces are washed off hard surfaces such as pavement, carried down storm drains, and piped into the Bay. The problem is made far worse by a lack of public understanding. Most people don't know that cleaning up after pets and properly disposing of the waste (not dumping it down a storm drain) and not feeding waterfowl (which encourages them to stay in an area instead of migrating) can go a long way toward keeping the Bay clean and the beaches and shellfish beds open. Similarly, the real villains—the viruses that accompany the bacteria into the Bay—are poorly understood. No one knows for sure what the relationship is between bacteria levels and the presence of viruses. And people find it hard to associate water-borne viruses with cases of swimmer's ear or stomach flu. One thing most experts agree on: if storm water is not being treated, it's probably not a good idea to go swimming after it rains.

Other sources of fecal coliform bacteria contamination—in Buzzards Bay and elsewhere—are old septic systems and cesspools that are not performing properly. Cesspools, merely pipes connected to pits in the ground, are more apt to overload the ability of the surrounding soil to filter waste. Ideally, septic systems trap heavy waste in the tank, which can then be pumped out, and distribute and filter the rest of it more efficiently.

To ensure that septic systems are working properly, the state's sanitary code, Title V, requires that homeowners have their systems inspected prior to adding bedrooms or selling their home. If a system does not pass inspection, homeowners are required to install a new one. A septic system's ability to filter pollutants depends on placement at a sufficient distance from ground-water, an adequately sized leaching field, and timely pumping, every three to five years.

Boats that dump raw sewage into the Bay instead of using pumpout facilities are also contributing fecal coliform bacteria to the Bay. The U.S. Environmental Protection Agency designated Buzzards Bay a "No Discharge" area in 2002. Dumping of any sewage, even treated, is prohibited. Several pumpout facilities have been built around the Bay to facilitate this new regulation.

AS I LEFT ELECTRIC AVENUE, I gazed out over the cold blue waters of Buttermilk Bay. A few hundred feet from the beach a small white skiff bobbed, anchored only a short distance from the outfall pipe. In it, a figure in bright orange waders stood erect, tugging rhythmically on the long handle of a quahog rake. It was a timeless scene that formerly I would have taken for granted, but that day I learned that it's only cleanup and advocacy efforts like the Electric Avenue system that can promise it any future at all.

FOUR OPEN TRENCHES. Four open trenches draining toxic chemicals into the Acushnet River were all it took to foul the Bay's mightiest harbor.

IT WAS RAINING and gloomy the day I went to New Bedford to tour the Environmental Protection Agency's cleanup sites on the harbor. A uniformed guard admitted me into a compound of official-looking white trailers surrounded by a chain-link fence. Inside the trailer that served as an office, cardboard boxes of documents were stacked all about. Men sat around a table drinking coffee and speaking in even, deliberate tones about saving a majestic harbor that has become a Superfund site.

Dave Dickerson, a young and capable EPA project manager, began by showing me a public relations presentation on his laptop that was designed to emphasize the EPA's good work in the dirty New Bedford cleanup. I sensed that the agency was suffering from a public relations problem in this city.

New Bedford Harbor is a Superfund site because of pollution by a group of synthetic chemicals called polychlorinated biphenyls (PCBs). PCBs were heavily used by electrical equipment manufacturers following World War II. New Bedford Harbor is so contaminated by them that people aren't allowed to fish here. And if they know what's good for them, residents will think twice before allowing their children to play barefoot along the waterfront during summer vacation. PCBs cause cancer, among various other human health problems, and the muck in parts of this harbor is saturated with them—up to 4 percent of the sediment, or forty thousand parts chemical per million parts muck. For perspective, the EPA considers any sediments with concentrations of PCBs above one part per million unsafe for human contact. The heaviest concentrations of the chemicals lay in the inner harbor, or the area above the bridge spanned by Route 195. The worst contamination of all is at the mouth of the Acushnet River at the harbor's head.

Nobody around here knew much about PCBs until 1979, when the state and the EPA tested fish and sediments from the harbor and discovered high levels of the chemicals. PCBs accumulate in fish, particularly in game fish such as striped bass, blues, tuna, and swordfish. When the scope of the contamination was discovered, it was obvious that nobody but the federal government had the kind of cash it would take to clean it up, so the harbor was declared a Superfund site. The feds move slowly. To date, the EPA has taken six thousand samples of sediment from the harbor for testing and has spent about $180 million on the project. Amazingly, although an immense amount of groundwork has been laid, and several PCB "hot spots" removed, the main cleanup effort has yet to materialize. The EPA has been camped out in this city for twelve years; heavy equipment lumbers about, city lots are fenced off, and nobody gets to go fishing in the city once known as the whaling capital of the world. It is a textbook situation for a public relations problem. Meanwhile, each day about half a pound of PCBs migrates from the inner harbor above the bridge to the outer harbor. Nobody even knows how much of that toxic load reaches the rest of Buzzards Bay.

The EPA's goal is to restore the health of New Bedford Harbor, including about two miles of the Acushnet River, by 2008 or 2013. They intend to accomplish this feat by scraping up all the mud from the inner harbor, squeezing the water out of it, and either shipping it to off-site toxic waste dumps or using it to construct three new self-contained pieces of shoreline on the harbor. If they pursue the last option, the use of the new land will be restricted; for example, schools will not be allowed there.

To grasp the extent of this job, picture seventy-five football fields aligned end to end and covered in five feet of muck. That is about the amount of contaminated harbor bottom that needs to be excavated and disposed of. How long the job takes and where the sediment ends up depend entirely on how much funding Congress gives to the project. When they finally do pull out of town, the EPA hopes to leave not only a clean harbor, but one revitalized by the community projects that are already springing up around them. Positive initiatives that the EPA's presence has fueled are not as obvious as the numerous construction sites, but they are here nonetheless. One example I saw was a homeowner leveraging the beauty of an EPA-restored salt marsh by constructing new gardens and duck pens on an adjacent riverbank. And on the harbor, at a graveyard of scuttled fishing vessels that the EPA is disinterring, the city has accepted an offer by the feds to resurrect an old city rail line.

The most disturbing element of the New Bedford Harbor tragedy is that it is the legacy of one inner-harbor facility, alternately used by two corporations, AVX Corporation and Aerovox Incorporated. The Cornell Dubilier facility (located on the outer end of the harbor) also contributed to the pollution, but the vast majority of it came from the AVX/Aerovox site. On one fine day in the 1940s, with the wind gently rippling the flow of the Acushnet River outside the factory windows, somebody decided that the right way to dispose of the PCBs produced in manufacturing operations was to dig four open trenches, fill them with the chemicals, and allow them to drain directly into the river. Later, on second thought, they decided it would be more efficient to dispose of the chemicals through the sewer system, so they were dispersed all over the harbor.

That gloomy day in New Bedford, I drove to the factory so I could view firsthand the facility that fouled the grandest harbor on Buzzards Bay. It was abandoned. Aerovox, the last tenant, set up shop at another location in the city after the extent of the contamination became known. The factory site is still very heavily contaminated with PCBs; Aerovox was supposed to clean it up but recently filed for bankruptcy protection instead. (To their credit, the company did contribute around $66 million to the general cleanup effort.) A yellow metal sign hangs on the barbed-wire fence: WARNING . . . NO TRESPASSING, HAZARDOUS SUBSTANCES . . . PER ORDER OF THE EPA. The factory itself is horrid and depressing, a low-slung monotony of red brick and rusty metal pipes, left to fall into ruin at the edge of the harbor. Here, at ground zero, the soil crawls with PCBs. The earth beneath me was a thousand times more contaminated than other sediments down-harbor that were considered toxic. The facility is itself, quite literally, a Superfund site waiting to happen.

Over on the Fairhaven side of the river, sunlight branched through breaks in the cloud cover, and a scene of sublime beauty caught me by surprise. Shafts of golden light hung heavily in the still air as the broad river pulsed tranquilly by a great field of swaying green cordgrass on the far bank. Necks arched, a pair of pure-white mute swans tacked slowly upstream against the current, and nervous mallard ducks jetted haphazardly out into the flow. Farther down the opposing shoreline lay a classic Buzzards Bay beach: a deserted arc of coffee-colored stones littered with crushed white shells and boulders blackened up to the high-water mark, backed by hunched stands of cedar, scrub oak, and maple. At one time, this place must have been revered as one of the most subtly beautiful spots on the Bay. Four open trenches were all it took to steal away its purity and render the pastoral scene in front of me merely a beautiful veneer masking deadly contamination.

Fortunately, in New Bedford the EPA is closing in on what will someday be one of Buzzard Bay's great success stories. Even better, it appears that we have learned a lesson: PCBs are now banned in this country, although they continue to be dumped into embayments around the world. For our Bay, though, the worst is over, at least with respect to pollution from one class of chemicals.

PETER PAN HAS NOTHING on George Hampson, an expert on the effects of oil on the environment from the Woods Hole Oceanographic Institution (WHOI). The contents of his office in North Falmouth reveal him to be the boy who never grew up: a drum labeled FLAMMABLE LIQUID, microscopes, rubber boots, fuel tanks for small boats, mesh bags stuffed with scientific apparatus, wooden racks holding glass sampling bottles, fish tanks. George is one of the scientists at WHOI who has spent the better part of his life providing the rest of us with the scientific facts we need to protect Buzzards Bay from oil pollution.

MARINE PLANTS AND ANIMALS most affected by oil pollution include those that don't move about, those that have a particular sensitivity to oil, or those that are still developing. The oil that enters Buzzards Bay is eventually broken down by exposure to air, sunlight, waves, tides, and microscopic organisms. However, the speed at which this happens—and thus the severity of the oil's effects on the marine environment—depends on a complex physical and chemical process. Factors in this process include the type of oil, temperature, weather, water conditions, and the type of bottom and shoreline. Consequently, the effects of any one source of oil pollution on the Bay are extremely difficult, if not impossible, to define. About all we know for sure is that any source of oil pollution, when viewed cumulatively, is bad for Buzzards Bay.

ONCE WHEN I WAS A BOY, fishing with my father in his boat near the Cape Cod Canal, he said to me, "Never get in the way of a barge, son. They can't stop for miles. They will run you down." Recently, I watched what looked like the northern tip of Naushon Island slowly detach from itself, like a dividing amoeba, as a great barge slid out from behind it, and the old fear returned. A friend in the trucking business once told me, "On the road, stay as far away as possible from oil rigs, because if they are fully loaded they can't stop." That's the frightening thing about fuel oil. Its flow, like the procession of tankers up the Bay, is endless. It never stops.

BUZZARDS BAY IS a major route for tankers and barges transporting heating oil, industrial oil, and gasoline to Boston and northern New England. There was little public awareness around the Bay about oil pollution until one of these ships, the *Florida*, went aground off West Falmouth in the fall of 1969 and belched 185,000 gallons of number 2 fuel oil, one of the most destructive types, into the surrounding waters. Hardest hit was the neighboring shoreline of North Falmouth, particularly the marsh at Wild Harbor River. Locals as far as three miles inland caught the reek of fuel oil in the air. The first sign of the tragedy were fish washing up on New Silver Beach, drifting, no longer able to swim. In the marsh at Wild Harbor River, the oil dived like an army of eels down fiddler crab holes, and clams mysteriously surfaced and bobbed about in tidal pools. Lobstermen shook their heads in disgust and wonder as they hauled dead lobsters in their traps. Two days later, when the scientists from WHOI motored a half-mile offshore and tested the sediments, they struck oil.

The oil company responsible for the mess didn't want to hear that it was their oil trapped in the bottom sediments. "Everybody knows," they crowed, "that oil floats." Unfortunately for them, they underestimated the scholarship of the scientists at Woods Hole. Max Blumer, a brilliant Swiss scientist, used a process called gas chromatography to "fingerprint" the oil from the spill and trace it to the *Florida,* something that had never been done before. And Howard Sanders, a world-renowned benthic biologist (that is, a scientist who studies bottom-dwelling organisms), produced a report on the damaging effects of the spill that was so loaded with convincing data, it would choke anyone intent on discrediting it. Today, more than thirty years later, Chris Reddy of WHOI has proved that oil still exists in the sediments of the marsh and that it has not been significantly broken down by bacteria and other environmental forces, as was expected, a discovery that is helping redefine public perception of oil spills worldwide.

The next major wreck was in 1974, when the *Bouchard 65* hit a submerged object at the southwest entrance to the Bay and was towed to an anchorage off Scraggy Neck in Cataumet. On nearby Bassetts Island, surf clams— seldom seen before in the area—washed ashore by the hundreds, dead. Near the island's south channel, in tiny Windsor Cove, the emerald saltmarsh cordgrass withered and disappeared and did not fully recover until the 1990s. The peat below it, which acts as topsoil for the marsh, and which was bound together by the roots of the grass, eroded and is gone forever. Unbelievably, the same ship, the *Bouchard 65*, ran aground again four years later, oozing another 81,000 gallons of oil into the eastern waters of the Bay.

A relatively quiet period followed this spill, until 1990, when the 617-foot *Bermuda Star* cruise ship, drifting in a dense fog, grounded on Cleveland Ledge in twenty feet of water. It spilled 7,000 gallons of oil, 3,000 gallons of which fouled the pristine shores of Naushon Island. Just eight days later, yet another *Bouchard*, the *145*, went up on the same ledge and spilled 100 gallons of the dreaded number 2 fuel oil before it was released from the rocks. This was a close call, because the ship contained over 5 million gallons of oil. These spills were instrumental in focusing the public's attention on the problem. It helped that the press reported that the cruise ship pilot had been socializing while waiting for the fog to break so the ship could enter the Cape Cod Canal.

Meanwhile, the team at Woods Hole was simultaneously fighting the oil companies and trying to make the public aware of the threat. It was no easy job. "A bunch of pit bulls we were," George Hampson admitted triumphantly. "We just didn't let go." Others who fought on the side of the Bay included Fred Grassle, a marine ecologist, and George Souza, the Falmouth Shellfish Officer. The oil companies harassed them, pressuring individuals instead of standing up to WHOI. They also tried to discredit the scientists' research.

But the tide of public opinion was turning against the oil companies. In 1980, passage of the U.S. Comprehensive Environmental Response, Compensation, and Liability ("Superfund") Act had put financial responsibility for cleanup costs squarely on the shoulders of the responsible party. This legislation provides a strong financial incentive for oil companies not to spill; it might still be the Bay's best protection. Next, motivated by a rash of similar spills around the country, including the *Exxon Valdez* spill in Alaska in

1989, Congress passed the Oil Protection Act of 1990. This legislation set broad federal safety requirements for the marine transport of oil, including double hulls on tankers. (Oil companies are not required to fully comply with the double-hull regulation until 2015.)

Locally, Marion "Mimi" McConnell of the Coalition for Buzzards Bay became incensed upon learning that the piloting requirements for the Bay were lax and antiquated. The eighteenth-century piloting law actually contained references to whaling ships. The coalition joined forces with other concerned groups to shepherd through modern piloting legislation. Today, any ship of 350 gross tons or more traveling through the Bay must be boarded by a state-certified pilot. Usually a local, such as a tug captain, the pilot is familiar with the waters of the Bay and is armed with a laptop computer loaded with state-of-the-art navigation software. Typically, the pilot clambers up the ship's gangway ten miles south of Cleveland Ledge and stays with the captain on the bridge to ensure the ship's safe passage through the Bay. Although overall the piloting requirements for the Bay are better, there is still significant room for improvement. One glaring loophole is the insufficient piloting requirements for barges being towed by tugs. The coalition also pushed through improvements to aids to navigation after the 1990 spills, including a new Buzzards Bay Light Tower, realigned channel buoys at the southwest end of the Bay, and a radar beacon on deadly Cleveland Ledge.

THE COAST GUARD enforces the pilotage requirements and ensures that the aids to navigation stay where they are supposed to be. They also maintain boxcars loaded with absorbent booms that can be used to clean ships or contain oil at strategic locations such as Otis Air Force Base.

Because of the press coverage spills receive, many people assume that tanker spills are the major cause of oil pollution in the Bay. They are not. Small, cumulative spills from a wide variety of sources in and around the Bay contribute far more oil than all the tanker spills combined. These range from routine marine operations, such as tank cleanings, to fueling spills and the improper disposal of engine oil in the watershed. These sources of pollution are called "nonpoint" because, unlike a tanker spill, you can't point a finger at their source.

Drip, drip, drip. The single greatest source of oil pollution to the Bay from the surrounding watershed is the oil dripping from underneath our cars, visible as black spots on the pavement below them. Washed off the pavement by rain, these drops form tributaries that descend into storm drains and combine into a river of oil that flows straight into the Bay. In general, older cars tend to drip more than newer ones. Diesel-burning trucks and cars are the worst offenders because they drip diesel, which is nothing more than number 2 fuel oil with a dye added to it for identification purposes. This type of fuel is more toxic to the environment than the lubricating oil dripped by gas-burning vehicles.

Storm-water treatment systems, like those used to treat fecal coliform bacteria contamination, can effectively prevent runoff oil from entering a harbor. Ultimately, however, the solution is proper vehicle maintenance. One good way to ensure this would be to require as part of the annual state inspection that a vehicle be drip-free.

The commercial fishing fleet, most of it based out of New Bedford and Westport, is believed to be a significant contributor to oil pollution on the Bay. Many of these fishermen change their engine oil after every trip, generating up to 120 gallons of waste oil. Because disposing of this oil is difficult and expensive, some fishermen have resorted to dumping it directly into the Bay. They accomplish this by setting adrift five-gallon buckets with holes chopped in the covers, which allow the ship's used oil to seep out inconspicuously. These white, blue, and brown buckets drift on the currents of the Bay and wash up on its beaches. The Coast Guard can fingerprint the oil in these buckets to the bilge of a particular boat, but without an onboard informant they have no place to start. We need to make it easier for these hardworking men to do the right thing and dispose of their oil responsibly on shore.

IF YOU KNOW HOW to look for it, you can find oil all over the Bay. You must search for it on rainy or overcast days. For some reason, oil carries its own unnatural luminescence and, like a vampire, will seldom reveal itself in the glare of sunlight. I once watched oil make its way across a parking lot during a rainstorm. It moved independently over a clear sheet of storm water, like a writhing, metallic-blue serpent, before slithering down a storm drain. I have encountered it on the banks of a remote tidal river in South

Dartmouth, transforming raccoon tracks pressed deep in black mud into glowing stars of cobalt blue. Oil is everywhere, sunk deep into the tissues of the Bay.

GLOBAL WARMING, sea-level rise, and coastal erosion are interrelated processes that together pose a threat to the coastal communities of Buzzards Bay. All are natural forces; all whittle away at the shoreline. Human activities have accelerated these processes, however, so that their effects now threaten lives and property in coastal areas worldwide. The Bay is particularly prone to land loss from their effects because it is low-lying and sandy. Most important, coastal communities on the upper reaches of the Bay are vulnerable to storm surges and flooding during hurricanes, a weakness that will be thoroughly exploited by the unnatural acceleration of these processes.

Most scientists now believe that the massive amounts of fossil fuels we have burned since the industrial revolution have loaded the atmosphere with carbon dioxide and caused the temperature to rise, contributing to the natural process of global warming. Jeff Williams of the U.S. Geological Survey recently announced at a presentation at WHOI, "There is new and stronger evidence that some portion of the global warming over the last fifty years is due to human activities." Scientists now estimate that between 1990 and 2100, the average global temperature will rise by 2.5 to 10.4 degrees Fahrenheit. One of the numerous implications of this change that is already occurring is sea-level rise.

The sea is rising because water expands when it is heated and because ice on the shores of the sea, such as the great West Antarctic ice sheet, is melting. The level of the sea has been rising at a highly variable rate for the last twenty thousand years, since the end of the Pleistocene ice age. We know from remains found there that mastodons once strode across Georges Bank, when it was connected by a land bridge to Cape Cod and the mainland. The geologic record shows that over the past hundred years, the sea in our region has risen one foot, and we have lost sixty-five acres of the Massachusetts coastline.

The land lost in Buzzards Bay goes largely unnoticed for two reasons. First, the coastline is highly irregular, twisted and curved into harbors and coves. A retreating shoreline is less obvious on this type of coast than on one that is relatively straight. Second, most of the land loss occurs where the mainland meets wetland, a place seldom inhabited by people.

Sea-level rise is a passive process. Picture the water level creeping up as you fill your bathtub. The disappearing walls of the tub are the shoreline. Now, to visualize the effect of global warming on sea-level rise, set a fifty-pound block of ice on the edge of the tub and crank up the heat in the bathroom.

Exactly how high the Bay will rise in the next hundred years is still a matter of uncertainty and speculation. From a countrywide perspective, we know we won't be the most heavily impacted: Chesapeake Bay will fare worst, and New Orleans will most likely have to be relocated or refortified with higher flood-control levees. All we know for sure is that the Bay will rise, and that some coastal towns stand to lose a significant amount of land in the process. According to Graham Giese at WHOI, even if we continue to lose land only at the current sea-level rise rate of one foot per hundred years and don't experience any additional loss because of an increased rate of global warming, towns will lose the following percentages of their land: Marion, 3.1 percent; Wareham, 2.4 percent; Fairhaven, 2.0 percent; Falmouth, 1.6 percent; Gosnold, 1.3 percent; and Mattapoisett, 1.2 percent. Bourne, Dartmouth, and New Bedford all stand to lose about 0.6 percent, with lessening amounts for the remaining coastal towns on Buzzards Bay.

Another long-term problem associated with sea level rise on the Bay may be the loss of salt marshes. Salt marshes filter toxins that would otherwise enter the Bay, act as nurseries for two-thirds of our coastal fish, and provide habitats for birds and countless other species. They can withstand moderate rises in sea level, but if the sea rises too quickly, they will be submerged.

Erosion is the active process of wind and water eating away at the shoreline. It is largely the result of storms. Massachusetts routinely loses just over half a foot of shoreline a year to erosion, in addition to the land lost to the passive process of sea-level rise. This figure is quite low compared to other parts of the Eastern Seaboard, many of which have an erosion rate of three feet per year. Over two-thirds of the Massachusetts coastline is eroding, at various rates. The worst damage occurs along the south-facing coastline of Nantucket, which loses twelve feet a year, and Martha's Vineyard, which loses five to six. In general, Buzzards Bay's rate of land loss is probably slightly lower than the Massachusetts average of half a foot per year, although certain vulnerable places such as Allens Pond and Horseneck Beach erode faster because of their extremely low, sandy composition and local currents.

Like global warming and sea-level rise, erosion is a natural process that has been accelerated by human activities. In fact, human activities have caused more erosion in some areas over the past fifty to a hundred years than natural processes. Built to combat erosion in the 1950s, jetties, groins, and seawalls turned out to be a bust. Instead of slowing down the natural process of erosion, they often speed it up. These artificial structures scallop the sand from beaches on their down-current side, and jettison it from their tips on their up-current side. (Current flows from the direction of the prevailing wind, which on Buzzards Bay generally means the southwest.) The armoring of coastal bluffs can also increase beach erosion by cutting off natural sand supplies to the beach. The heaviest land loss around these structures occurred in the years immediately following their construction and presently continues at a lesser rate. Today, "soft engineering" techniques that attempt to mimic the natural processes of the coastline are the trend in coastline preservation. A well-known example of the success of this kind of engineering is Miami Beach, which was severely eroded until the 1970s. The Army Corps of Engineers removed the jetties and created the beach using a technique called beach nourishment, importing sand from activities such as dredging.

The greatest hazard Buzzards Bay faces is that the accelerated processes of global warming, sea-level rise, and erosion will produce a stronger storm surge in a major hurricane. A storm surge is a massive dome of water created by the winds around a hurricane's eye. As described in the chapter on hurricanes, this dome, which is funneled ashore by the rising sea bottom as the storm approaches land, is the most life-threatening part of a hurricane, the primary reason coastal areas are evacuated. Some communities in the upper reaches of the Bay, such as Wareham, already experience terrific storm surges as high as twenty-five feet. A higher water level on the Bay will fuel an even stronger surge, resulting in greater flooding and higher rates of coastal erosion. To further complicate matters, some scientists believe we are entering, globally, a twenty- to thirty-year cycle of increased hurricane activity.

To visualize the mechanics of this situation, picture once again your bathtub. The block of ice you set on the edge has now melted and flowed into the tub, raising the water to a level disturbingly close to the rim—sea-level rise. This is not, in itself, a crisis. Now picture a ten-year-old boy leaping haphazardly into the tub—the hurricane. The wall of water that lunges over the rim is the storm surge, the damage it causes to the bathroom is erosion, and the two inches of water left saturating the floor is the flood. The moral of the story, which we all know from childhood, is "Don't fill the tub too high." The real-life consequences we can expect from a storm surge of this magnitude include increased damage to residences and businesses and higher casualty rates. Higher flood levels will expose septic systems and sewer pipes and contaminate sources of fresh water such as wells. Toxins such as gasoline will escape into the environment.

One way to avoid some of these consequences is to use scientific data to determine appropriate sites for coastal development now. The long-term solution involves combating global warming, because ultimately the crux of the problem is a higher water level on Buzzards Bay. Our government's continued refusal to support the international Kyoto Treaty, which sets targets for reductions in greenhouse gas emissions, is a major stumbling block. Let's hope that the communities on the low, vulnerable shores of Buzzards Bay will not end up serving as a tragic consequence—canaries in the coal mine—of our country's failure to address the very potent dangers of global warming.

Afterword

I WAS STANDING on the shoreline of the cove where I grew up, at the very spot where my grandfather had launched his skiff. Formerly stony ground, the area has since filled in with spartina grass, but the tall pipe that anchored the rope-and-pulley system that my grandfather used to run his boat out beyond the low-tide mark is still there, rusted and leaning over, unnoticeable in the tall grass. It was winter, a cold blue December morning with slanting bright sunshine, and all was dead quiet. The surface of the cove was motionless, like glass. I like to look at the Bay in winter because, free of boats, I imagine that it looks as it did in Gosnold's day or before. A pair of mallards erupted from the shoreline, feathers whistling rhythmically, and I watched their crisp, colorful reflections move across the open waters. All around me songbirds sang cheerily; I recognized the calls of chickadees, song sparrows, and blue jays. Black crows cawed loudly to each other and drove their beaks up to the hilt into the wet sand. Beside the road ringing the cove, two pairs of cardinals, brilliant red and muted brown, hopped about, quietly feeding in the orange needles scattered beneath green cedars.

All the magic of Buzzards Bay was embodied here: the picturesque, sheltered harbor; the clean water hosting a variety of birds, plants, and animals; the scalloped white beaches striped by rocky cobble and backed by hunched dark cedars. Many of the challenges facing the Bay were represented here as well: the brown tidal pond up behind the road, choked by nitrogen; the soft-shelled clam beds, closed because of fecal coliform bacteria contamination; the residential development of large, year-round homes replacing modest cottages.

I adjusted the blanket wrapped around my baby son in my arms. He woke up, squinted, and turned sharply away from the brilliant rays of the low winter sun. My son is big for his age, and he laughs a lot, like his great-grandfather. Some day, I hope that he will launch his own boat from this spot. By the time my son has children of his own, I realized, the fate of the Bay will be determined, for better or worse. The game will be over. Much of the unprotected land in its watershed will be developed. Will the nitrogen from septic systems have wrung the oxygen out of the Bay, leaving the waters of coves like this one murky and lifeless? Will a devastating oil spill have occurred? Will my son have any reason to carry a fishing rod or a shellfish basket? Countless generations have lived and died on the shores of this beautiful place. It is astonishing that after so very long, the Bay's fate has come to rest squarely on our own.

At the waterline, I stooped and plucked a quahog shell from the clear icy water. Its inner edge, splashed with deep purple, shone in the morning sunlight as if newly painted. "Hey, Wes," I said to my son, "take a look at this!" He stared at the shell intently but didn't look impressed. After a while, I noticed a jerking motion under the tightly wrapped blanket. I loosened it, and a tiny white hand, fingers outstretched, stole forth and seized the purple edge of the shell. Then, in the manner that babies do, he began to pull the shell ever so slowly toward his open mouth.

References

EPIGRAPHS THROUGHOUT BOOK

Brereton, John. *Brereton's Relation.* Third Series of the Collections of the Massachusetts
    Historical Society, Vol. VIII, pp. 83 – 103.

Archer, Gabriel. *Archers Relation.* Third Series of the Collections of the Massachusetts
    Historical Society, Vol. VIII, pp. 72 – 81.

NATIVE AMERICANS

Bingham, Amelia G. *Mashpee, Land of the Wampanoags.* 1981.

Burrell, Chris. "Wompanoag business record raises doubts on casino." *Boston Sunday Globe,* 5
    January 2003.

"District Attorney seeks to 'clarify' fishing rights." *Cape Cod Times,* 8 April 1999.

Doherty, Katherine M., and Craig A. Doherty. *The Wampanoag.* New York: F. Watts, 1995.

Forbes, Alan. *Other Indian Events of New England.* Boston: State Street Trust Company, 1941.

Gookin, Daniel. *Historical Collections of the Indians of Massachusetts.* 1674 (published 1792).

Hare, Lloyd C. M. *Thomas Mayhew, Patriarch to the Indians.* New York and London: D. Appleton
    and Company, 1932.

Keene, Betsey D. *History of Bourne from 1622-1937.* Bourne, Mass.: Bourne Historical Society, 1975.

Marshall, Glenn. Personal interview, 29 January 2003.

Peters, Russell M. *The Wampanoags of Mashpee.* Boston: Nimrod Press, 1987.

Plymouth Archaeological Rediscovery Project. http://plymoutharch.tripod.com.

Russell, Howard S. *Indian New England Before the Mayflower.* Hanover, N.H.: University Press
    of New England, 1980.

Silverberg, Robert. *Home of the Red Man.* Canada, N.Y.: Graphic Society Publishers, 1963.

Simmons, William S. *Spirit of the New England Tribes.* Hanover, N.H., and London: University
    Press of New England, 1986.

Travers, Milton A. *The Wampanoag Indian Federation of the Algonquin Nation.* New Bedford,
    Mass.: Reynolds-De Walt, 1957; rev. ed. Boston: Christopher Publishing House, 1961.

Vuilleumier, William.S. *Indians on Olde Cape Cod.* Taunton, Mass.: Sullwold Publishing, 1970.

Weinstein-Farson, Laurie. *The Wampanoag.* New York: Chelsea House, 1989.

Wilbur, Keith C. *The New England Indians.* Chester, Conn.: Globe Pequot Press, 1978.

BIRDS

Nisbet, Ian. Personal interview, 7 October 2003.

Perkins, Simon. Personal interview, 4 and 5 November 2003.

Sibley, David Allen. *The Sibley Guide to Birds.* New York: Alfred A. Knopf, 2000.

WILDLIFE

"Diamondback Terrapin (*Malaclemys terrapin*)." University of Delaware Graduate College of
    Marine Studies, http://www.ocean.udel.edu/kiosk/terrapin.html.

"Harbor Seals." SeaWorld/Busch Gardens Animal Information Database, http://
    www.seaworld.org/infobooks/HarborSeal/.

Hurley, Steve. Personal communication (at Marys Pond), 27 March 2003.

—. *Southeast Wildlife District Trout Stocking Program 2003.* Buzzards Bay Office, Commonwealth
    of Massachusetts Division of Fisheries and Wildlife, 2003.

—. *Stocked Trout Ponds of Southeastern Massachusetts 2003*. Buzzards Bay Office, Commonwealth of Massachusetts Division of Fisheries and Wildlife, 2003.

Lazell, James D. *This Broken Archipelago: Cape Cod and the Islands, Amphibians, and Reptiles*. New York: Quadrangle Press, New York Times Book Company, 1976.

Lewis, Don. "Death in the Marsh. Diamondback Terrapins Die in Large Numbers on Cape Cod." Diary of a Terrapin Researcher, http://terrapindiary.org/die-offs.

Mello, Marc. Personal interview, 19 March 2003.

Mills, Tony. "Diamondback Terrapin: Malaclemys terrapin." Savannah River Ecological Laboratory Outreach and SPARC. http://www.uga.edu/srel/outreach.htm.

HURRICANES

And Bob Was His Name. Sun City West, Ariz.: C. F. Boone Publishing Company, 1991.

Atlantic Oceanographic and Meteorological Laboratory, Hurricane Research Division (NOAA). "Frequently Asked Questions." http://www.aoml.noaa.gov/hrd/tcfaq/tcfaqHED.html.

Cape Cod Standard-Times. Hyannis, Mass. 23 and 24 September 1938.

Cape Cod Times. 2 September 1954; 20 August 1991.

Falmouth Enterprise. 23 and 30 September 1938; 3 September 1954; 20 August 1991.

Ghiorse, John. Personal interview, 11 March 2003.

Gray, Dr. William. "The Tropical Meteorological Project." Colorado State University, http://hurricane.atmos.colostate.edu/Forecasts/.

Howes, Brian L., and Dale D. Goehringer. *Ecology of Buzzards Bay: An Estuarine Profile. Biological Report 31*. National Biological Service, U.S. Department of the Interior, 1996. http://www.savebuzzardsbay.org/bay-info/ecology.htm.

Hurricane 1954. Special report of *New Bedford Standard Times*, 11 September 1954.

Miller, Alice, and Frank Miller. Personal interview, 25 March 2003.

Tripp, Bradford. Personal interview, 18 March 2003.

Vallee, David R. *A Centennial Review of Major Land Falling Tropical Cyclones in Southern New England*. Taunton, Mass.: NOAA/National Weather Service Forecast Office. www.erh.noaa.gov/er/box/tropical_cyclones.htm.

ELIZABETH ISLANDS

Buckley, I. Thomas. *Penikese, Island of Hope*. Stony Brook Publishing, 1997.

"The Cuttyhunk Fishing Club." Literature from the Cuttyhunk Fishing Club, Cuttyhunk, Mass.

Cuttyhunk Historical Society. *Images of America: Cuttyhunk and the Elizabeth Islands*. Charleston, S.C.: Arcadia Publishing, 2002.

Howland, Alice Forbes. *Three Islands—Pasque, Nashawena, Penikese*. Privately printed, 1964.

Humphrey, Peter. "Little folk part of island lore." *Boston Globe*, 17 March 1995.

Lepers of Buzzards Bay. Videorecording. Boston: WGBH Educational Foundation, 1994.

O'Brien, Greg. *O'Brien's Original Guide to Cape Cod and the Islands*. Hyannis, Mass.: Parnassus Imprints, 1996.

Teller, Walter. *Cape Cod and the Offshore Islands*. Englewood Cliffs, N.J.: Prentice Hall, 1970.

PLANTS

Amos, William Hopkins. *Atlantic and Gulf Coasts*. Audubon Society Nature Guides Series. New York: Knopf, 1985.

Backus, Dick. Personal interview (on tour of Penikese Island), 17 September 2003.

Backus, Richard H., Pamela T. Polloni, Brian L. Reid, Paul Somers, and Theodore O. Hendrickson. "The Flora of Penikese Island, Massachusetts: The Fifth Survey (1998 – 1999), with Emphasis on the Woody Vegetation." *Rhodora*. 104, No. 919 (2002): 219 – 252.

Costa, Joe. Personal communication, 2003.

Digregorio, Mario. Personal interview (on salt marsh and bog outing), 14 September 2003.

Digregorio, Mario, and Jeff Wallner. *A Vanishing Heritage: Wildflowers of Cape Cod*. Lebanon, N.H.: University Press of New England, 2003.

Duncan, Wilbur Howard. *The Smithsonian Guide to Seaside Plants of the Gulf and Atlantic Coast from Louisiana to Massachusetts, Exclusive of Lower Peninsula Florida*. Washington, D.C.: Smithsonian Institution Press, 1987.

Giambarba, Paul. *Cape Cod Seashore Life*. Barre, Mass.: Scrimshaw Press, Barre Publishers, 1968.

Hampson, George. Personal communication, 2003.

Massachusetts Division of Marine Fisheries, Southeast Marine Fisheries Station. *Submerged Aquatic Vegetation: Essential Fish Habitat*.

O'Brien, Greg. *A Guide to Nature on Cape Cod and the Islands*. New York: Penguin Books, 1990.

BOATING

Baker, Ben. Personal communication, 2003.

Bailey, Anthony. *The Coast of Summer*. New York: Harper Collins, 1994.

Buzzards Bay. http://www.impulz.net/buzzardsbay.

Community Boating Center. http://www.communityboating.org.

Community Boating Center, Inc. "Testimonials." Unpublished handout. P.O. Box 41021, New Bedford, Mass., 02744.

Massachusetts Maritime Academy. http://www.mma.mass.edu/.

Muldoon, John. Personal interview, 22 November 2003.

Schooner Ernestina. http://www.ernestina.org/index2.html.

Vaitses, Steve. Personal interview, 20 September 2003.

Veneri, Barbara. "Community Boating Center offers valuable resource." *New Bedford Standard-Times*, 17 May 1998.

—. "Joining Forces: NBH, Community Boating Center come together." *New Bedford Standard-Times*, 11 May 2003.

—. "Sailing School: Community Boating Center puts kids at the helm, building water—and life—skills." *New Bedford Standard-Times*, 24 July 2001.

White, Marion Jewett. *Eldridge Tide and Pilot Book*. Boston, Mass, 2001.

FISHERIES

Cebula, Henry. Personal communication, 18 December 2002.

Commonwealth of Massachusetts Division of Fisheries, Wildlife, and Environmental Law Enforcement. *Massachusetts Marine Recreational Fishing Information*. Boston, Mass., 2002.

Commonwealth of Massachusetts Division of Marine Fisheries. *Sanitary Survey of New Bedford. A chronology of Buzzards Bay bacterial shellfish closures from 1900*. Pocasset, Mass.

Dean, Micah J., Kimberly A. Lundy, and Thomas B. Hoopes. *2001 Massachusetts Lobster Fishery Statistics*. Technical Report TR-13. Gloucester, Mass.: Annisquam River Marine Fisheries Station, 2002.

Estrella, Bruce. Personal communication, 11 December 2002.

Garfield, Seth. Personal communications, 12 and 20 December 2002.

Howes, Brian L., and Dale D. Goehringer. *Ecology of Buzzards Bay: An Estuarine Profile. Biological Report 31*. National Biological Service, U.S. Department of the Interior, 1996. http://www.savebuzzardsbay.org/bay-info/ecology.htm.

Kolek, Andrew. Personal communication, 5 December 2002.

Leavitt, Dale. Personal communication, 2 December 2002.

Moore, Hillary B. *Marine Ecology*. Commonwealth of Massachusetts Division of Marine Fisheries, 2002.

Whittaker, David. *Quahog Standing Crop Survey: New Bedford/Fairhaven Inner and Outer Harbors*. Pocasset, Mass.: Commonwealth of Massachusetts Division of Marine Fisheries/New Bedford Harbor Trustee Council, June 6, 1999.

—. Personal communications, 2002 – 2003; personal interview, 10 December 2002.

Woods Hole Oceanographic Institution Sea Grant Program. "Fisheries and Aquaculture." http://www.whoi.edu/seagrant/research/fa/fatheme.html.

CONSERVATION

Buzzard Bay Project. "The Massachusetts Alternative Septic System Test Center." http://www.buzzardsbay.org/etimain.htm.

Buzzards Bay Project, Town of Bourne. *Buttermilk Bay Stormwater Remediation Project*. Prepared for Massachusetts Department of Environmental Protection and U.S. EPA Region I. 1996 – 2000.

Buzzards Bay Project National Estuary Program. *Buzzards Bay Comprehensive Conservation and Management Plan*. 1991. http://www.buzzardsbay.org/ccmptoc.htm.

Coalition for Buzzards Bay and School for Marine Science and Technology, UMass-Dartmouth. *Baywatchers III: Nutrient Related Health of Buzzards Bay Embayments 1992-2001*. New Bedford: Coalition for Buzzards Bay, 2003.

Dickerson, David. Personal communication (on New Bedford Harbor PCB tour), 17 May 2002.

Giese, Graham S. "Sea Level Rise." Woods Hole Oceanographic Institution. Coalition for Buzzards Bay Lecture. Woods Hole, Mass., 10 April 2002.

Giese, Graham S, D. G. Aubrey, and P. Zeeb. *Passive Retreat of Massachusetts Coastal Upland Due to Relative Sea-Level Rise*. Woods Hole, Mass.: Woods Hole Oceanographic Institution, 1987.

Hampson, George. Personal communications, 2002 – 2003.

Heufelder, George. Personal communication (at Massachusetts Alternative Septic System Test Center), 14 May 2002.

Howes, Brian L., and Dale D. Goehringer. *Ecology of Buzzards Bay: An Estuarine Profile*. Biological Report 31. National Biological Service, U.S. Department of the Interior, 1996. http://www.savebuzzardsbay.org/bay-info/ecology.htm.

Howes, Brian, Tony Williams, and Mark Rasmussen. *Baywatchers II: Nutrient Related Water Quality of Buzzards Bay Embayments: A Synthesis of Baywatchers Monitoring 1992–1998*. New Bedford: Coalition for Buzzards Bay, 1999.

McConnell, Marion (Mimi). Personal communication, 26 September 2002.

O'Connell, James F., Robert E. Thieler, and Courtney Schupp. *New Shoreline Change Data and Analysis for the Massachusetts Shore with Emphasis on Cape Cod and the Islands: Mid-1800s to 1994*. Woods Hole Oceanographic Institution Sea Grant Program. Woods Hole Oceanographic Institution, Cape Cod Cooperative Extension, U.S. Geological Survey, 2002.

Reddy, Christopher. Personal communication, 2004.

Rocha, Bob. Personal communication, 2002.

Rockwell, John, David S. Janik, and Bernadette Taber. *Unified Rules and Regulations for Stormwater Management for Use by Planning Boards, Boards of Health, and Conservation Commissions*. Buzzards Bay Project, Massachusetts Office of Coastal Zone Management, 1996.

Taber, Bernadette. Personal communication (at Electric Avenue storm-water management site), 7 May 2002.

Tripp, Bruce. Personal communication, 9 September 2002.

Williams, Jeff. *Global Warming, Coastal Erosion, and Sea Level Rise*. United States Geological Survey. Coalition for Buzzards Bay Lecture. Woods Hole, Mass., 10 April 2002.

Williams, Tony. Personal communication, 2002.

Index